Understanding the Stigma of Mental Illness

Understanding the Stigma of Mental Illness: Theory and Interventions

Edited by

Julio Arboleda-Flórez
Queen's University, Ontario, Canada

and

Norman Sartorius
University of Geneva, Switzerland

John Wiley & Sons, Ltd

Other Wiley Editorial Offices

John Wiley & Sons Inc., 111 River Street, Hoboken, NJ 07030, USA

Jossey-Bass, 989 Market Street, San Francisco, CA 94103-1741, USA

Wiley-VCH Verlag GmbH, Boschstr. 12, D-69469 Weinheim, Germany

John Wiley & Sons Australia Ltd, 33 Park Road, Milton, Queensland 4064, Australia

John Wiley & Sons (Asia) Pte Ltd, 2 Clementi Loop #02-01, Jin Xing Distripark, Singapore 129809

John Wiley & Sons Canada Ltd, 6045 Freemont Blvd, Mississauga, Ontario, L5R 4J3, Canada

Wiley also publishes its books in a variety of electronic formats. Some content that appears in print may not be
available in electronic books.

Library of Congress Cataloging-in-Publication Data

Understanding the stigma of mental illness : theory and interventions/edited by Julio Arboleda-Florez and
   Norman Sartorius.
        p. ; cm.
   Includes bibliographical references and index.
   ISBN: 978-0-470-72328-9 (alk. paper)
   1. Mental illness–Public opinion.   2. Mental illness–Social aspects.   3. Schizophrenia–Public opinion.
4. Schizophrenia–Social aspects.   5. Stigma (Social psychology)   I. Arboleda-Flórez, J. (Julio),
1939– II. Sartorius, N.
   [DNLM: 1. Mental Disorders.   2. Cross-Cultural Comparison.   3. Health Policy.
4. International Cooperation.   5. Prejudice.   6. Stereotyping.   WM 140 U558 2008]
   RC455.2.P85U53   2008
   362.2′6–dc22   2007047643

British Library Cataloguing in Publication Data

A catalogue record for this book is available from the British Library

ISBN: 978-0-470-72328-9

Typeset in 10/12pt Times by Aptara Inc., New Delhi, India
Printed and bound in Great Britain by Antony Rowe Chippenham, Wiltshire
This book is printed on acid-free paper responsibly manufactured from sustainable forestry
in which at least two trees are planted for each one used for paper production.

Cover illustration: Holly Nielson

Contents

List of contributors

Josef Aldenhoff,   Center for Integrative Psychiatry , ZIP gGmbH, Niemannsweg 147, 24105 Kiel, Germany

Matthias Angermeyer,   Centre for Public Mental Health, Untere Zeile 13, 3482 Gösing am Wagram, Austria

Julio Arboleda-Flórez,   Department of Psychiatry, Queen's University, 99 University Avenue, Kingston, ON K7L 3N6, Canada

Anja E. Baumann,   Department of Psychiatry and Psychotherapy, Heinrich-Heine-University, Bergische Landstraβe 2, Düsseldorf 40629, Germany

Romain Beitinger,   BASTA Bündnis für psychisch erkrankte Menschen, Möhlstr. 26, 81675 Munich, Germany

Thomas Bock,   Department of Psychiatry and Psychotherapy, University of Hamburg, Martinistraβe 52, 20246 Hamburg, Germany

Olga Cuenca,   Llorente & Cuenca , Hermanos Bécquer 4, Madrid 28006, Spain

Petra Decker,   Department of Psychiatry and Psychotherapy, LMU University of Munich, Nussbaumstraβe 7, 80336 Munich, Germany

Arno Deister,   Clinic for Psychiatry, Psychotherapy and Psychosomatic Medicine, Robert-Koch-Str. 2, 25524 Itzehoe, Germany

Wolfgang Gaebel,   Department of Psychiatry and Psychotherapy, Heinrich-Heine-University, Bergische Landstraβe 2, Düsseldorf 40629, Germany

Werner Kissling,   Department of Psychiatry and Psychotherapy, Technical University of Munich, Möhlstrasse 26, 81675 Munich, Germany

Michelle Koller,   Department of Community Health and Epidemiology, Queen's University, 2nd Floor, Abramsky Hall, Arch Street, Kingston, ONK7L 3N6, Canada

Bruce G. Link,   Department of Epidemiology, Columbia University, 722 West 168 Street, New York, NY 10032, USA

J. Scott Long,   Department of Sociology, Indiana University, 1020 E. Kirkwood Ave, Bloomington, IN 47405, USA

Juán José López-Ibor,   Psychiatry Department, Faculty of Medicine, Ciudad Universitaria s/n, Madrid, 28040, Spain

María Inés López-Ibor,   Department for Psychiatry and Medical Psychology , Faculty of Medicine, Complutense University of Madrid, Ciudad Universitaria, Madrid, 28040, Spain

Jack K. Martin, Karl F. Schuessler Institute for Social Research, Indiana University, 1022 E. Third St., Bloomington, IN 47405, USA

Roumen Milev, Department of Psychiatry, Queen's University, 99 University Avenue, Kingston, ON K7L 3N6, Canada

Hans-Jürgen Möller, Department of Psychiatry and Psychotherapy, LMU University of Munich, Nussbaumstraße 7, 80336 Munich, Germany

Dieter Naber, Department of Psychiatry and Psychotherapy, University of Hamburg, Martinistraße 52, 20246 Hamburg, Germany

Sigrun Olafsdottir, Dept. of Sociology, Boston University, 96 Cummington St., Boston, MA 02215, USA

Bernice A. Pescosolido, Department of Sociology, Indiana University, 1022 E. Third St., Bloomington, IN 47405, USA

Jo C. Phelan, Department of Sociomedical Sciences, Columbia University, 722 West 168 Street, New York, NY 10032, USA

Manuela Richter-Werling, Irrsinnig Menschliche.V, Verein für Öffentlichkeitsarbeit in der Psychiatrie, Johannisallee 20, 04317 Leipzig, Switzerland

Norman Sartorius, University of Geneva, 14 Chemin Colladon, Geneva 1209, Switzerland

Beate Schulze, Department of General and Social Psychiatry, University of Zurich, Rämistrasse 71, Zurich, CH-8006, Switzerland

Hugh Schulze, c/Change Inc, 1052 W. Fulton Market 2e, Chicago, IL 60607, USA

Heather Stuart, Department of Community Health & Epidemiology, Queen's University, 99 University Avenue, Kingston, ON K7L 3N7, Canada

Alp Üçok, Department of Psychiatry, Faculty of Medicine, Istanbul University, Millet Street , Istanbul 34390, Turkey

Richard Warner, Mental Health Center of Boulder County, 330 17th St., Boulder, CO 80302, USA

Kerstin Wundsam, BASTA Bündnis für psychisch erkrankte Menschen, Möhlstr. 26, 81675 Munich, Germany

Lawrence H. Yang, Department of Epidemiology, Columbia University, 722 West 168th Street, New York, NY 10032, USA

Harald Zäske, Department of Psychiatry and Psychotherapy, Heinrich-Heine-University, Rhineland State Clinics Düsseldorf, Bergische Landstraße 2, 40629 Düsseldorf, Germany

Foreword

The World Health Organization has estimated that 450 million people today suffer from mental or behavioural disorders, or from psychosocial problems such as those related to alcohol and drug abuse. Many of them suffer alone and in silence. Many never receive treatment of any kind. Between them and the prospect of care stand the barriers of stigma, prejudice, shame and exclusion.

In Latin America and the Caribbean, as everywhere else in the world, the burden of mental disorders has become too large to ignore. Current data likely underestimate the numbers of untreated people but even for the acknowledged numbers, there is a wide gap between the need for and provision of mental health care. Changes in the population structure will only widen this treatment gap unless remedial policies can be formulated and implemented.

The World Health Organization and the Pan American Health Organization have issued this emphatic statement: *Mental Health, neglected for far too long, is crucial to the overall well-being of individuals, societies and countries and must be universally regarded in a new light.*

The stigmatizing of, and discrimination against, people with mental disorders is as old as humanity, but there has never before been a Zeitgeist, a moment, a social group, or the political will to focus on finding solutions, such as there is today. This new determination to resolve problems may be related to the realization that mental illness does not respect age, race or socio-economic status and that, in any country, a large proportion of the population will be affected by mental health. Mentally ill people and their families need treatment, social services and enlightened policies to manage their conditions; their needs can no longer be ignored. Moreover, the economic impact of stigmatization upon medical resources, as well as upon absenteeism in the labour force, also demands attention. Researchers, clinicians, policy makers, those affected and their families seem to be of one mind–it is time to find solutions.

That stigma and discrimination exist is not in question. It is known that stigma and discrimination negatively affect the treatment and recovery of people with mental illness. There are moves to combat these but such interventions themselves require evaluation so that we can learn what has an effect and what does not. What need to be more clearly elucidated are ways to measure stigma and discrimination and then ways to determine which treatment strategies are most effective. Scales to measure stigma have to be devised and tailored to measure this social construct among the stigmatizers, which might be the whole of the society, including even the mentally ill themselves (for self-stigma is a major block to recovery). Four intervention methods are commonly recognized – literacy campaigns, protest actions, contact enhancements and political activism to protect the civil and political rights of patients. The impact and effectiveness of these methods need to be evaluated.

This book is utopian in the sense that it has been conceived as a way to start doing more about measuring stigma and discrimination and about intervening to break the cycle of despair that these produce. The book, therefore, is not about what stigma and discrimination are, or their impacts, but about the best ways to measure them and how to reduce them. The book contains theoretical chapters to frame the issue, but most address measurement and interventions. As such, the book is directed at anti-stigma practitioners, researchers and clinicians. It should be a resource for academics and students intent on learning more about these issues and, last but not least, a guide for policy makers and administrators interested in improving the way people with mental illness are managed in clinical settings and in the community. The book is a call to action and a cry for the inclusion of the mentally ill in our society.

I am pleased to present this book to you and to recommend it to the public health community and other members of society involved in this subject. The Pan American Health Organization acknowledges and appreciates the contribution of this distinguished group of experts. I hope that this excellent and useful book will help hasten the urgent changes that are needed in our region.

Dr. Mirta Roses Periago
Director, Pan American Health Organization

Preface

The editors and the majority of those who contributed chapters to this volume worked together for a number of years in the largest ever international programme to combat stigma and discrimination caused by a disease. The programme, initiated as an Institutional Programme of the World Psychiatric Association (WPA) in 1996, assembled teams in some twenty countries, and experts from many more[1] to fight stigmatization and discrimination against schizophrenia sufferers. The programme was highly successful in many of its settings and is still running in a number of the countries originally involved, as well as in others that joined later.

Reflecting these origins, this volume contains two types of chapters: those dealing with theoretical issues (chapters by Arboleda-Flórez, Stuart, B. Schulze, H. Schulze, and Yang and his colleagues), and those reporting on experience from some of the settings of the WPA programme – the chapters by López-Ibor and colleagues, Baumann and colleagues, and Üçok and Warner. Sartorius describes the WPA programme as a whole and summarizes some of the main lessons learned during its first 10 years. One chapter has been contributed by an author who did not participate in the WPA programme – Pescosolido discusses a major investigation of attitudes to people with mental illness, bringing together data from a variety of countries.

In the chapters dealing with theoretical issues, emphasis has been placed on problems of measurement in anti-stigma programmes, starting with an historical overview of measurement approaches. These chapters describe the assessment of the needs which an anti-stigma programme should attempt to address, strategies for evaluating such efforts and the use of advanced information technology in their conduct. Of the chapters reporting country-specific issues, two address an issue that has received insufficient attention in the past – the role of health care staff in stigmatization – while one reviews the way in which a number of centres collaborated in establishing anti-stigma initiatives simultaneously over several locations in Germany.

The main message of the volume is that it is possible to carry out successful programmes against stigma and that a robust collection of interventions has been developed in parallel with the relevant technology of measurement and evaluation. The question today is no longer whether we should fight stigma – we must because stigma remains the main obstacle to any mental health programme – nor even how this should be done. The focus has shifted to the choice to be made, by individuals and societies– to do something about stigma or to close their eyes both to the need to act and to the options for effective intervention that are at their disposal.

The authors and editors hope that this volume will spur individuals and societies to act.

Julio Arboleda-Flórez
Norman Sartorius
December 2007

---

[1] Sartorius N. and Schulze H.: *Reducing the Stigma of Mental Illness - A Report from a Global Programme of the World Health Organization*. Cambridge: Cambridge University Press, 2005

1 The rights of a powerless legion

Julio Arboleda-Flórez

Department of Psychiatry, Queen's University, Kingston, ON K7L 3N6, Canada

Introduction

The most frequent contact the general public has with mental illness is through the media or by direct observation in the busy streets of large cities of derelicts, most of whom are mentally ill. Unfortunately, media portrayals of mental patients usually relate to them as unpredictable, violent and dangerous. The association between mental illness and violence is only one of the many negative stereotypes and prejudicial attitudes held by the public about persons with a mental illness. Direct observation of mentally ill persons in the streets further cements the stereotype that mental illness causes an inevitable downward spiral for those who are affected. These impressions help to perpetuate stigmatizing attitudes against mental conditions and discriminatory practices against mental patients.

Findings of the landmark psychiatric epidemiological study of Stirling County in Nova Scotia, Canada, are described in a classic book entitled *My Name is Legion* [1].[1] This biblical quote [2] is used by many writers and, as used in the Stirling County study, it conveys the large number of those affected. Years after this study and on observing how mental patients are treated, managed or disposed of in many countries, it is obvious that their numbers do not change their plight in society. Despite their numbers, mental patients do not count politically, they are powerless. It is the thrust of this chapter that whereas attitudes such as stigma might be endured, discrimination has to be counteracted; rights have to be fought for.

This chapter contains a historical overview on matters of stigma and includes a review of theoretical elements that lie at the foundations of stigma as a social construct and its negative impacts on patients and their families as well as a dissection of common elements of programmes aimed at combating the stigma of mental illness. The chapter also contains a review on the matter of discrimination which is considered to be the most pernicious aspect of stigma as it impacts on the political and civil rights of mental patients.

Historical elements

Stigma, a tattoo or brand in Greek (from the verb stizein), was a distinguishing mark burned or cut into the flesh of slaves or criminals by the Ancient Greeks so that others would know

---

[1] This is a quote from the Bible relating how Jesus is said to have cast the demons out of a possessed individual. Pigs ate the demons and proceeded to drown themselves in the Sea of Galilee.

Understanding the Stigma of Mental Illness: Theory and Interventions   Edited by Julio Arboleda-Flórez and Norman Sartorius
© 2008 John Wiley & Sons, Ltd

who they were and that they were less valued members of society. Although the Greeks did not use the term 'stigma' in relation to mental illness, stigmatizing attitudes about the illnesses were already apparent in the sense that mental illness was associated with concepts of shame, loss of face, and humiliation [3], as in Sophocles' *Ajax* or in Euripides' *The Madness of Heracles*.

Later, and throughout the Christian world, the word *stigmata* became associated with peculiar marks on individuals re-presenting the wounds of Christ on their bodies, mostly on their palms and soles [4]. This religious connotation is not the same as the other derivative of the Greek word *stigma*, which is a form of social construction to indicate a distinguishing mark of social disgrace that, at the same time, conveys a social identity. The inquisitorial attitude toward witches, as dictated in the *Malleus Maleficarum (The Witches' Hammer)* [5], apart from being highly misogynous, also represents a negative and condemning attitude toward mental illness. This attitude might have been the origin of the stigmatizing attitudes held toward persons with mental illness from the rise of rationalism in the 17th century to the present day in Christian cultures [6]. 'Madness' has long been held among Christians as being a form of punishment inflicted by God on sinners [7].

Recent movements to advance the human rights of mentally ill persons have their genesis in the appalling abuses suffered by generations of mental patients, both before and after the birth of the asylum. Paradoxically, however, the birth of the asylum was in many respects the product of compassion: although the story may be apocryphal, the establishment of the first European asylum for the insane in Valencia in 1409 by Father Gilabert Jofré is said to have been motivated by Jofré's witnessing of the abuse suffered by a mental patient [8]. However, what began as a refuge quickly developed into a prison, and resulted in what Luis Vives in the 16th century was already describing as institutionalized social exclusion [9]. But, as Sebastian Brant pointed out [10], banishment through institutionalization was just a continuation of a more pernicious model of social management prevalent before the advent of the asylum in Valencia. In his *Stultifera Navis (Ship of Fools)* Brant tells us how, before the *Narrenhaus* (madhous), mental patients were condemned to navigate the waters of the rivers of Europe in *Narrenschiffes* that never found a port as they were banished from town to town.

Socio-politically, the asylums replaced the leprosariums. But whereas the latter were exclusively for lepers, asylums became places for all sorts of undesirables, not just those affected by mental conditions: institutions made for their time and aptly described as the 'great confinement' [11]. In fact, the *lettres de cachet* contemplated in the French *Loi sur les aliénés* of 1838 [12] gave the 'hospital archers' (*gardiens de l'Hôpital*) authority to round up and lock up, among others, 'beggars, vagabonds, the chronically unemployed, criminals, rebel politicians, heretics, prostitutes, syphilitics, alcoholics, madmen and idiots'. These orders became the blueprint for similar institutions all over the Western world [13]. The characterization of the mentally ill as 'wild beasts' left no alternative but to put them away [14].

It has been a long struggle for the mentally ill to return from their banishment. Even gestures such as that of Pinel who, imbued with the libertarian ideals of the French Revo-lution, publicly cut the chains that held the mentally ill to their posts at La Saltpêtrière in 1795, have been insufficient, as old and decrepit mental hospitals are still the preferred, and often only, model of care in many countries [15]. And yet, the opposite, allowing patients to return to their communities, has not resulted in meaningful liberation for most persons with mental disabilities. In most countries, even the most advanced and prosperous, men-tal patients are no longer in asylums, but in prisons, which have become veritable mental hospitals [16]. Criminalization of persons with mental disorders is regulated and overseen by courts of law and forensic psychiatrists who, in concert, have become the gatekeepers, or modern-day superintendents [17]. The process of forensic evaluations has become another filter for treatment that keeps mentally ill persons in limbo, ensconced among three seemingly inimical systems – health care, justice and corrections. In the end, the impacts of many forensic evaluations amount to the same reality – loss of liberty in a hospital for the criminally insane or deprivation of liberty in a jail pending legal dispositions. As asked by one commentator, what have the mental patients gained? [18].

Theoretical considerations

Stigma has been thought of as an attribute that is 'deeply discrediting' so that stigmatized persons are regarded as being of less value and 'spoiled' by three different kinds of stigmatizing conditions: 'abominations' of the body, such as physical deformities, 'tribal identities' such as race, sex or religion, and 'blemishes of individual character', such as mental disorders or unemployment [19]. *Stigma,* however, is not a static concept, but a social construction that is linked to values placed on social identities, a process consisting of two fundamental components: the recognition of the differentiating 'mark', and the subsequent devaluation of the bearer [20]. Thus, stigma could be conceived of as a relational construct that is based on attributes, which may change with time and from one culture to another. Stigma develops within a social matrix of relationships and interactions so that new conditions could become stigmatizing and conditions that may be stigmatizing at one time or within a given culture could come to be accepted later so that their bearers stop being stigmatized.

Furthermore, stigma can be understood within a three-dimensional axis involving perspective, identity and reactions. *Perspectives* pertain to the way the stigma is perceived. Stigma is different, whether it be perceived by the person who does the stigmatizing (perceiver) or by the person who is being stigmatized (target). *Identities* relate to group belongingness, and they lie in a continuum from entirely personal to group-based identifications. *Reactions* are the ways the stigmatizer and the stigmatized react to the stigma and its consequences; reactions could be measured at the cognitive (knowledge), affective (feelings, tones and attitudes), and behavioural levels.

Along with these three dimensions it is also important to distinguish three major characteristics of the stigmatizing mark: 'visibility', or how obvious the mark is, 'controllability', which relates to the origin or reason for the mark and whether it is under the control of the bearer, and 'impact' or how much those who do the stigmatizing fear the stigmatized [21]. The more visible the mark, the more it might be perceived to be under the control of the bearer, and the more feared the impact, such as conveying an element of danger, the more pronounced the stigma.

Mental patients who show visible signs of their conditions because their symptoms or the side effects of medications make them appear abnormal, who are socially construed as being weak of character or lazy, and who display threatening behaviours, usually score high on any of these three dimensions. By a process of association and class identity, all mental patients are equally stigmatized; individual patients, regardless of level of impairment or disability, are lumped together into a class; class belongingness reinforces the stigma against the individual.

Unfortunately, a definition of stigma, what it is and how it develops, still leaves unanswered the question of *why* it develops. However, a theory has been advanced although little is known about this, that three major components are required – function, perception and social sharing [22]. An original 'functional impetus' would be accentuated through 'perception', and subsequently consolidated through social 'sharing' of information. The sharing of stigma becomes part of a society that creates, condones and maintains the stigmatizing attitudes and behaviours. These authors further indicate that the most likely candidate for the initial 'functional impetus' is the goal of avoiding threat to the self.

Initial perception of tangible or symbolic threat

↓

Perceptual distortions that amplify group differences

↓

Consensual sharing of threats and perceptions[2]

Tangible threats are 'instrumental' in the sense that they threaten a material or concrete good, while those that are symbolic threaten beliefs, values, ideology or the way in which the group ordains its social, political or spiritual domains.

Cultural perceptions of mental illness consider it as posing a tangible threat to the health of society because it engenders two kinds of fear: the fear of potential immediate physical threat of attack and the fear that we may all share in losing our own sanity. Furthermore, to the extent that mentally ill persons are stereotyped, conceptualized and labelled [23] as lazy, unable to contribute, and hence, a burden to the system, mental illness may also be perceived as posing a symbolic threat to the beliefs and value system shared by members of the group. At a more practical level, the stigma associated with mental illness can also be attributed to the traditionally different venue for treatment for the mentally ill. For whereas persons affected by a physical condition, with the exception of leprosy and tuberculosis, have always been cared for and treated in general hospitals in their own communities, mental patients were for centuries sent away to mental institutions or asylums that were usually situated far away from their communities. The decision to send persons with mental illness to far-away mental hospitals, although well intentioned in its origins, contributed to their dislocation from their communities, and the loss of their community ties, friendships and families. At an academic level, the segregation between the two systems of health also meant the banishment of mental illness and of psychiatry from the general stream of medicine. Psychiatry had no cures to offer and, being away from academic centres led it to stagnation in research and development. The few therapeutic successes, such as the cures for pellagra and for syphilis, were accomplished out of the mental hospitals. Worse, as those conditions ceased to be reasons for mental hospitalization, the idea was reinforced that the patients that remained in the mental hospitals suffering from other mental illnesses were incurable. The lack of effective therapies that influenced most of psychiatric work for centuries not only contributed to the asylum mentality, but was also a result of the academic banishment of psychiatry.

Myths and stigma

Stigma is a negative differentiation attached to some members of society who are affected by some particular condition or state. This negative *attitude* that dictates that those members

---

[2] Adapted from Stangor and Crandall [22], p. 73

be maintained at a distance is related to negative stereotyping and *prejudicial* attitudes that, in turn, lead to *discriminatory* practices. Thus, whereas stigma is an attitude, *discrimination* is behaviour aimed at depriving the stigmatized person of legal rights and legally recognized entitlements. Stigma, prejudice and discrimination are, therefore, inextricably related. Unlike prejudice, however, stigma involves definitions of character and class identification, so it has larger implications and impacts.

Prejudice most often stems from ignorance, or unwillingness to find the truth. For example, a study conducted by the Canadian Mental Health Association [24] found that the most prevalent misconceptions about mental illness included that mental patients were dangerous and violent (88%), that they had a low IQ or were developmentally handicapped (40%), that they could not function, hold a job, or have anything to contribute (32%), that they lacked will power or were weak or lazy (24%), that they were unpredictable (20%), and, finally, that they were to be blamed for their own condition and should just shape up (20%). In a survey among first-year university students in the United States, it was found that almost two-thirds believed that 'multiple personalities' were a common symptom of schizophrenia, and on a different poll conducted among the general public 55% of respondents did not believe that mental illness existed and only 1% acknowledged that mental illness was a major health problem [24]. Some of these myths also surfaced in a study conducted in Calgary, Alberta, Canada, during the pilot study for the World Psychiatric Association (WPA) programme 'Open the Doors'. In this study [25], it was found that respondents believed that persons with schizophrenia could not work in regular jobs (72%), had a split personality (47%), or were dangerous to the public because of violent behaviour (14%). In Africa, conceptions of mental illness are strongly influenced by traditional beliefs in supernatural causes and remedies. Even policy makers frequently hold the opinion that mental illness is often incurable and unresponsive to accepted medical practices [26]. Thus, high levels of knowledge could coexist with high levels of prejudice and negative stereotypes. For while most of the myths about mental illness could be traced down to prejudice and ignorance of these conditions, enlightened knowledge does not necessarily translate into less stigma unless the tangible and symbolic threats that it poses are also eradicated.

Violence and mental illness

An association between mental illness and violence, specifically schizophrenia, although confirmed epidemiologically, remains unclear and seems to flow not so much through direct links of causality, but through a series of confounders and covariates [27]. These facts, however, do not deter the media from their penchant to portray mental patients as unpredictable, violent and dangerous [28, 29]. This portrayal is reinforced by movies in which a popular plot, long exploited by the cinematographic industry, is that of the 'psycho-killer' [30]. Movies about 'mentally ill killers' have been identified by 85.6% of relatives of persons with mental illness as the most important contributor to the stigma of the illness [31]. Movies have not only stigmatized those with mental illness, their negative stereotypes have extended also to psychiatrists who are often portrayed as libidinous lechers, eccentric buffoons, vindictive, repressive agents of society, or evil minded; and in the case of female psychiatrists, as loveless, sexually frustrated and unfulfilled [32]. In fact, the media and movies may just be reflecting on what the public feels and believes about mental illness. This would be hardly surprising when the public is bombarded with factual information of mayhem and gore in horrendous crime committed by an alleged mental patient. At times, the story also mentions that the culprit is suspected to be 'psycho', 'paranoid', 'depressed' or 'schizophrenic'. This type of news, even when reported conscientiously and accurately, arouses fear and apprehension and pushes the public to demand measures to prevent further crimes. Fear is the primary impulse to the development of stigma. The fear of mental illness, and the subsequent stigmatization of those with mental illness, is largely based on fears that they are unpredictable and dangerous. One single case of violence is usually sufficient to counteract whatever gains mental patients have made to be accepted back into the community. Persons with mental illness in general bear the brunt of impact because of the actions of the few. Unfortunately, the media do not inform the public that only a very small minority of mental patients commits serious crimes, or that the percentage of violence that could be attributed to mental illness as a portion of the general violence in the community is also small [33].

Human rights infringements

Outright discriminatory policies ending in abuses of human rights and denial of legal entitlements can often be traced to stigmatizing attitudes, plain ignorance about the facts of mental illness, or lack of appreciation of the needs of persons with mental illness. These policies and abuses are not the preserve of any country in particular.

Modern mental health systems do not depend on mental hospitals, but on psychiatric units in general hospitals and on an array of community mental health agencies. These systems need a different level of discourse on human rights from the discourse attached to institutions. Economic discrimination and the disparities in access to care as well as the systemic, structural violence to which mental patients are subjected in the community are the major issues in modern mental health systems. The human rights discourse has to evolve from over-preoccupation with basic rights to freedom and autonomy to protection of citizen entitlements denied to the mentally ill as a class within the larger social system. The struggle for those who care about them is to gain for them the same rights and entitlements that other citizens enjoy [34].

A distinction must be drawn between negative rights and positive rights or entitlements. International sources of human rights recognize both negative and positive rights. Negative or 'first-generation' rights include those which preclude interference with a protected freedom, and prevent the state from certain proscribed action. Positive or 'second-generation' rights impose mandatory obligations upon states. Although the national systems of many countries, especially democratic ones, provide significant civil and constitutional protections with respect to the negative rights of its citizens, including those who suffer from mental disorders, the same cannot be said with respect to entitlements to the provision of social services [35]. Legal activism in mental health should aim at remedying these shortcomings.

Most legislation that deals with the mentally ill reflects the realities of the past when they were forced to remain in institutions; thus, it focuses on traditional political rights such as liberty, due process, protection against abuses and the authoritarian imposition of treatment [36]. While it is very important to keep these protections in place, in the majority of countries where deinstitutionalization policies have been implemented mental patients are no longer in mental hospitals, but in the community. Most of them do not have access to a bed in any type of hospital. The challenge facing many mental patients is the obverse of what preceded the current model; where systemic abuse and deprivation of freedom constituted the greatest weakness under prior regimes, mental patients in modern models of care face structural and systemic neglect. This neglect has had a profound impact on all mental patients, as an unprotected social underclass. In this regard, the question whether mental patients have gained anything may appear to be rhetorical, but looking at the plight of the mentally ill in the mental health ghettos of any large city, or in the prisons, makes the question practical, obligatory and immediate and one that demands answers from legislators and policy makers and from society in general.

High levels of stigmatizing attitudes among the general public and even among clinicians may be at the base of what Kelly calls 'structural violence', a pernicious and insidious form of discrimination and abuse, the resolution of which is translated into a deprivation of rights [37]. In fact, mental patients seem to have obtained the 'anti-right' to remain homeless on the streets where they might freeze to death on winter nights, to be unemployed, or to be confined to a permanent existence of poverty and charity. On the basis that an existence on the street for lack of proper accommodation increases the risk of victimization, it may be that mental patients are disproportionately robbed, mugged, raped, beaten up or murdered in the streets where they sleep. Should they react violently, many times in self-defence, they are labelled dangerous and sent to prison. Mental patients have in effect been granted the anti-right to be criminalized and to receive treatment, if any, in prisons and penitentiaries, as opposed to hospitals, where most citizens expect to go if they fall ill [38]. The facile manner in which mental patients have been criminalized reinforces the stigmatizing attitudes in society. This has fuelled further fears that they are dangerous and unpredictable, and has led to further calls for expansion of controls via commitment legislation [39, 40]. In turn, the harshness of their existence has a negative impact on their illness as biological, psychological and social elements are in close interplay to reinforce aetiological factors and to maintain disease status.

Unfortunately, mental patients are caught in a tetrad of misfortunes – poverty, disenfranchisement, powerlessness and championlessness – that conspire to make impossible any improvement of their situation.

Mental patients are usually found on the lowest rungs of the socio-economic scale. Mental illness seems practically a synonym for *poverty*. Their illness impacts heavily on their employability as it attacks before many of them achieve their developmental potential, thereby truncating their education and reducing their marketability. To complicate matters, accessing prompt treatment is difficult for young persons. Poor knowledge of the nature and presentation of mental conditions, confusion as to the nature of the symptoms, fear of stigma among family members, lack of financial resources, and a health system that does not provide sufficient treatment options for the young unnecessarily prolong the period between the appearance of the illness and the first opportunity for treatment. For others who become ill later in life, the illness often leads to unemployment and catastrophic loss of income with a rapid fall in the socio-economic scale. Oftentimes, even claiming disability insurance, which has been paid for eventualities of this nature, becomes a nightmare. Insurance companies tend to regard mental health claims suspiciously, curtailing treatment options, and causing the person to incur unnecessary legal costs for experts to redress the injustice.

Politically, mental patients are *disenfranchised*. They have no voice. In some countries, they have no right to vote and in those where they can, because of their mental condition, they find it difficult to enter the electoral registries; many simply have no address and, having no home address, they cannot vote. In comparison with other patient groups, such as those for breast cancer, prostate cancer, AIDS, heart disease, chronic obstructive pulmonary disease (COPD), which are capable of mounting lobbies and carrying out political activism in order to improve their access to better health care, lobbying and political mobilization are hard to organize among the mentally ill. The families of mental patients are themselves affected. Many live in poverty, so that they too have little political influence. *Disenfranchisement* and lack of voice render social problems invisible so that the plight of the mentally ill or their families seldom enters the sphere of political debate. This results in neglect of mental health systems, poor budgetary allocations, inadequate facilities and utter disregard for their social situation.

Powerlessness of the mentally ill often stems from the nature of the symptoms that consume their energies and compromise their ability to participate in social and political activities. Seriously ill mental patients are too preoccupied with their delusions and hallucinations, may be too paranoid to even consider trusting others in any form of group action, too disordered because of manic behaviour, or too depressed to even care, and the chronically ill are too preoccupied with their own conditions and about surviving to be able to mount any concerted political action. Serious mental conditions are incapacitating and disturb the appropriate modulation of affects and behavioural controls. These conditions also alter cognitive processes that are necessary to make sense of complex issues and to express opinions in a coherent fashion, especially if speaking in public, as most political actions require. The mentally ill are not just disenfranchised, they are totally alienated from the political system; they are powerless.

Finally, *championlessness* completes the misfortunes, for besides lacking a political voice of their own, the mentally ill also lack political champions. Even when a leader or advocate surfaces and argues for the mentally ill, the motivating force is not infrequently outrage stemming from a personal situation, for example – oftentimes a close relative has succumbed to mental illness and the champion politician has to face the reality of inadequate services. Unfortunately, fear of negative repercussions in political capital has led politicians to hide the mental illness of their relatives or among themselves. A history of mental illness is a major roadblock to seeking or remaining in public office. In regard to clinicians who often feel that they have to confront the social reality of their patients and who have a duty to advocate for them, if they do, they are seen as self-serving. If they gain political office, they move on to other issues as they do not wish to be typecast as a single-issue politician hammering at something for which there is no political resonance.

Over the past several years, however, states have come to realize the depth and cost of mental health conditions within their populations; this awareness has accelerated the momentum for mental health law reform. Such reforms, however, ought not to be restricted to operational questions on the adequate level of services, nor to the problem of financing, but should include a review of the human rights dimension of such systems. For, while the protection of the human rights of mental patients seems to have become a priority in the international arena, as evinced from the growing body of international law in this area, the actual plight of mental patients does not seem to have improved, and in fact, seems to be getting worse, largely as a result of neglect at the national level

In her 15 January 2005 statement to the Open-Ended Working Group of the UN Commission on Human Rights, the UN High Commissioner for Human Rights underscored the importance of expanding our vision, both nationally and internationally, of the scope of fundamental human rights:

> *Recognizing the status of economic, social and cultural rights as justifiable entitlements is crucial to honouring the political, moral and legal commitments undertaken by States when the international bill of rights was adopted* [41].

Her comments reaffirmed the conception of positive social entitlements as justiciable human rights under international law (as enshrined in such conventions as the *International Convention on Social, Economic and Cultural Rights*) [42] and underscored the failure of states to give meaningful effect to 'second-generation' rights. International law has, in many respects, led the way in advancing the rights of mentally ill persons. This advancement has taken the form of both binding and non-binding international norms, as well as proposals for domestic legislative reform. International law finds its expression in either treaties or customary norms. It is under these treaties that human rights, including a right to health and social services, have figured prominently under international law.

Human rights under international law, however, have made the furthest progress with respect to negative rights (that is, relative to states) than to citizens' entitlements. Thus, the *International Covenant on Civil and Political Rights* (ICCPR) [43] has had a great impact on the promotion of negative rights with respect to persons with disabilities. This covenant, which has been ratified by 151 countries, is among the most important multilateral treaties advancing first-generation human rights. The covenant extends a number of protections to the individual that are particularly relevant to mentally ill persons, in particular, Article 9 which extends rights to individuals with respect to liberty and security of the person, and prohibits state action which arbitrarily restricts those rights [44].

On matters of secondary rights, Article 12 of the *International Covenant on Economic, Social and Cultural Rights* (ICESCR) is perhaps the most significant international source of a 'right to health care' as it enjoins the *States parties to the present Covenant* (to) *recognize the right of everyone to the enjoyment of the highest attainable standard of physical and mental health* (see [43]). Unfortunately, this covenant is subject to the limitation that, in order to be effective for any citizen worldwide, its principles have to be given expression and individually enacted by each country in its national legislation.

Another significant development with respect to the development of positive rights to health care is UN Resolution 46/119, the *Principles for the Protection of Persons with Mental Illness and for the Improvement of Mental Health Care* (the 'MI Principles') [45]. These Principles specifically recognize the positive right of persons with mental illnesses to treatment. For example, Principle 1.1 specifies that *"[a]ll persons have the right to the best available mental health care, which shall be part of the health and social care system'*. Although it may be true that Principle 1.1, and the *MI Principles* generally, may be incapable of grounding any positive rights claim against an individual state, it is nevertheless expressive of a growing international recognition of the importance of positive rights, particularly where the rights of the mentally disabled are concerned.

Notwithstanding the existence of a growing body of international law both prohibiting discrimination and limiting state interference with respect to people with disabilities, as well as positive entitlements with respect to the provision of medical services, it is unclear what practical impact these resolutions have in the domestic sphere. As indicated, implementing negative rights is, in general, not too difficult as derelict states that do not comply are usually identified and even sanctioned, but not so in regard to positive rights whose absence is the most appalling in regard to mental patients. For example, in countries with established economies, health insurance companies openly discriminate against persons who acknowledge that they have had a mental problem [46]. Life insurance companies, as well as income protection insurance policies make a veritable ordeal out of collecting payments due to temporary disability caused by mental conditions such as anxiety or depression. Many patients see their payments denied or their policies discontinued. Government policies sometimes demand that mental patients be registered in special files before pharmacies could dispense needed psychiatric medications. At a larger level, many countries dedicate only a pittance of their health budgets to mental health and most developed countries provide only a modicum of funds from their national research budgets for research into mental conditions [47].

In developing countries, beliefs about the nature of mental conditions, sometimes enmeshed with religious beliefs and cultural determinants, tend to delay needed treatment by penalizing and stigmatizing not only the patients, but also their families, even when they are entitled to access treatment opportunities [26]. Within the Chinese culture, mental illness is highly stigmatizing for the whole family, not just the individual afflicted. The emphasis on collective responsibility leads to the belief that mental illness is a family problem. Thus, Chinese care givers may prefer to cope with mental illness within the context of the family as long as possible. The downside to this approach is unnecessary delays in treatment and worsening of the mental condition [48].

In general, illness and disability due to mental disorders have received little attention from governments in developing countries. Mental health services have been poorly funded and most countries lack formal mental health policies, programmes and action plans. In 1988 and 1990 two resolutions designed to improve mental health were adopted among African countries. However, a survey conducted two years later to follow up on what progress had resulted from these resolutions unfortunately showed disappointing findings [26].

In Uganda, per capita yearly expenditure for mental illness is only US $ 4.00, well below the US $10.00 recommended by the World Bank [49]. In Nigeria, excessive workloads, frequent transfers, responsibility without authority, and other inherently poor management practices are blamed for the poor mental health conditions of employees and the consequences if they happened to complain about their difficulties (50]. In the words of the World Health Organization, mental patients are 'denied citizens' [51].

Three levels of social interaction – stigmatizing attitudes, lack of or failure to implement positive rights, and the tetrad of poverty, disenfranchisement, powerlessness and championlessness – are essential to understand the vacuum that exists between official documents and good intentions of the law against discrimination and the realities in the lives of mentally ill persons in modern-day society.

Consequences of stigma

The stigma of mental illness affects the requirements for care of good quality in mental health, compromising access to care through perceptions among policy makers and the public that persons with mental illness are dangerous, lazy, unreliable and unemployable. Eventually, these attitudes impact on the willingness of authorities to provide proper financial resources for their care so that a vicious circle forms, entrapping the mentally ill person and the family [52].

There may be some controversy about whether what is stigmatized is not the mental condition as such or the mental patient, but the behaviours that they tend to display [53]. On the assumption that objectionable behaviours are part and parcel of the mental condition, this controversy appears Byzantine. Real-life perceptions and patients' estimonials tell a different story about how it feels to have a mental illness.

> Michelle, a vivacious 25-year-old office worker, tells about her major disappointment with her family and family friends who simply expected her to have an abortion when she announced that she was pregnant. They assumed that her schizophrenia would incapacitate her to deliver and to care for her baby. They were also afraid that her

medications could have teratogenic effects on the baby. She carried her baby to term and is taking care of it despite the opposition of family and friends.

Michelle's experience is not uncommon. For many persons with mental illness, the stigma of their illness is worse than the disease and it spreads a cloud over every aspect of their lives and further on the lives of other members of the family.

John, a 19-year-old university student, had to accept the termination of a relationship he had just started with a girl from his neighbourhood. Her parents objected to the relationship and decided to send her to another city for her education, in part in an attempt to break up the relationship, once they knew that John's mother's frequent hospitalizations for the past several years were not due to 'diabetes', but to a manic depressive illness. John described the experience with some resignation, 'it seems as if I have to carry the sins of my parents'.

In the study by the Canadian Mental Health Association quoted above [23], mental patients felt that social and family life (84%), along with employment (78%) and housing (48%), were the areas most commonly affected by stigma. In that survey respondents also felt excluded from the community (22%) and complained that stigma has a negative impact on their self-esteem (20%).

In a survey conducted among members of their own support organization by 'survivors'[3] of mental illness in Thunder Bay, Ontario, Canada [54], housing, employment, and transportation in public buses were described as degrading and outright discriminatory.

'I have to lie to my landlord to get a place to live, like tell him you are on disability, if it is not visible or physical, they don't take you. Even slumlords won't take you because they don't want psychiatrically ill people living in their buildings.'

In this Report, 'survivors' found that 'mental health barriers' among the public often led to stigmatization, prejudice and stereotyping and that they were not listened to, or understood. They also felt ignored, avoided or treated without respect and sensitivity. They reported that these attitudes could also be found during their interactions with social assistance personnel and with clinical staff.

'At the agency the staff talk about patients and how crazy they are. No wonder there is such stigma in the community.'

And another patient commented poignantly about health personnel:

'At the hospital, they take your clothes away. They put you in pyjamas ... it strips away your identity. You know, we are not all crazy. We don't all see the boogieman around the corner. Some of us have legitimate complaints. But if you are always told "oh, you are just overreacting, you know, you don't know what you are talking about" or stuff like that, after a while you start to believe that yeah, maybe I am. And you know, there

---

[3] Some mental patients' self-help support groups in Canada and in other countries have used this term to bring attention to their struggle for a more compassionate mental health system and better social acceptance.

*are some doctors who don't know anything about mental illness and who cannot tell
an oesophagus from an asshole.'*

One newspaperman [55] describes his feelings after a bout of major depression:

*Stigma was, for me, the most agonizing aspect of my disorder. It cost friendships,
career opportunities, and – most importantly – my self-esteem. It wasn't long before I
began internalizing the attitudes of others, viewing myself as a lesser person. Many of
those long days in bed during the depression were spent thinking, 'I'm mentally ill. I'm
a manic-depressive. I'm not the same anymore'. I wondered, desperately, if I would
ever again work, ever again be 'normal'. It was a godawful feeling that contributed
immensely to the suicidal yearnings that invaded my thoughts.*

Strategies to combat the stigma of mental illness

Four strategies have been identified as appropriate to combating stigma and discrimination:
stigma-busting, education, contact and political activism to diminish or stop abuse of civil
and human rights of mental patients.

- *Stigma-busting activities* are usually undertaken by mental patient lobby groups or
  support family groups and aim at identifying and denouncing negative and highly
  stigmatizing portrayals of mental patients in movies and the media. Often, letters
  are written to the media or producers and, on occasions, rallies are mounted in front
  of movie houses to protest. These groups, therefore, should remain vigilant and be
  ready to denounce local or national news, advertisements or movies that stigmatize,
  ridicule or demonize people with mental illness as violent, unpredictable or dangerous.
  No evaluations have been conducted about the effectiveness of these confrontational
  activities, but from the point of view of lending a voice and undertaking political action
  they can be seen as serving a major need for mental patients themselves to let their
  voices be heard.

- *Educational activities* usually take the form of massive national campaigns aimed at
  increasing knowledge in the general population about mental illness, its treatment and
  the prospects for recovery. They can also be aimed at smaller audiences of identified
  stakeholders or groups with influence via pamphlets, conferences, presentations, and
  so on, on the nature of mental illness and the treatments available. National and
  international organizations and associations as well as national and local governments
  have come to appreciate the need to change attitudes toward persons with mental
  illness and to sensitize the public to the notion that mental conditions are no different
  than other conditions in their origin and that diagnosis and treatments are available
  and effective.

  Campaigns like *Changing Minds*, organized by the Royal College of Psychiatrists
  in the UK [56], are based on providing information to the public so as to dispel myths
  and stereotypes about those with mental illness. This campaign has used leaflets,
  pamphlets, films and other ways of mass communication.

  In one well-known film, *1 in 4*, the message is direct and pithy; it emphasizes that
  mental health problems can touch anyone, proclaiming that '1 *in 4 could be your
  Brother, your Sister. Could be your Wife, your Girlfriend... 1 in 4 could be your
  Daughter... 1 in 4 could be me... it could be you!'*

Pamphlets produced for this campaign emphasize messages indicating that social despair and isolation have replaced old methods of physical isolation:

> *For centuries people with mental illness were kept away from the rest of society, sometimes locked up, often in poor conditions, with little or no say in running their lives. Today, negative attitudes lock them out of society more subtly but just as effectively.*

Similarly, a campaign in Australia by the National Mental Health Promotion and Prevention Action Plan [57] through the *Community Awareness Program* (CAP) and the Australasian *Psychiatric Stigma Group* aimed at improving mental health literacy in the population. CAP was a four-year programme liberally funded to increase community awareness of all mental conditions. Specifically, it had three goals: to position mental health on the public agenda, to promote a greater understanding and acceptance of those experiencing mental illness, and to dispel myths and misconceptions about mental illness. The programme had a built-in evaluation based on a benchmark survey and pre-/post-test tracking design. The most significant results include the fact that while tolerant attitudes were consolidated, they did not increase; that there was a slight increase in the awareness of services; and that there was no clear evidence of behaviour change [58]. The Australasian Psychiatric Stigma Group has more modest goals, mostly by linking consumers, providers, and many other interested groups in a public evaluation of the impact of stereotyping and stigma on the lives of psychiatric service-users, their carers, and the lives of providers [59].

SANE Australia is a national charity that helps people affected by mental conditions. One major and famous feature of this group is the popular TV soap opera *Home and Away* in which one storyline is about a young character who develops schizophrenia [60]. SANE has a function similar to NAMI (National Alliance for the Mentally Ill) in the United States [61] and CAMIMH (Canadian Alliance on Mental Illness and Mental Health) [47]. They are all umbrella family groups that lobby for better education, more research funding, and more accessible treatment opportunities for persons with mental illness.

Similar programmes and groups can be found in other countries such as Germany [62], the United States [61] and most recently, in Canada a newly established Mental Health Commission [64] has announced the possibility of mounting a major national campaign and programmes to combat stigma and discrimination. Two international programmes are those of the World Health Organization [65] and the World Psychiatric Association [66].

- *Contact* refers to increased visibility of mental patients among particular audiences in order to convey a sense that they are not always deranged, psychotic or seriously depressed and suicidal, and that they can act as normally as anybody else. Contact and educational strategies are found in the two international programmes. The WHO programme *'Stop exclusion. Dare to care'* follows mostly an educational strategy with elements of legal activism, at local levels and through local organizations. This programme aims at combating stigma and at rallying support for more enlightened and equitable structures for the care of those with mental illness and the acceptance of mental health as a major topic of concern among member states. This programme brings timely information to correct the myths surrounding mental conditions such as the beliefs that they affect only adults in rich countries, that they are not real illnesses but incurable blemishes of character, or that the only alternative would be to lock mental patients in institutions. The programme also invites individuals, families, communities, professionals, scientists, policy makers, the media and NGOs to join forces and to share a vision where individuals recognize the importance of their own mental health; where patients, families and communities will feel sufficiently empowered to act on their own mental health needs; where professionals will not only treat those with mental illness, but will also engage actively in mental health promotion and preventative activities; and where policy makers will plan and devise policies that are more responsive to the needs of the entire population. Methodologies of this programme include the distribution of pamphlets, posters, booklets and stickers, and through the many collateral organizations and distribution channels open to WHO contact with patients and their families.

On its part, the WPA initiated in 1998 its Global Programme against Stigma and Discrimination because of Schizophrenia. Full information on this programme including training modules, and a full annotated bibliography can be found at the site *Open the Doors* (www.openthedoors.com) some attached as appendix to this book. Although circumscribed to schizophrenia, the results of the programme in the different countries where it has been implemented are equally applicable to any other mental condition. The programme was first pilot-tested in Calgary and Alberta, Canada, in 1998, and has now been established in over 27 countries in all continents. This programme targets different audiences according to location, but depends heavily on local action groups that organize themselves to plan and initiate projects that mobilize local resources into action to combat the stigma associated with this disease. Education at a local level is a major element of this programme, but it is possible that contact is its main characteristic as patients and their families are co-participants and active players in all activities. Contact is also encouraged through special programmes such as *Partnership* where mental patients are coached to go to schools or to businesses to speak about their conditions or theatre activities where again mental patients are the actors and perform in front of live audiences.

- *Political activism* includes a systemic and concerted effort to bring to the attention of society and various levels of government the plight of mental patients and to lobby for better access to care and other services while promoting changes in practices, laws or regulations considered discriminatory against mental patients. Political activism forms part of the two international programmes. The WHO programme *Stop exclusion. Dare to care* aims at providing incentives to national governments and health care organizations to change policies and to become actively involved in the reorganization of services and in the development of appropriate mental health policies. The WPA programme *Open the Doors* also has a major political activism component. The programme in Calgary lobbied the National Hospital Accreditation agency to change its best practices requirements regarding management of mental patients at Emergency Departments in general hospitals and has managed through presentations of its members to be active in the Federal Government lobbying for a National Commission on Mental Health.

Conclusions

Empowerment is intrinsic to the mental health of communities. The support and involvement of communities in the development, implementation and organization of their own health structures and programmes has led to the realization at the community level of the impact and the ramifications to health of social scourges such as drug and alcohol abuse, family and social violence, suicide and homicide, and mental illness.

Centuries of prejudice, discrimination and stigma, however, cannot be changed solely through government pronouncements and legislative fiats, important as they are. The successful treatment and community management of mental illness relies heavily on the involvement of many levels of government, social institutions, clinicians, care givers, the public at large, the patients or 'consumers' and their families. Successful community reintegration of mental patients and the acceptance of mental illness as an inescapable fact of our social fabrics can only be achieved when communities take control and become masters of their own mental health structures, programmes, services and organizational arrangements.

There is a need, therefore, to engage the public in a dialogue about the true nature of mental illnesses, their devastating effects on individuals, their families and society in general, and the promises of better treatment and rehabilitation alternatives. An enlightened public working in unison with professional associations and with lobby groups on behalf of persons with mental illness can put pressure on national governments and health care organizations to provide equitable access to treatment and to develop legislation against discrimination. With these tools, communities could then enter into a candid exchange of ideas about what causes stigma and what are the consequences of stigmatizing attitudes in their midst. Only these concerted efforts will, eventually, dispel the indelible mark, the stigma caused by mental illness and the associated discrimination that is the basis for the denial of rights and entitlements to mental patients.

References

1. Leighton, A.H. (1959) *My Name is Legion*, New York: Basic Books.
2. The Bible: Mark 5.9/Luke 8.30 ('*My name is Legion: for we are many*').
3. Simon, B. (1992) Shame, stigma, and mental illness in Ancient Greece. In P.J. Fink and A. Tasman (eds) *Stigma and Mental Illness*. Washington, DC: American Psychiatric Press.
4. The Bible: Paul. Gal 6: 17 ('*I bear on my body the stigmata of Christ*').
5. Kramer, H. and Sprenger, J. (1486) *Malleus Maleficarum*. English translation by M Summers. New York: Dover Publications, 1971.
6. Mora, P. (1992) Stigma during the Medieval and Renaissance periods. In P.J. Fink and A. Tasman (eds) *Stigma and Mental Illness*. Washington DC: American Psychiatric Press, pp. 41–57.
7. Neaman, J.S. (1975) *Suggestion of the Devil: The Origin of Madness*. Garden City, NY: Anchor Books/Doubleday.
8. Pinel, P. (1801) *Tratado Medico-filosófico de la enajenación mental o manía*. Madrid: Editorial Nueva, 1988.
9. Vives, J.L. (1526) *De subventione pauperum – Antología de Textos de Juan Luis Vives* (trans. F. Tortosa). Valencia: Universitat de Valencia, 1980.
10. Brant, S. (1497) *Stultifera Navis*. Website, retrieved 14 December 2005 from www.spamula.net/blog/archives/000429.html.
11. *Loi sur les aliénés* n° 7443 du 30 juin, 1838, J.O., 6 July 1838.
12. Foucault, M. (1988) *Madness and Civilization* (trans. Richard Howard). New York: Vintage Books.
13. Dórner, K. (1969) *Bürger und Irre* (transl. *Ciudadanos y locos*). Madrid: Taurus.
14. Gracia, D. and Lázaro, J. (1992) Historia de la psiquiatría. In J. Ayuso Gutiérrez and L. Carulla (eds) *Manual de Psiquiatría*. Bogotá: Interamericana-McGraw-Hill.
15. Häfner, H. (1991) The concept of mental illness. In A. Seva (ed.) *The European Handbook of Psychiatry and Mental Health*. Barcelona: Editorial Anthropos.
16. Konrad, N. (2002) Prisons as new hospitals. *Curr. Opinion Psychiatry*, **15**, 583–587.
17. Arboleda-Flórez, J. (2005) Forensic psychiatry: two masters, one ethics. *Die Psychiatrie*, **2**, 153–157.

18. Weisstub, D. (1985) Le droit et la psychiatrie dans leur problématique commune. *McGill Law Journal*, **30**, 221–265.
19. Goffman, E. (1963) *Stigma: Notes on the Management of Spoiled Identity*. Englewood Cliffs, NJ: Prentice-Hall.
20. Dovidio, J.F., Major, B. and Crocker, J. (2000) Stigma: introduction and overview. In T.F. Heatherton, R.E. Kleck, M.R. Hebl and J.G. Hull, *The Social Psychology of Stigma*. New York: Guilford Press.
21. Crocker, J., Major, B. and Steele, C. (1998) Social stigma. In D.T. Gilbert, S.T. Fiske and G. Lindzey (eds) *Handbook of Social Psychology* (4th edn., Vol. 2) Boston: McGraw-Hill.
22. Stangor, C. and Crandall, C.S. (2000) Threat and the social construction of stigma. In T.F. Heatherton, R.E. Kleck, M.R. Hebl and J.G. Hull, *The Social Psychology of Stigma*. New York: The Guilford Press, p. 73.
23. Link, B.G. and Phelan, J.C. (2001) Conceptualizing stigma. *Annual Review of Sociology* **27**, 363–385.
24. Canadian Mental Health Association, Ontario Division (1994): *Final Report. Mental Health Anti-Stigma Campaign Public Education Strategy*.
25. Stuart, H. and Arboleda-Flórez, J. (2001) Community attitudes toward people with schizophrenia. *Canadian Journal of Psychiatry*, **46**(3), 55–61.
26. Gureje, O. and Alem, A. (2000) Mental health policy development in africa. *Bulletin of the WHO* 2000, **78**(4), 475–482.
27. Arboleda-Flórez, J. (1998) Mental illness and violence: an epidemiological appraisal of the evidence. *Canadian Journal Psychiatry*, **43**, 989–996.
28. Steadman, H. and Cocozza, J. (1978) Selective reporting and the public misconceptions of the criminally insane. *Publ. Opinion Q.* **41**, 523–533.
29. Rovner, S. (1993) Mental illness on TV. *Washington Post*, 6 July, Sect. A:3.
30. Byrne, P. (1998) Fall and rise of the movie 'psycho-killer'. *Psychiatric Bulletin*, **22**: 174–176.
31. Wahl, O.F. and Harman, C.R. (1989) Family views of stigma. *Schizophrenia Bulletin*, **15**, 131–139.
32. Gabbard, G.O. and Gabbard, K. (1992) Cinematic stereotypes contributing to the stigmatization of psychiatrists. In P.J. Fink and A. Tasman (eds) *Stigma and Mental Illness*. Washington DC: American Psychiatric Press.
33. Monahan, J. (1997) Clinical and actuarial predictions of violence. In D. Faigman, D. Kaye, M. Saks, and H. Sanders (eds) *Modern Scientific Evidence: the Law and Science of Expert Testimony*. Chicago: University of Chicago Press.
34. Farmer, P. (1999) Pathologies of power: rethinking health and human rights. *American Journal of Public Health* **89**(10), 1486–1496.
35. Hirschl, R. (2002) 'Negative' rights vs 'positive' entitlements: a comparative study of judicial interpretations of rights in an emerging neo-liberal economic order. *Human Rights Quarterly*, **22**, 1060–1085.
36. Laing, R. (1971) *Psychiatry and Anti-Psychiatry*. London: Tavistock Publications.
37. Kelly, B.D. (2005) Structural violence and schizophrenia. *Social Science and Medicine*, **61**, 724–730.
38. Arboleda-Flórez, J. and Weisstub, D.N. (1997) Epidemiological research with vulnerable populations. *Acta Psychiatrica Belgica*, **97**, 125–165.
39. Appelbaum, P. (1997) Almost a revolution: an international perspective on the law of involuntary commitment. *Journal of American AcademicPsychiatry Law*, **25**, 135–147.
40. Durham, M. and LaFond, J. (1985) The empirical consequences and policy implications of broadening the statutory criteria for civil commitment. *Yale Law and Policy Review*, **3**, 395–446.
41. Arbour, L. Statement by Ms. Louise Arbour, High Commissioner for Human Rights to the Open-Ended Working Group established by the Commission on Human Rights to consider options regarding the elaboration of an optional protocol to the International Covenant on Economic, Social and Cultural Rights, available online at www.unhchr.ch/huricane/huricane.nsf/0/ECAE2629449C1EBCC1256F8C0035047D?opendocument.
42. United Nations (1966) *International Covenant on Economic, Social and Cultural Rights*, 16 December, 2200A UNTS.
43. United Nations (1966) *International Covenant on Civil and Political Rights*, 19 December, 9999 UNTS 171, arts. 9–14, Can T.S. 1976 No. 47, 6 I.L.M. 368.

44. Gostin, L.O. and Gable, L. (2004) The human rights of persons with mental disabilities: a global perspective on the application of human rights principles to mental health. *Md. L. Rev.* **20**:30–63 *at 34*.

45. United Nations (1991) Principles for the Protection of Persons with Mental Illness and for the Improvement of Mental Health care, GA Res. 46/119, UN GAOR, 46th Sess.,188.

46. Weisstub, D.N. and Arboleda-Flórez, J. (in press) *Canadian Mental Health Rights in an International Perspective. Book to honour Professor Davic C. Thomasma.* London: Elsevier.

47. Canadian Association of Mental Illness and Mental Health (2000) *Building Consensus for a National Action Plan on Mental Illness and Mental Health.* Toronto: CAMIMH Publications.

48. Ryder, A., Bean, G. and Dion, K. (2000) Caregiver responses to symptoms of first-episode psychosis: a comparative study of Chinese and Euro-Canadian families. *Transcultural Psychiatry*, **37**(2), 255–265.

49. *The Monitor* (Kampala) (1998) *Five million Ugandans 'mentally sick'.* 29 October.

50. *Vanguard Daily* (Lagos) (2000) *Don't ask employers to pay attention to workers' mental health.* 11 October.

51. World Health Organization (2007) *Denied Citizens – Mental Health and Human Rights.* Website accessed on 8 September 2007. www.who.int/mental_health/en/

52. Sartorius, N. (1999) One of the last obstacles to better mental health care: the stigma of mental illness. In J. Guimón, W. Fischer and N. Sartorius (eds) *The Image of Madness.* Basel: Karger.

53. Link, B.G., Phelan, J.C., Bresnahan, M., Stueve, A. and Pescosolido, B.A. (1999) Public conceptions of mental illness: labels, causes, dangerousness, and social distance. *American Journal of Public Health* **89**(9), 1328–1333.

54. People Advocating for Change through Empowerment – PACE (1996) *Surviving in Thunder Bay: An Examination of Mental Health Issues.* Thunder Bay, Ontario, Canada.

55. Simmie, S. and Nuñes, J. (2001) *The Last Taboo – A Survival Guide to Mental Health Care in Canada.* Toronto: McClelland & Stewart, pp. 308–309.

56. The Royal College of Psychiatrists – United Kingdom: *Changing Minds* Campaign. Site 102 posted 01/10/2001. www.changingminds.co.ok/whatsnew/pr/pr.

57. Commonwealth Department of Health and Aged Care – Commonwealth of Australia (1999) Australian National Mental Health Strategy – *National Mental Health Promotion and Prevention National Action Plan, under the Second National Mental Health Plan,* 1998–2003.

58. Rosen, A., Walter, G., Casey, D. and Hocking, B. (2000) Combating psychiatric stigma: an overview of contemporary initiatives. *Australasian Psychiatry* **8**(1), 19–26.

59. Mental Health Commission of New Zealand (1998) *Blueprint for Mental Health Services in New Zealand.* Wellington.

60. SANE (1999) SANE's new Helpline. *SANE News*: 10.

61. NAMI (2001) Wilson Boulevard, Arlington, VA, 22201, USA

62. Wölwer, W., Buchkremer, G., Häfner, H., Klosterkötter, J., Maier, W., Möller, H.J. and Gaebel, W. (eds) (2003) German Research Network on Schizophrenia. Bridging the gap between research and care. *European Archives of Psychiatry and Clinical Neuroscience* **253**, 321–329.

63. The Report of the Surgeon General of the United States (1999) Website posted 3/8/2000. www.mentalhealth.about.com/health/mental/health/library/blsurgeon.htm.

64. Government of Canada (2005) Minister Dosanjh announces that the government of Canada will establish a Canadian Mental Health Commission. Website accessed on 8 September 2007 at www.hc-sc.gc.ca/ahc-asc/media/nr-cp/2005/2005_130_e.html.

65. World Health Organization (2000) Mental Health Programme – *Stop exclusion – Dare to care.* Geneva.

66. World Psychiatric Association (2000) Global Programme to Reduce the Stigma and Discrimination because of Schizophrenia, *Open the Doors.* Accessed through site www.openthedoors.com.

2 Cross-Cultural Aspects of the Stigma of Mental illness

Bernice A. Pescosolido[1], Sigrun Olafsdottir[2], Jack K. Martin[1,3] and J. Scott Long[1]

[1] *Department of Sociology, Indiana University, Bloomington, IN 47405, USA*
[2] *Department of Sociology, Boston University, Boston, MA 02215, USA*
[3] *Karl F. Schuessler Institute for Social Research, Indiana University, Bloomington, IN 47405, USA*

Prepared for *Stigma in Mental Health: Interventions to Reduce the Burden*, J. Arboleda-Florez and H. Stuart (eds.) John Wiley & Sons, Ltd. Based on a presentation at the World Psychiatric Association International Congress, October 2006, Istanbul. We acknowledge support from the Fogarty International Center, the National Institute of Mental Health and the Office of Behavioral and Social Science Research, all of the U.S. National Institutes of Health (Grant No.5 R01 TW006374). We also acknowledge financial support for the Icelandic data from the Icelandic Centre for Research and the University of Iceland.

Introduction

As noted in *Healthy People* 2010 [1], a striking finding of the landmark Global Burden of Disease Study [2] lies in the world-wide impact of mental illness on overall health and productivity. Profoundly under-recognized, mental illness constitutes 11% of the global burden of disease, with major depression alone currently ranking fourth and expected to rise to second by 2020. In some regions of the world (e.g., Western Pacific), mental disorders already represent the largest contributor to the total disease burden, and there is great concern with the "mortality crisis" related to mental illness in Eastern Europe [3].

In the face of these concerns, the World Health Organization's (WHO) International Pilot Study of Schizophrenia (IPSoS), the International Study of Schizophrenia (ISoS) and the Study of the Determinants of Outcomes of Severe Mental Disorders (DOSMD) have all documented enormous heterogeneity in the outcomes of mental illness within and across countries [4–7]. While it is generally agreed that the reasons for these differences are "far from clear" [5], one predominant explanation revolves around culturally defined processes. Scholars and policymakers alike suggest that stigma may be the reason behind such findings and lies at the root of recovery from mental illness [8]. As such, understanding the cultural contexts that facilitate good outcomes may offer a lever for stigma reduction. In particular, whether individuals and others around them recognize mental illness, stigmatize these conditions and support seeking care is critical, since each represent key aspects of culture that can influence the outcome of mental illness [9,10].

Not surprisingly, there have been calls for systematic, comparable studies of stigma within and across social and cultural contexts in order to understand its origins, meanings and consequences [3, 4, 11–13]. Despite these calls and findings that document the pervasive existence and impact of stigma in different countries [14–18], we know relatively little about the cross-cultural distribution of stigma. Researchers across the globe have collected data on stigma, but differences in samples (often student or provider samples) and instrumentation make it difficult, if not impossible, to compare findings. Thus, questions about whether and how the social reaction to mental illness varies across countries, whether the underlying operative processes are similar, and whether it maps onto the distribution of outcome heterogeneity remain unanswered. Not surprisingly, then, the important question of whether these differences can offer a wedge into decreasing stigma's negative impacts, also remains unanswered.

In sum, while the influence of cultural context on health and well-being is widely acknowledged, the empirical literature on the cross cultural nature of stigma remains underdeveloped [19]. The World Psychiatric Association's (WPA) Global Programme Against Stigma and Discrimination Because of Schizophrenia [20] has encouraged the development of a comparative catalogue of information and, to date there have been only a few large-scale studies (e.g., in Canada, the U.K., the U.S. and Germany). Even recent cross-national efforts, while springing from and being influenced by the WPA initiative, have not been linked in practice, making inference about comparative influences difficult. Moreover, there has never been, to our knowledge, a methodologically coordinated attempt to understand the extent to which mental illness is understood and stigmatized across countries (e.g., as an exception, see [21] for a comparison of the attitudes of German and U.S. high school students and mental health staff).

To answer this call and begin to explore the insights that differences across societies might offer to combat the stigma of mental illness, the Stigma in Global Context – Mental Health Study (SGC-MHS) was launched with the support of the U.S. National Institutes of Health (through the Fogarty International Center in collaboration with the National Institute of Mental Health and the Office of Behavioral and Social Science Research) and the Icelandic Centre for Research. The SGC-MHS is a theoretically based and methodologically coordinated collaborative study of the levels and correlates of the stigma of major depression and schizophrenia in 15 nations around the world.

Our goal here is to introduce the SGC-MHS by presenting early results from five European countries (Bulgaria, Germany, Hungary, Iceland, and Spain), focusing on three issues closely related to recovery – work, marriage and community acceptance. Since the ISoS found that the greatest differences in recovery across countries align with a nation's level of development, the descriptive findings presented here may offer a conservative view of cross-national variation. By focusing on one continent, albeit with countries with varying GDPs and political and health care systems, this first exploration provides only an indicator of the potential for comparative analyses to assist the development of stigma-reduction efforts.

We begin by reviewing what we know about stigma from the wide range of studies that have been done. We then focus on studies of the outcomes of mental illness, first targeting the shift in emphasis from symptoms to "recovery" in its current usage, and then laying out arguments that have been made about the role of stigma in understanding outcomes. A brief description of WHO efforts on outcomes and some conclusions that appear in the scientific literature follows. After providing the background orientation for the SGC-MHS, we lay out the design and methods for the study and present descriptive findings on Europe as outlined above. We conclude by discussing the next steps for the SGC-MHS and its implications for stigma reduction.

Taking Stock: Stigma in Cross-Cultural and Historical Frames

Stigma is an attribute that marks a person as tainted, calls their identity into question, and allows them to be devalued, compromised, and considered "less than fully human" [22, 23]. Thus, stigma deprives people of their dignity, challenges their humanity, and interferes with their full participation in society [24]. Fabrega [15] describes the pervasiveness of stigma historically and cross-culturally, and empirical studies reveal both the similarities across countries and changes over time. Importantly, the focus of the impact of stigma has broadened as research has continued, and as "recovery" has become the primary goal for practitioners, consumers, and advocacy groups. As Ware and colleagues have noted, too often persons with mental illness are "in the community, but not of it." To increase social integration, they argue that both professionals and policymakers should focus on "connectedness" and "citizenship" [25, p. 469].

Below, we describe the widening concerns, the range of cross-national findings, and what we have begun to learn about large-scale changes in stigma.

Domains and Domain Shifts in the Study of the Outcomes of Mental Illness

Etiological issues aside, earlier work from the medical sciences focused on basic issues related to the "success" of the treatment of mental illness. Symptom reduction, rehospitalization, mortality, and debates about the course of diseases such as schizophrenia [26, 27] dominated the research discourse in psychiatry, psychology and mental health services research. Goffman's 1963 classic work [28] put stigma at the forefront of most social science discussions of the outcomes of mental illness and received at least a passing mention in most other research. Social scientists, including those in public health, tended to focus more intensely on broader, community-based issues including lower quality of life, well-being, marriage and work possibilities, persistent social stress and low self-esteem [29–34].

However, with deinstitutionalization, the shift to community-based care, and growing calls for multidisciplinary work, outcome studies have become more integrated, inclusive, and multi-faceted, documenting the profound effects of stigma, including interference with the process of recovery [18, 35], the loss of legal rights [36], and discrimination, even among practitioners in both the general and mental health system [37, 38]. Researchers documented distressingly poor outcomes for mental illness cross-nationally. In Hong Kong, Mak and Gow [39] found former psychiatric patients living in deprived conditions regarding housing and social life, and reported that the lives of these people existed on the margins of society [31] in Austria; also [40] in Canada). In Singapore, former patients reported that stigma affected their self-esteem, relationships and job opportunities [41]. In Israel [42] and Australia [43], stigma resulted in an avoidance of mental health services [43]. Finally, these studies, as well as one from Nigeria, reported a greater social and medical vulnerability of persons with mental illness, compared to individuals with coronary disease, tuberculosis or cancer [44].

Only recently have we begun to get a picture of the larger, temporal dynamics of stigma. Pioneering survey work, begun in the U.S. in the 1950s [45–48] and continued in the decades that followed, documented both the lack of understanding of mental illness, negative attitudes surrounding issues of cause, treatment and outcome, and a high level of public sentiment that favored the social rejection of persons with mental illness [21, 49–52]. However, innovations in treatment, advances in scientific knowledge, shifts in the locus and philosophy of treatment, and growth of a consumer advocacy movement shaped professional perceptions of stigma, and were often hailed as decreasing community-based stigma. Yet, such conclusions were based, almost exclusively, on personal observation and anecdotal evidence ([53–58]; see [59] for a review).

In the 1990s, researchers took up the challenge of collecting contemporary evidence, and where possible, matching it to data from the past. This growing body of empirical studies gives cause for both hope and despair. Several high-quality, representative regional and national studies report remarkably consistent findings, at least in Western nations. They indicate that the American, British, Irish and Canadian publics display a high level of acceptance of scientific advances marking biological and genetic causes of mental health problems; an acknowledgement of, and differential response to types of mental health and substance abuse problems (e.g., depression, schizophrenia, addictions); and a recognition of the existence of (and support for) effective treatments [14, 16, 17, 60]. Contact with persons with mental health problems was broadly in evidence. About half of those studied across surveys reported knowing someone with a mental health problem or someone who had used services or received some kind of treatment. In fact, in the American case, the MacArthur study was able to mark a real increase in public sophistication and knowledge of these matters over the last 40 years [59, 61, 62].

Coupled with these positive findings, other data revealed a darker side to cultural changes. A majority of the American and Canadian publics reported an unwillingness to work alongside or have intimate connections with persons with mental illness [17, 61, 63]. Many also agreed with images of persons with mental illness as unpredictable and dangerous. For example, in the U.S., where comparable data over time were available, Phelan et al. [59] reported an actual doubling, since the 1950's, in spontaneous mentions of violence as descriptive of persons with mental illness. Further, a majority of respondents appeared to be quite willing to use legal means to coerce individuals into a range of treatments (e.g. doctors, clinics, hospitals), with near unanimous support for this approach when persons, despite the description of their problems, were labeled as "dangerous to themselves or others" [64].

Similarly, studies in other countries that targeted shorter time frames also reported mixed findings. In Hong Kong, public concerns decreased and knowledge of mental illness increased, but attitudes toward persons who had been treated in the mental health system had become slightly more negative [65]. In Canada, Brockman and D'Arcy's [66] restudy of the classic Cumming and Cumming study [47] found only slight improvements. In Greece, among a very select sample, Lyketsos and colleagues [67] found little change over a 2-year period. However, Paykel et al. [68] found significant and positive changes regarding public attitudes toward depression in Great Britain from 1992 to 1996. In sum, this body of existing research shows deep and widespread negative attributes, reactions, and affect toward people with mental illness, together with increasing sophistication regarding causes and treatment.

In tandem with these research efforts, a set of clinically-based studies of the treated population of persons with schizophrenia and other serious mental illnesses has raised intriguing questions about stigma and its influence on outcomes. We turn to these studies.

Stigma and the International Study of Schizophrenia: The Paradox of Development

Technically, the WHO's efforts to study schizophrenia represent a sustained research agenda which began in the late 1960s and has spanned 30 research sites in 19 countries. According to Hopper and his colleagues [69], the initial effort, the International Pilot Study of Schizophrenia (IPSS), helped establish the feasibility of such large scale studies while the second, the Determinants of Outcomes of Severe Mental Disorder (DOSMeD) replicated the initial IPSS finding that individuals who had more positive outcomes were likely to be found in those countries crudely classified as "developing". Further, the most recent study, the ISoS, attempted to follow-up on this striking finding while correcting, where possible, for earlier methodological limitations which hindered claims of generalizability. Like the studies that came before, the ISoS continued to document better outcomes for those outside of the "developed" world [6].

Given that a country's participation in these studies is voluntary and unfunded through a central source, the range and depth of these studies is truly impressive. That said, even with the ISoS, the set of sites involved is neither representative of existing countries nor large in number. What becomes remarkable in the face of limitations is the robustness of the finding noted above: Individuals who have been diagnosed as having schizophrenia or other serious mental illnesses appear to report better outcomes if they live in regions of the world considered to be "developing," rather than those considered to be "developed." Although social scientists have been increasingly skeptical of this particular conceptual distinction, the finding that individuals in Latin America, Africa or Asia seem to "do better" than those who live in the United States or Western Europe has been called "durable" [4, p. 836] and "the single most important finding" in comparative mental health services research [70].

To evaluate this finding in the context of the strengths and limits of the studies, Hopper and Wanderling [4] have provided the most thorough consideration and analysis of the developed-developing difference in the ISoS. Following up on the initial findings with data 13 years later and with two additional samples, they find that the outcomes of illness trajectories for study participants continue to favor the developing world. They go further to assess specific sources of potential bias including differences in follow-up methods, the grouping of data, ambiguities in diagnosis, selective outcome measures, and sociodemographic differences (i.e., gender, age) among the study participants. Finding that none of these can explain the differences in illness course and outcomes, they suggest that further research needs to focus on "the cultural", including "auspicious or alternative beliefs" [4, p. 843].

While Hopper and Wanderling are clear about the complexity of what "culture" means to the entire course of an illness and the illness career it shapes, they nonetheless suggest that it is the local context that matters. And, while they are skeptical about the ability of structured questionnaires to get at the "local", particularly everyday experiences, we believe that such approaches can at least explore, if not capture, the local cultural context of attitudes, beliefs, hopes and fears that surround the onset, recognition and response to mental illness. Such aspects of the non-material culture, according to the "new" sociology of culture, represent tools in a cultural toolkit that individuals can draw from as necessary to face life situations [71, 72]. This toolkit, shaped by the larger cultural climate, holds the resources that individuals, their families and others in the community use to understand the experience of mental illness; categorize problems, prospects and sources of care, and make decisions about their own behavior and, often, that of others [73, 74].

In sum, whether these beliefs, attitudes and opinions reveal concern, fear, or treatment efficacy, they reflect the prejudice and the potential for discrimination which fits our common understanding of the stigma that surrounds mental illness. The SGC-MHS was designed to take advantage of the opportunity to examine cross-national variation in cultural context and begin to calibrate how this one aspect of culture aligns with or contradicts our concerns about the differences in outcomes. In the next section, before we describe the specifics of the SGC-MHS, we discuss how the WHO paradox, coupled with other theoretical and empirical work on stigma and outcomes, motivated the specific study goals.

The Cultural Context of Stigma: How Do Countries Differ?

In the previous section, we brought together existing evidence of the breadth and depth of stigma across countries and provocative cross-national findings in what empirical work exists. Thus, while stigma is seen as "cross culturally ubiquitous" [24, 75], the earliest work [28] to the most recent [15, 24] conceptualizes stigma as a phenomenon shaped by cultural and historical forces. Early on, anthropologists described the different ways that cultures shape how individuals with mental illness are viewed and treated (e.g., [21, 76]). More recently, Lefley [77] contends that chronicity, itself, is a cultural artifact based, at least in part, on differing worldviews, religious traditions, the role of alternative healing systems, and differences in the cultural value of interdependence.

Even studies that have documented differences in outcomes for persons with mental illness across countries point to and call for further investigations across cultural contexts (see also [12, 24]). They suggest that future research must identify the collective properties of social, cultural, economic and physical environments that influence health and disease outcomes. And, the sheer range of differences that Lefley [77] describes above can be enormous. For example, Sartorius [78] reports that the ratio of psychiatrists to the population ranges from 1:1,000-5,000 in the more developed societies (e.g., Europe) to 1: 50,000-100,000 in the developing world to only 1:5,000,000 in some African countries. Of course, this is not independent of the availability of economic capital in a society which needs to be considered as well. For example, the WHO reports that countries in the Western Pacific Region devote less than 5% of their small health budgets to mental health and neurological disorders [79, p. 121]. Thus, existing research suggests that we need to examine cross-cultural issues directly, rather than making assumptions about their correlation with broad categories.

Even under the best designs, the ability to examine all of these issues fully is limited by funding and by the willingness and ability of researchers in different countries to mount a study to provide information about cross-national differences. Indeed, the existence of sufficient research infrastructure to mount such research reflects both happenstance (e.g., whether any individuals were trained in survey research methodology), and the existing resources of a country that enable a national-level study. Thus, as we undertook the SGC-MHS, we sought to focus on coverage, comparability, and representativeness. We describe the end result next.

The Stigma in Global Context – Mental Health Study: Foundations

The SGC-MHS basic questions are, at base, descriptive: Do people's attitudes, beliefs and behavioral predispositions vary in response to descriptions of persons with symptoms/

behaviors that meet criteria for two major mental illnesses – schizophrenia and depression? And if so, how do they vary? The study does not target only conventional measures of stigma, per se, but seeks to understand what cross-national differences exist across a number of cultural factors that may play a role in shaping the response to mental illness. These include the profiles/levels of knowledge of mental illness, assessments of severity, recognition of and attribution for the profiles provided, the degree of prior contact with persons with mental illness, stigmatizing responses such as negative characterizations (e.g., dangerousness, long term negative impact) or rejection (e.g., a desire for social distance), and evaluations of the need for and utility of treatment, including specific provider types (e.g., "doctors", psychiatrists).

At this writing, we are still in the field for many countries. So, we focus on our basic question with a broad-brush, inductive look at one continent, Europe. However, even with this preliminary look, we pay attention to the findings of the WHO studies: Does it appear, even at this point, that countries with higher levels of economic capital vary systematically in public attitudes toward mental illness?

The Design of the SGC-MH Project

Critical to a sound cross-national study is the assurance that, to the degree possible, each country will approach the collection of data in the same way, both logistically and culturally. To help ensure this, the SGC-MHS was based on an existing infrastructure with a history of cross-national collaboration and strict rules for the data collection of their own projects. The "platform" for the SGC-MHS is *The International Social Survey Program* (ISSP). The ISSP is an on-going, annual program of cross-national collaboration that brings together an international cadre of leading social scientists and expert survey researchers.

The SGC-MH study is not a part of the standard ISSP research program which involves modules developed and approved by the participants. Rather, we used the ISSP as an organizing platform to ensure the collection of high quality data, to select survey organizations with an established record of routine and successful cross-national collaboration, and to ensure a set of agreed-upon principles relative to sampling, data collection procedures, fielding guidelines, codebook construction, data sharing, and archiving.

We established a translation procedure which began with ISSP standard approaches but was supplemented with an in-house "cultural" review with a native speaker who was asked to give an oral translation of the target language instrument without having seen the original English language instrument. This allowed both an extra eye to culturally relevant language usage that enabled us to correct poorly worded items caused by too literal translation, and an opportunity to ask people from that country questions about local idioms, the nature of the mental health treatment system, and their perceptions about cultural differences that could potentially affect data collection. These individuals were not experts in the field of mental health and illness, nor were they professional translators; rather the primary criteria were fluency in both English and the target language, and cultural fluency gained from recent experience living in that country. With the information gathered during these sessions, which averaged in length from 3 to 4 hours, we returned to each country's survey team with a set of questions, suggestions and concerns to negotiate a final instrument that was tailored for naturalness while maintaining the meaning necessary for comparability across countries.

Sampling and Fielding

Eligible respondents were non-institutionalized adults (i.e., eighteen years of age or older). Individuals who resided in institutional settings (e.g., hospitals, prisons, etc.) were not included in the sample frame. The selection of sample elements across all national cross-sections was based on multi-stage probability methods. Within each nation, sample weights were computed to offset any potential biases; however, analyses of the weighted and unweighted data revealed few systematic differences. Therefore, we utilize the unweighted data, unless otherwise indicated.

The complexity of the vignette strategy required face-to-face personal interviews conducted by trained interviewers. In line with ISSP procedures, all field data collection efforts were closely monitored by survey center employees who also served as liaisons to the SGC-MH team for translation, data coding and preparation and delivery of the data file.

Interview Schedule

The SGC-MH interview schedule consisted of two parts. The first 15 minutes tapped substantive issues related to the stigma of mental illness, with reference to the vignette person and more generally with regard to mental illness. These questions were asked in a single block, and in identical order for each country. The second part of the interview schedule consisted of an agreed upon set of background variables that have been tailored to each nation by the ISSP. The Zentralarchiv (the ISSP designated Archive in Germany; www.issp.org) holds a volume describing these background and socio-demographic variables which provide the basis for a comparable, but tailored, approach. To respond to specific theoretical, ethical, or cultural issues, any individual question was omitted after negotiation between the SGC-MHS team and survey center liaisons.

Vignettes

As discussed earlier, much of the SGC-MHS instrument involved assessing respondents' reactions to and evaluations of the individual described in the hypothetical scenario. These vignettes described a person meeting criteria for a DSM-IV diagnosis of major depression, schizophrenia, or a physical health problem – in this case, asthma. Within vignettes, the individual's race or ethnicity and gender were randomly assigned. Previous research suggests that this strategy avoids the problem of identifying and labeling a "case" for the respondent as someone who is "mentally ill", and allows for better data collection on issues of knowledge and labeling [63]. In the current study we relied on two such unlabelled mental health vignettes (schizophrenia and major depression), and one physical health problem (asthma). Wording for the mental health problem vignettes was evaluated for accuracy by members of the nation-specific research teams and an international psychiatrist. Vignettes were randomly assigned to respondents.

Unlike the ISSP where non-literal translations are discouraged, and in addition to the second step cultural translation described above [82], the instrument was culturally tailored on two distinct issues. First, the SGC-MHS is primarily vignette-based, describing (but not categorizing) a person who meets clinical criteria for schizophrenia or depression. The vignettes were initially developed in accordance with the DSM-IV but were revised for cross-cultural applicability by the group of survey research experts leading each country's effort in an early international meeting in Madrid in 2004. Indeed, even the selection of which disorders to include was decided during the Madrid meeting. The vignettes were examined; rewritten for cultural applicability by a psychiatrist who had been involved in the WHO studies; and approved by the larger group. Second, the labels applied in the interview schedule were modified to include and/or substitute culturally relevant idioms (see below for a description of the vignette strategy). In addition, the list of "providers," particularly regarding traditional or indigenous healers, was matched to parameters of the local formal and informal health care systems in each country.

The Present Analysis

For the analyses we present here, data came from 5 European countries and were collected by five survey organizations: 1) The Agency for Social Analysis, Sofia (Bulgaria); 2) Zentrum für Umfragen, Methoden und Analysen (ZUMA), Mannheim (Germany); 3) TARKI, Social Research Center, Budapest (Hungary); 4) Félagsvísindastofnun, Reykjavik (Iceland); and 5) Analisis Sociologicos, Economicos Y Politicos, S.A. Madrid (Spain). The sampling procedures described earlier yielded samples of 1,121 respondents in Bulgaria, 1,255 respondents in Germany, 1,252 respondents in Hungary, 1,033 respondents in Iceland, and 1,206 respondents in Spain. Thus, the combined five nation sample we examine here is comprised of 5,867 respondents. Also, for the purposes of the current study, we only examined responses to the mental illness vignettes (i.e., major depression and schizophrenia). Thus, by eliminating respondents who received the asthma vignette, we reduced the nation-specific sample sizes by roughly one-third. The resultant samples that provide the data for our subsequent analyses are comprised of 764 respondents in Bulgaria, 847 in Germany, 840 in Hungary, in 673 for Iceland, and 847 in Spain. Thus, the total effective sample for the analyses reported here is comprised of 3,971 respondents, and includes only those who were asked to assess the depression and schizophrenia vignettes.

Measures: Stigmatizing Attitudes

In the analysis presented here, our dependent variables were cross-national public endorsements of stigmatizing attitudes toward persons with mental illness across three venues important for recovery: the community, the workplace, and the family. Each dimension is captured by a single-item, coded such that higher scores on each item indicated the endorsement of more stigmatizing sentiments. First, *community stigma* was tapped by the question, "A person like NAME has little or no hope of being accepted as a member of his/her community", coded 1=strongly agree, 2=agree, 3=disagree, 4=strongly disagree. Second, *workplace stigma* was measured by the question, "If a person like NAME is qualified for a job, he or she should be hired like any other person", also coded 1=strongly agree, 2=agree, 3=disagree, 4=strongly disagree. Third, *relational/family stigma* was indexed by the question, "How willing would you be to have NAME marry someone related to you?", coded as 1=definitely willing, 2=probably willing, 3=probably unwilling, 4=definitely unwilling.

Results: What are the Levels of Stigma Across Five European Nations?

The presentation of our analysis proceeds in two steps. First, we examine the distribution on levels of the endorsement of the three stigmatizing attitudes for depression and schizophrenia combined, and by condition, without regard to nation. Second, we examine the distributions for each condition for the five European nations individually.

Stigma in Europe

Table 2.1 displays the percentage of respondents residing in five European nations who endorsed stigmatizing attitudes relative to the hiring, community acceptance, and marriage of persons described with behaviors meeting DSM-IV criteria for depression and schizophrenia. Several notable patterns emerge from these data. First, without regard to nation, over half of respondents (56.4%) report being unwilling to have a person with depression or schizophrenia marry into his or her family, and more than a third (33.7%) believe that persons with depression or schizophrenia have little hope of being accepted in their respective communities. However, respondents report lower levels of rejection with respect to the workplace. Overall, only about 1 in 5 respondents (23.5%) reported that a qualified person with a mental health problem should not be hired.

The data in Table 2.1 also reveal a pattern reported in previous studies of public preferences for social distance from persons with mental health problems (see, for example, [63]) that suggest that the public clearly distinguishes between persons described with symptoms of depressive disorders or schizophrenia. Regardless of the interactional venue (i.e., community, work, or family [marriage]), across the board, respondents in our five European nations are significantly more likely to report rejection of a person with schizophrenia, relative to a person with depression.

Table 2.1 Distributions on Stigma Attitudes for Five European Nations

	Combined		Depression		Schizophrenia	
	%	N	%	N	%	N
Don't Hire, Even if Qualified						
Strongly Agree	5.0	183	4.3	80	5.8	103
Agree	18.5	674	15.2	285	21.9	389
Disagree	54.4	1,985	56.9	1,065	51.7	920
Strongly Disagree	22.2	810	23.6	442	20.7	368
N		3,652		1,872		1,780
Unlikely to Be Accepted in Community						
Strongly Agree	4.6	171	4.2	78	5.1	93
Agree	29.1	1,079	24.7	465	33.6	614
Disagree	47.6	1,769	48.7	325	46.6	852
Strongly Disagree	18.7	692	22.5	422	14.8	270
N		3,709		1,880		1,829
Willingness to Have Marry Into Family						
Definitely Unwilling	27.2	963	23.0	408	31.4	555
Probably Unwilling	29.2	1,032	26.4	469	31.9	563
Probably Willing	31.0	1,096	35.4	628	26.5	468
Definitely Willing	12.7	448	15.2	269	10.1	179
N		3,539		1,774		1,765

Stigma Differences Across Europe

Table 2.2 reports the percentage of respondents, by country, who endorsed stigmatizing attitudes with regard to depression and schizophrenia for the same three items. For the most part these nation-specific estimates mirror the patterns observed in Table 2.1. Specifically, in each nation, regardless of the interactional venue (i.e., work, community, or family), respondents are more likely to prefer social distance from a person described as having symptoms of schizophrenia when compared to a person described as meeting criteria for depression. Also as before, regardless of nation or disorder type, the lowest levels of rejection are observed in the workplace setting, with higher levels of rejection reported in community and family settings.

However, the findings suggest that there are distinctions that can be drawn between the proportions of respondents in the five nations who are likely to endorse stigmatizing responses. Indeed, for each social venue and both disorder types, the proportion of stigma-tizing attitudes differs significantly across the five nations. One the one hand, the highest levels of rejection are reported by respondents from the two Eastern European nations (i.e., Bulgaria and Hungary) and Spain. On the other hand, respondents in both Germany and Iceland report substantially lower levels of rejection. More specifically, almost one third to one half of the respondents in Bulgaria, Hungary and Spain believe that the individual de-scribed with schizophrenia should not be hired, compared to only 10 to 20 percent of those in Iceland and Germany, respectively. A similar pattern, although with fewer individuals

Table 2.2   Percentage of Respondents Endorsing Stigmatizing Attitudes With Regard To Depression and Schizophrenia Across Five European Nations Arranged by Level of Development (GDP per capita, low to high)

	Depression %	Schizophrenia %
Don't Hire, Even if Qualified		
(Strongly Agree/Agree, combined)		
Bulgaria	17.6	32.5
Hungary	26.1	31.7
Spain	29.8	43.1
Germany	13.1	20.6
Iceland	8.1	10.0
Unlikely to Be Accepted in Community		
(Strongly Agree/Agree, combined)		
Bulgaria	35.2	49.0
Hungary	26.3	36.1
Spain	30.4	40.2
Germany	34.1	45.6
Iceland	17.6	23.0
Willingness to Have Marry Into Family		
(Definitely/Probably Unwilling, combined)		
Bulgaria	56.4	73.7
Hungary	61.6	70.6
Spain	47.2	67.4
Germany	46.8	54.9
Iceland	38.0	50.2

expressing rejection, is reported for those who received the depression vignette. The percentage endorsing social distance is generally higher for acceptance in the community and even more so for marriage; but even here, one country stands out. In Spain, about 43% of respondents indicated an unwillingness to see individuals described with schizophrenia to be hired; about 30% express similar concerns about those described with depression. So, while the pattern is not exactly the same across all venues and across the disorders, there are clear national differences, with Icelanders always anchoring the bottom. Here, the lowest proportion of respondents endorses stigmatizing responses.

Discussion: Preliminary Insights and Next Steps

As Link and Phelan [85] point out, stigma matters for public health because it is a social cause of disease which compromises a person's ability to cope with mental illness, produces stress, and exposes them to other disease-producing conditions. The disadvantages with regard to power, prestige and social connections translate into the possibility that individuals with mental illness will have restricted life styles and life chances, including but not limited to social relationships, community living options, and citizenship rights [86].

The SGC-MHS was designed to follow up on insights of the WHO studies which suggested that a lever for stigma reduction might be found in understanding whether there are places across the globe offering more auspicious settings for recovery from the challenges of mental illness. Are there cultures which can be characterized as less stigmatizing, that is, offering more community inclusion and less rejection across critical arenas of life? The early picture that we report here from five European countries offers both encouragement for cross-national differences but greater complexity than suggested by the original WHO studies. That is, we do find overarching differences, both by disorder and by country. In general, respondents report more stigma regarding schizophrenia than for depression.

Perhaps more surprising is the way the different European nations "stack up." There are clear and significant national differences. But, these differences do not suggest that same direction for level of development that the larger WHO studies suggested. Within Europe, in post-communist countries which have a lower level of development based on GDP per capita, more respondents perceive rejection for mental illness, while those in the more economically advanced nations, particularly Iceland, report less rejection. These results point to the need for a consideration of many other potential conditions that shape stigma; for example, the tradition of social welfare in democracies.

As a first step, our analysis is intriguing but raises more questions than answers for understanding the cross-national dimensions of stigma. Considerations that are aligned along an illness career model will shape our analyses of whether the assessment and recognition of mental illness differs cross-nationally and whether labeling has differential effects on rejection. By having asked about issues from onset to recovery, we will have the possibility of seeing where and how nations differ. Following up on these initial findings will likely present an even more complex picture, as more nations and more issues such as recognition are added. But even these first analyses suggest that unscrambling the patterns in these data may help tailor stigma reduction efforts.

The public health ramifications of not knowing the underlying workings of stigma are costly. According to the U.S. Surgeon General, stigma is the "most formidable obstacle to future progress in the arena of mental illness and health" [87, p. 3]. Similarly, the WHO and the World Psychiatric Association mark public stigma and discrimination as *the* critical barriers to the appropriate care and inclusion of persons with mental illness in society, and as the "chief nemesis" to improving and assuring the quality of life for persons with severe mental illness [79, 88]. The existing gaps in scientific knowledge leave little room to estimate the malleability of stigma by marking its cross-national variation and to offer science-based approaches that attempt to change the larger culture and climate of communities. The SGC-MHS attempts to address the important goal of understanding the etiology of stigma to assist in the development of "evidence-based interventions to prevent or mitigate stigma's negative effect on the health of individuals, families and societies worldwide" ([89]; http://www.nih.gov/news/pr/aug2002/fic-28.htm). Along with the WHO efforts and those of the Institute of Medicine, we agree that research on both the individual and collective properties associated with health communities is expected to provide opportunities for prevention and/or intervention at lower cost than traditional individual level strategies [90, p. 91].

References

1. U.S. Department of Health & Human Services (2000) *Healthy People 2010: Understanding and Improving Health*. 2nd ed. Washington, DC: U.S. Government Printing Office.
2. Murray, C.J.L. and Lopez, A.D. (eds) (1996) *Global Burden of Disease: a Comprehensive Assessment of Mortality and Disability from Disesases, Injuries, and Risk Factors 4 in 1990 and Projected to 2020*. Harvard School of Public Health, Cambridge, MA
3. Rutz, W (2001). Mental health in Europe: problems, advances and challenges. *Acta Psychiatrica Scandinavica* Supplementum (410), 15–20.
4. Hopper, K. and Wanderling, J. (2000) Revisiting the developed versus developing distinction in course and outcome in schizophrenia: results from ISoS, the WHO Collaborative Follow-up Project. International Study of Schizophrenia. *Schizophrenia Bulletin* **26**(4), 835–846.
5. Kulhara, P. and Chakrabarti, S. (2001) Culture and schizophrenia and other psychotic disorders. *Psychiatric Clinics of North America* **24**(3), 449–464.
6. Sartorius, N., Gulbinat, W., Harrison, G., Laska, E. and Siegel, C. (1996) Long-term follow-up of schizophrenia in 16 countries. A description of the international study of schizophrenia conducted by the World Health Organization. *Social Psychiatry and Psychiatric Epidemiology* **31**(5), 249–258.
7. Sartorius, N., Jablensky, A. and Shapiro, R. (1978) Cross-cultural differences in the short-term prognosis of schizophrenic psychoses. *Schizophrenia Bulletin* **4**(1), 102–113.
8. Remschmidt, H., Nurcombe, B., Belfer, M.L., Sartorius, N. and Okasha, A. (2007) *The Mental Health of Children and Adolescents: An Area of Global Neglect*. Chichester: Wiley.
9. Pescosolido, B.A. (1991) Illness careers and network ties: a conceptual model of utilization and compliance. In G.L. Albrecht and J.A. Levy (eds) *Advances in Medical Sociology* (pp. 161–184). Greenwich, CT: JAI Press.
10. Pescosolido, B.A. (2006) Of pride and prejudice: the role of sociology and social networks in integrating the health sciences. *Journal of Health and Social Behavior* **47**(September), 189–208.
11. Caracci, G. and Mezzich, J.E. (2001) Culture and urban mental health. *Psychiatric Clinics of North America* **24**(3), 581–593.
12. Ng, C.H. (1997) The stigma of mental illness in Asian cultures. *Australian and New Zealand Journal of Psychology* **31**(3), 382–390.
13. Slu, T. (1989) Short-term prognosis of schizophrenia in developed and developing countries. WHO international study program. *Zhurnal Nevropatologii I Psikhiatrii Imeni S - S - Korsakova* **89**(5), 66–72.
14. Crisp, A.H., Gelder, M.G., Rix, S., Meltzer, H.I. and Rowlands, O.J. (2000) Stigmatization of people with mental illness. *British Journal of Psychiatry* **177**(1), 4–7.
15. Fabrega, H., Jr. (1991) The culture and history of psychiatric stigma in early modern and modern western societies: a review of recent literature. *Comprehensive Psychiatry* **32**(2), 97–119.

16. Pescosolido, B.A., Martin, J.K., Link, B.G., Kikuzawa, S., Burgos, G. and Swindle, R. (2000) Americans' views of mental illness and health at century's end: continuity and change. Public report on the MacArthur Mental Health Module, 1996 General Social Survey. Bloomington, IN: Indiana Consortium for Mental Health Services Research.

17. Stuart, H. and Arboleda-Flórez, J. (2001) Community attitudes toward persons with schizophrenia. *Canadian Journal of Psychiatry* **46**(3), 245–252.

18. Wahl, O.F. (1999) Mental health consumers' experience of stigma. *Schizophrenia Bulletin* **25**(3), 467–478.

19. National Research Council and Institute of Medicine (2000) *From Neurons to Neighborhoods: The Science of Early Childhood Development*. Committee on Integrating the Science of Early Childhood Development. Jack P. Shonkoff and Deborah A. Phillips, eds. Board on Children, Youth, and Families, Commission on Behavioral and Social Sciences and Education. Washington, D.C.: National Academy Press.

20. Sartorius, N. (1997) Fighting schizophrenia and its stigma. A new World Psychiatric Association educational programme. *British Journal of Psychiatry* **170**(4), 297.

21. Townsend, J.M. (1975). Cultural conceptions, mental disorders, and social roles: a comparison of Germany and America. *American Sociological Review* **40**(6), 739–752.

22. Crandall, C.S. (2000) Ideology and lay theories of stigma: the justification of stigmatization. In T.F. Heatherton, R.E. Kleck, M.R. Hebl and J.G. Hull (eds), *The Social Psychology of Stigma* (pp. 126–152). New York: Guilford Press.

23. Crocker, J., Major, B. and Steele, C.M. (1998). Social stigma. In D. Gilbert, S.T. Fiske and G. Lindzey (eds), *The Handbook of Social Psychology* (pp. 504–553). New York: McGraw-Hill.

24. Dovidio, J.F., Major, B. and Crocker, J. (2000) *The Social Psychology of Stigma*. New York: Guilford Press.

25. Ware, N.C., Hopper, K., Tugenbert, T., Dickey, B. and Fisher, D. (2007) Connectedness and citizenship: redefining social integration. *Psychiatric Services* **58**(4), 469–474.

26. Farnham, C.R., Zipple, A.M., Tyrell, W. and Chittinanda, P. (1999) Health status risk factors of people with severe and persistent mental illness. *Journal of Psychosocial Nursing and Mental Health Services* **37**, 16–21.

27. Harding, C.M., Brooks, G.W., Ashikaga, T., Strauss, J.S. and Breier, A. (1987) The Vermont longitudinal study of persons with severe mental illness, II: Long-term outcome of subjects who retrospectively met *DSM-III* criteria for schizophrenia. *American Journal of Psychiatry* **144**(6), 727–735.

28. Goffman, E. (1963) *Stigma: Notes on the Management of Spoiled Identity*. Englewood Cliffs, NJ: Prentice-Hall.

29. Markowitz, F.E. (1998) The effects of stigma on the psychological well-being and life satisfaction of persons with mental illness. *Journal of Health and Social Behavior* **39**(4), 335–347.

30. Link, B.G., Struening, E.L., Rahav, M., Phelan, J.C. and Nuttbrick, L. (1997) On stigma and its consequences: evidence from a longitudinal study of men with dual diagnoses of mental illness and substance abuse. *Journal of Health and Social Behavior* **38**(2), 177–190.

31. Katsching, H. (2000) Schizophrenia and the quality of life. *Acta Psychiatrica Scandinavica* **102** (Suppl.), 33–37.

32. Mechanic, D., McAlpine, D., Rosenfield, S. and Davis, D. (1994) Effects of illness attribution and depression on the quality of life among persons with serious mental illness. *Social Science and Medicine* **39**(2), 155–164.

33. Wright, E.R., Gronfein, W.P. and Owens, T.J. (2000) Deinstitutionalization, social rejection, and the self-esteem of former mental patients. *Journal of Health and Social Behavior* **41**(1), 68–90.

34. Myers, J.K. and Bean, L.L. (1968) *Decade Later*. New York: John Wiley & Sons.

35. Markowitz, F.E. (2001) Modeling processes in recovery from mental illness: relationships between symptoms, life satisfaction, and self-concept. *Journal of Health and Social Behavior* **42**(1), 64–79.

36. Burton, V.S.J. (1990) The consequences of official labels: a research note on rights lost by the mentally ill, mentally incompetent, and convicted felons. *Community Mental Health Journal* **26**(3), 267–276.

37. Bailey, S.R. (1998) An exploration of critical care nurses' and doctors' attitudes towards psychiatric patients. *Australian Journal of Advanced Nursing* **15**, 8–14.

38. Scholsberg, A. (1993) Psychiatric stigma and mental health professionals (stigmatizers and destigmatizers). *Medicine and Law* **12**, 409–416.
39. Mak, K.Y. and Gow, L. (1991) The living conditions of psychiatric patients discharged from half-way houses in Hong Kong. *International Journal of Social Psychiatry* **37**(2), 107–112.
40. Chernomas, W.M., Clarke, D.E. and Chisholm, F.A. (2000) Perspectives of women living with schizophrenia. *Psychiatric Services* **51**(12), 1517–1521.
41. Lai, Y.M., Hong, C. and Chee, C.Y. (2001) Stigma and mental illness. *Singapore Medical Journal* **42**(3), 111–114.
42. Ben Noun, L. (1996) Characterization of patients refusing professional psychiatric treatment in a primary care clinic. *Israel Journal of Psychiatry* **33**, 167–174.
43. Fuller, J., Edwards, J., Procter, N. and Moss, J. (2000) How definition of mental health problems can influence help-seeking in rural and remote communities. *Australian Journal of Rural Health* **8**(3), 148–153.
44. Ohaeri, J.U. (2001) Caregiver burden and psychotic patients' perception of social support in a Nigerian setting. *Social Psychiatry and Psychiatric Epidemiology* **36**(2), 86–93.
45. Star, S.A. (1952) What the public thinks about mental health and mental illness. National Association for Mental Health.
46. Star, S.A. (1955) The public's ideas about mental illness. National Opinion Research Center, Chicago, IL.
47. Cumming, E. and Cumming, J. (1957) *Closed Ranks: An Experiment in Mental Health Education.* Cambridge, MA: Harvard University Press.
48. Gurin, G., Veroff, J. and Feld, S. (1957) Americans view their mental health, 1957 [computer file]. Conducted by University of Michigan, Institute for Social Research, social science archive. ICPSR ed. Ann Arbor, Mi: Inter-university consortium for political and social research [producer and distributor], 1975.
49. Rabkin, J. (1974). Public attitudes toward mental illness: a review of the literature. *Schizophrenia Bulletin* **10** (Fall), 9–33.
50. Armstrong, B. (1976) Preparing the community for the patient's return. *Hospital and Community Psychiatry* **27**, 349–356.
51. Roman, P.M. and Floyd, H.H. (1981) Social acceptance of psychiatric illness and psychiatric treatment. *Social Psychiatry* **16**(1), 21–29.
52. Link, B.G., Yang, L., Phelan, J.C. and Collins, P. (2004) Measuring mental illness stigma. *Schizophrenia Bulletin* **30**(3), 511–541.
53. Baxter, W.E. (1994) American psychiatry celebrates 150 years of caring. *Psychiatric Clinics of North America* **17**(3), 683–693.
54. Dain, N. (1994) Reflections on antipsychiatry and stigma in the history of American psychiatry. *Hospital and Community Psychiatry* **45**(10), 1010–1014.
55. Hyman, S.E. (2000) The millennium of mind, brain and behavior. *Archives of General Psychiatry* **57**(1), 88–89.
56. Pang, J.J. (1985) Partial hospitalization: an alternative to inpatient care. *Psychiatric Clinics of North America* **8**, 587–593.
57. Rose, R. (1988) Schizophrenia, civil liberties and the law. *Schizophrenia Bulletin* **14**(1), 1–15.
58. Swan, J. (1999) Wearing two hats. Consumer and provider. *Journal of Psychosocial Nursing and Mental Health Services* **37**(7), 20–24.
59. Phelan, J.C., Link, B.G., Stueve, A. and Pescosolido, B.A. (2000) Public conceptions of mental illness in 1950 and 1996: what is mental illness and is it to be feared? *Journal of Health and Social Behavior* **41**(2), 188–207.
60. McKeon, P. and Carrick, S. (1991). Public attitudes to depression: a national survey. *Irish Journal of Psychological Medicine* **8**, 116–121.
61. Link, B.G., Phelan, J.C., Bresnahan, M., Stueve, A. and Pescosolido, B.A. (1999) Public conceptions of mental illness: Labels, causes, dangerousness and social distance. *American Journal of Public Health* **89**(9), 1328–1333.
62. Swindle, R., Heller, K., Pescosolido, B.A. and Kikuzawa, S. (2000) Responses to nervous breakdowns in America over a 40-year period: mental health policy implications. *American Psychologist* **55**(7), 740–749.

63. Martin, J.K., Pescosolido, B.A. and Tuch, S.A. (2000). Of fear and loathing: the role of disturbing behavior, labels and causal attributions in shaping public attitudes toward persons with mental illness. *Journal of Health and Social Behavior* **41**(2), 208–233.
64. Pescosolido, B.A., Monahan, J., Link, B.G., Stueve, A. and Kikuzawa, S. (1999) The public's view of the competence, dangerousness, and need for legal coercion of persons with mental health problems. *American Journal of Public Health* **89**(9), 1339–1345.
65. Chou, K.L. and Mak, K.-Y. (1998). Attitudes to mental patients among Hong Kong Chinese: a trend study over two years. *International Journal of Social Psychiatry* **44**(3), 215–224.
66. Brockman, J. and D'Arcy, C. (1978) Correlates of attitudinal social distance toward the mentally ill: a review and resurvey. *Social Psychiatry* **13**(1), 69–77.
67. Lyketsos, G., Mouyas, A., Malliori, M. *et al.* (1985) Opinion of public and patients about mental illness and psychiatric care in Greece. *British Journal of Clinical Social Psychology* **3**, 59–66.
68. Paykel, E.S., Hart, D. and Priest, R.G. (1998) Changes in public attitudes to depression during the Defeat Depression campaign. *British Journal of Psychiatry* **173**(6), 519–522.
69. Hopper, K., Harrison, G. and Wanderling, J. (2007) An overview of course and outcome in ISoS. In K. Hopper, G. Harrison, A. Janca and N. Sartorius (eds), *Recovery from Schizophrenia: An International Perspective: A Report from the WHO Collaborative Project, the International Study of Schizophrenia* (pp. 23–38). New York: Oxford University Press.
70. Lin, K.M. and Kleinman, A.M. (1988) Psychopathology and clinical course of schizophrenia: a cross-cultural perspective. *Schizophrenia Bulletin* **14**(4), 555–567.
71. DiMaggio, P.J. (1997) Culture and cognition. *Annual Review of Sociology* **23**, 263–287.
72. Swidler, A. (2001) *Talk of Love: How Culture Matters*. Chicago: University of Chicago Press.
73. Pescosolido, B.A., Brooks-Gardner, C. and Lubell, K.M. (1998). How people get into mental health services: stories of choice, coercion and 'muddling through' from 'first-timers'. *Social Science and Medicine* **46**(2), 275–286.
74. Pescosolido, B.A., Wright, E.R., Alegria, M. and Vera, M. (1998) Social networks and patterns of use among the poor with mental health problems in Puerto Rico. *Medical Care* **36**(7), 1057–1072.
75. Neuberg, S.L., Smith, D.M. and Asher, T. (2000) Why people stigmatize: toward a biocultural framework. In T.F. Heatherton, R.E. Kleck, M.R. Hebl and J.G. Hull (eds) *The Social Psychology of Stigma* (pp. 31–61). New York: Guilford Press.
76. Benedict, R. (1934) Anthropology and the abnormal. *Journal of General Psychiatry*, **10**(1), 59–80.
77. Lefley, H.P. (1990) Culture and chronic mental illness. *Hospital and Community Psychiatry* **41**(3), 277–286.
78. Sartorius, N. (1998) Stigma: what can psychiatrists do about it? *The Lancet* **352**(9133), 1058–1059.
79. World Health Organization (2005) *Mental Health Atlas*. Geneva: World Health Organization.
80. Inglehart, R. and Baker, W. (2000) Modernization, globalization, and the persistence of tradition: empirical evidence from 65 societies. *American Sociological Review* **65**(1), 19–55.
81. Inglehart, R. (1997) *Modernization and Postmodernization: Cultural, Economic and Political Change in 43 Societies*. Princeton, NJ: Princeton University Press.
82. Thakker, J. and Ward, T. (1998) Culture and classification: the cross-cultural application of the DSM-IV. *Clinical Psychology Review* **18**(5), 501–529.
83. Jenkins, J.H. (1988) Ethnopsychiatric interpretations of schizophrenic illness: the problem of nervios within Mexican-American families. *Culture, Medicine and Psychiatry* **12**(3), 301–329.
84. Guarnaccia, P.J., Rivera, M., Franco, F. and Neighbors, C. (1996) The experiences of ataques de nervios: towards an anthropology of emotions in Puerto Rico. *Culture, Medicine and Psychiatry* **20**(3), 343–367.
85. Link, B.G. and Phelan, J.C. (2001). Conceptualizing stigma. *Annual Review of Sociology* **27**, 363–385.
86. Failer, J.L. (2002) *Who Qualifies for Rights? Homelessness, Mental Illness, and Civil Commitment*. Ithaca, NY: Cornell University Press.
87. U.S. Department of Health and Human Services (1999) *Mental Health: A Report of the Surgeon General*. Rockville, MD: U.S. Department of Health and Human Services, Substance Abuse and Mental Services Administration, Center for Mental Health Services, National Institutes of Health, National Institute of Mental Health.

88. Sartorius, N. and Schulze, H. (2005) *Reducing the Stigma of Mental Illness: A Report from a Global Association*. New York: Cambridge University Press.
89. Keusch, G.T. (2002) Fogarty International Center announces new research program in stigma and global health. National Institutes of Health (http://www.nih.gov/news/pr/aug2002/fic-28.htm).
90. Singer, B. and Ryff, C. (2001) *New Horizons in Health: an Integrative Approach*. Washington DC: National Academy Press.

3 The WPA Global Programme against Stigma and Discrimination because of Schizophrenia

Norman Sartorius

University of Geneva, Switzerland

The World Psychiatric Association (WPA) Global Programme against Stigma and Discrimination because of Schizophrenia was started in 1996, when I became President of the WPA. Initially, we saw it as an opportunity (and a necessity) to produce a policy document, a declaration similar to the Madrid Declaration and other official statements of the WPA.

From initial reactions of many with whom this idea was discussed it became clear that it would be better to develop a programme to fight stigma rather than to make a statement about the need to remove it. It seemed that such a programme was timely, that it would attract collaboration from many countries and that it would bring together mental health professionals and others who need to be involved in mental health care and are often working apart. We were fortunate to obtain an unrestricted educational grant from Eli Lilly and Company that made it possible to start the programme without delay and support its early development.

Thus, in 1996 we brought together a group of people whom we felt could help in the development and implementation of a programme against stigma. The group that met in Geneva included psychiatrists, social scientists and communication experts as well as representatives of governments and of family and patient organizations. It reviewed the preliminary plans for the programme and identified individuals and organizations that could be focal points for its development at country level. It also confirmed that the proposals about the development and structure of the programme were reasonable and likely to be successful.

Canada was the first country to implement the programme and served as its pilot site. Spain and Austria were the next two countries to join and, soon after, a number of other sites followed in other countries (see Table 3.1).

As time went by, the level of activity in the sites varied. Activities were reduced in some of them for a host of reasons – political, personal and institutional. In others, action grew stronger and the programme that was initially restricted to a limited community expanded

Understanding the Stigma of Mental Illness: Theory and Interventions   Edited by Julio Arboleda-Flórez and Norman Sartorius
© 2008 John Wiley & Sons, Ltd

Table 3.1   List of countries participating in the programme

The Americas	Europe	Asia*
Brazil	Austria	India
Canada	Czech Republic	Japan
Chile	Germany	
United States	Greece	
	Italy	
Eastern Mediterranean	Poland	
and North Africa	Romania	
Egypt	Slovakia	
Morocco	Spain	
Turkey	Switzerland	
	United Kingdom	

* SANE Australia (formerly Schizophrenia Australia Foundation) is
working in partnership with the WPA programme.

and covered the whole country (e.g. Spain). The involvement of a large number of groups
proved to be invaluable for the programme because it ensured that at any given time there
were a number of sites with lively and vigorous action that permitted the programme as a
whole to continue its robust existence over a long period.

The results of the pilot project in Canada were immensely helpful for the further development of the programme. They showed that it is of central importance to involve people
with schizophrenia and their families in selecting targets for the programme. They also
indicated that the success of the programme should not be judged by changes of attitude
alone; changes in the behaviour of all concerned were a much more difficult but also more
worthy objective.

The programme adopted an operational model of development of stigma and its consequences [1, 2] (see Figure 3.1). The model implies that a marker (a visible abnormality, a diagnostic label, the colour of skin) that allows the identification of a person can be loaded with
negative contents by association with previous knowledge, information obtained through
the media, memories of unpleasant incidents, heard or seen. Once the marker is loaded in
this way, it becomes a stigma and anyone who has it will be stigmatized. Stigmatization
may lead to negative discrimination which, in turn, leads to numerous disadvantages in
terms of access to care, poor health service, frequent setbacks that can damage self-esteem,
and additional stress that might worsen the condition of the person who is ill or otherwise
stigmatized, and thus amplify the marker, making it even more likely that the person will
be identified and suffer from discrimination and other consequences of stigma.

This cyclical model also implies that an intervention at any point might stop that process.
Thus, if it proves impossible, for example, to remove stigma, it is often possible to focus
on removing discrimination by legal and other means. In other instances, it might become
possible to improve treatment and rehabilitation services to a level at which they can offer
help to the persons who have the disease and their families and support them in living with
the illness by protecting their self-esteem and functioning in social roles. Sometimes it
is possible to remove the marker – as in the case with extra-pyramidal symptoms that can
appear as side effects of certain types of medications but do not appear with other treatments.

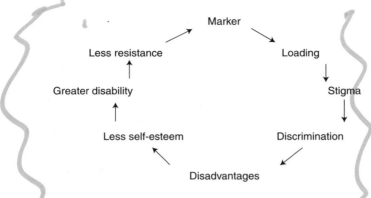

Figure 3.1 The vicious cycle of stigmatization

In some instances, there is enough time and opportunity to educate the community in a manner that will decrease the negative loading of the marker.

An important issue at the very beginning of the programme was its scope. Eventually, it was decided to concentrate on stigma linked to schizophrenia rather than to all mental illnesses. There are strong arguments for both of these two options. It could be argued that taking all mental illnesses as a target might – if the programme is successful – help incomparably more people than the prevention or removal of stigma concerning a single disease such as schizophrenia. A point in favour of the broad focus could also be that the general public does not make a distinction between mental illnesses and that, therefore, engaging support of a wide section of the population might be more difficult if a psychiatric label is used in defining the focus of action. Targeting many mental diseases, it was felt, might help to engage a larger number of patient and family organizations. The question of equity also arises if only one disease is selected as a target for action: why should other illnesses not receive the same benefits from such a programme?

The arguments for taking only schizophrenia as a focus are also numerous and seem to prevail over the reasons for taking all mental diseases as the target. Schizophrenia as a syndrome is a paradigm of mental illnesses and the general public, when asked to describe a mentally ill person, invariably lists symptoms such as delusions and hallucinations – hallmarks of schizophrenia – as the defining features of a 'madman'. Stigma related to schizophrenia is more pronounced than the stigma attached to, say, anxiety states or dementia of old age. Success in the prevention or removal of stigma related to schizophrenia would show the way to those fighting to remove stigma related to other mental illnesses and indeed to other stigmatizing illnesses, for example leprosy or syphilis.

The selection of schizophrenia as the central focus of the programme makes the definition of the programme activities less complicated and the evaluation of success easier. Although some non-governmental organizations – for example the World Schizophrenia Fellowship – did excellent work to help people with schizophrenia there was when the WPA programme was initiated no coordinated international project by a professional or governmental organization that dealt with the disease and could attract the attention of governments and other authorities to the need to support care for people with schizophrenia and their families – arguably the most wretched group among those struck by mental illness.

The structure of the programme was kept simple. A Steering Committee[1] guided the development of the programme and the office of the Scientific Director helped in the day-to-day operation of the programme. The Steering Committee made decisions about programme coordination, which was entrusted to its Scientific Director located in Geneva, Switzerland. The office of the Director maintained continuous communication with the heads of the collaborating sites whose representatives met annually to review progress and identify areas in which common action might be useful. The central office also established four working groups[2] that were entrusted with the development of documents, reviews and other materials supporting action at country level. The products of the working groups were used to build the programme or independently. Thus, for example, one of the groups has produced a description of schizophrenia written in simple language for use by the general public and the media. The book has been translated into a number of languages, e.g. Spanish [3] and published even in countries that did not participate in the programme.

At country level the programme was entrusted to a country action group. A rule of thumb was that the group should be of a size that would allow its members to go for a meal together in a single car. Such an action group was to ensure support of a larger group of patrons – persons of importance and influence – that could be invited to become members of the advisory group at country level and were likely to be willing to meet at regular intervals (say, every six months), to receive reports of the action group and to help it by advice, comment and influence to carry out the programme.

The decision to proceed in this way was based on experience from previous international collaborative work which strongly suggested that the guarantee of success for a study or other project at country level is not a strong commitment of the government or of an institution, but the decision of an individual or of a small group of people to carry out the project. Support by institutions and governmental agencies is helpful and often necessary, but never sufficient. The programme thus expanded to any country in which there was a small group of people willing to lead the action and maintain it over years.

The meeting held in Geneva in 1996 recommended that the office of the Scientific Director develop a set of specific plans that would be offered to the action groups in the countries together with an estimate of the time necessary and allowable for the execution of each activity in the plan. This would essentially be what has been described as a *collaborative project* [4], in which the steps in the programme are accepted and implemented by all the participating sites in the same manner. It was felt that this would help to maintain the identity of the programme and facilitate the exchange of experience and evaluation.

As it turned out this decision had to be modified. Consultations with the potential heads of action groups in the countries and the results obtained during the pilot programme in Canada led to the development of a strategy that seemed dangerously similar to a plan for confusion but, in time, proved its worth and became a hallmark of the programme.

In brief, rather than developing a detailed, comprehensive plan of action at the centre, the Scientific Director's office defined the general principles of the programme and suggested how the programme should be administered in order to support country activities, but allowed the sites to select specific targets for action and its speed. The targets at the country sites were chosen relying mainly on the advice of persons most directly concerned with

---

[1] Composition of the Steering Committee: Norman Sartorius (Switzerland), *Chairman 1996–1999, Scientific Director 1999–2005*; Juan J. López-Ibor (Spain), *Chairman 1999–2002;* Julio Arboleda-Flórez (Canada), Ahmed Okasha (Egypt), *Chairman 2002–2005;* Hugh Schulze (United States), Costas N. Stefanis (Greece), Narendra N. Wig (India).

[2] For the list of the members of working groups, see [2].

problems related to stigmatization and discrimination: in each of the sites the first step of the action groups was an exploration of the consequences of stigma and discrimination for people with schizophrenia, their families and others who were involved in the provision of care and in the rehabilitation of those disabled by schizophrenia and its consequences. This preliminary exploration usually resulted in a long list of complaints and problems reported by those concerned. The action groups then examined these complaints and problems and divided them into those due to stigma and discrimination and those that had little to do with them. From the former list of problems the action groups selected targets for using several criteria: the probability that the problem can be resolved relatively quickly, the likelihood that the problem can be tackled by the action groups (with the support of the local advisory group), the availability of support for work on that problem – either in the form of advocacy or concrete support of an institution or agency, and the likelihood that the action undertaken will help to attract attention and support from many sources and potential partners.

The results of proceeding this way were that the programme sites selected different targets for action (see Table 3.2) and that the speed of their progress varied. This might be seen as a disadvantage, particularly for reporting about the programme and for its evaluation. These shortcomings are, however, significantly outweighed by the facts that it is easier to find support for a programme that is locally relevant and that the Action groups and other participants in the programme knew that they were working on problems particularly important for their areas. A moral advantage of this way of proceeding was also that action was harmonious with one of the main objective of the programme – that of contributing to the self-esteem of the persons affected by schizophrenia by giving them an opportunity to decide on the course of action and to participate in it, thus treating them as equal and making them partners in programme development.

To maintain easy communication and an overall sense of the programme, the office of the Scientific Director drafted instruction guidelines giving a sequence of steps in programmes at country level. The sequence – for example, concerning the formation of the local Action group, the collection of information, the establishment of the advisory group – was the same for all sites, but the timing of the steps as well as the selection of activities at country level was left to the decision of the local Action groups and their partners. A website was established in 1998 to facilitate the spread of information and communication about the programme.

The question of evaluation of success attracted much attention during the first meeting in Geneva and on several occasions after that. The usual comparisons of achievements with the objectives seemed appropriate in some instances but not in others. The main objective of the WPA programme was not to carry out a multinational study but to develop an action programme of demonstrable usefulness and a model from which others could learn. The aim of being an action programme carries two other obligations with it: first, that progress should be measured by the extent to which activities against stigma and discrimination become part and parcel of the routine country health and mental health programmes; and second, that those who have identified problems and difficulties because of stigmatization and discrimination – persons suffering from schizophrenia and their carers – see that some of their difficulties diminish and some of their problems related to stigma vanish. It was thus a change of the behaviour of people, both of those who had the diagnosis of schizophrenia and of all others, a change of rules of law and similar indications that were selected rather than other earlier often used indications, e.g. changes in attitudes. The second of these obligations imposes the need for evaluation of the success of each of the component activities so that those who want to learn from the WPA effort can select those of proven usefulness in another setting.

Table 3.2   List of anti-stigma interventions by participating sites. Adapted with permission from table 19.2 of Sartorius N. and Schulze H. (2005), Copyright Cambridge University Press, 2005

	Austria	Brazil	Canada	Chile	Germany	Greece	Japan	Italy
Survey of Knowledge/Attitudes	×	×	×		×	×	×	×
Speaker's Bureau	×	×	×		×		×	×
School Education (Primary &/or Secondary)	×		×		×	×	×	×
Educating Psychiatrists	×	×	×	×	×		×	
Educating GPs	×		×	×	×			
Educating other Health Care Professionals	×	×	×	×	×	×	×	×
Educating Journalists	×	×	×		×	×	×	×
Stigma Busting/Stigma Watch*				×	×	×		×
Educating Clergy		×	×			×		×
Publications in Scientific Journals	×	×	×		×	×	×	×
Publications in Newspaper/Magazines	×	×	×		×	×	×	×
Radio Programs	×	×	×			×		
Television Programs	×	×	×		/×			
Anti-stigma Awards	×	×			×	×		
Theatre Presentations	×		×		×	×		
Story Workshops		×	×					
Art Presentations/Competitions			×		×	×		
Educating Families		×	×			×		
Other		Education with Public Movie Screening/Festival			Open-Door-Day in the Hospital Benefit Jazz Concert	Benefit concert with Nana Mouskouri		Focus Groups with Patients and Family Members

(*continued*)

Table 3.2   (*Continued*)

	Morocco	Poland	Slovakia	Spain	Turkey	UK	US
Survey of Knowledge/ Attitudes	×	×	×	×	×	×	×
Speaker's Bureau		×	×	×	×	×	×
School Education (Primary &/or Secondary)			×		×	×	
Educating Psychiatrist		×		×	×		
Educating GPs	×			×	×		
Educating other Health Care Professionals		×		×	×	×	
Educating Journalists		×		×	×		×
Stigma Busting/ Stigma Watch				×			×
Educating Clergy		×					
Publications in Scientific Journals	×	×		×	×	×	×
Publications in Newspaper/ Magazines	×	×	×	×	×	×	×
Radio Programs	×	×	×	×	×		×
Television Programs	×	×	×	×	×		
Anti-stigma Awards				×			×
Theatre/Dramaturgic Presentations							
Story Workshops			×				
Art Presentations/ Competitions		×				×	×
Educating Families	×	×	×	×		×	
Other	Educating Patients	Day of Solidarity with People Suffering from Schizophrenia	Media Cell	Website Educating Patients Public Lectures Media Guide	Short Films for TV		Books Cinema Slides Bus Ads Public Lectures

* Refers to arrangements that permitted identification of developments or events that could worsen the stigma of mental illness and its consequences and to express protest or undertake other steps to prevent harm from such an event (e.g. producing or showing a movie portraying a mentally ill person in a very negative manner).

The results of the programme and details about its implementation can be found in its overall report [2] and in the numerous publications produced by the Action groups in their respective countries.[3] Taking those results into account and recalling what the programme groups reported it is now, ten years after the initiation of the programme, possible to make recommendations concerning the development of a concerted effort to fight stigma because of an illness. These include the following.

First, an anti-stigma programme has to be long-lasting and not a campaign. Profoundly embedded attitudes and social arrangements including laws cannot be expected to change overnight. Short-lasting paroxysms of public education or other interventions often leave people who expected a great deal from a campaign more unhappy and dissatisfied after it than they were before it. Anti-stigma programmes must therefore – because they must last over time – devote a good part of their energy to becoming a routine part of health and social service plans and institutions.

Second, a programme against stigma must be successful if it is to retain the loyalty of those who work in it. This means that the goals of the programme have to be stated in broad, overarching terms but that specific plans for immediate application have to be modest in size and have good chances to succeed. This also means that the goals of the programme must have local relevance and that its success will serve as an argument helping to find further support and funding for the programme.

Third, the programme must deal with the problems experienced by the people who have the illness and by their family. While the process of stigmatization is similar in different settings, what bothers people is different. The best way to identify what is most disturbing – and should therefore be among the targets of the programme – is to ask those who are most directly affected about their experience and about changes that they would see as being important in terms of improving their situation.

In most parts of the world, there are no systematic studies that document the everyday problems and experiences of consumers (of mental health services); yet, without such data, it is likely that much energy will be spent in action that will give more satisfaction to those who have undertaken it than to those whom it was supposed to serve.[4]

Fourth, the programme should not be a programme of the mental health service system alone. The participation of others – representatives of different sectors of the government and of community members – is not only important because it strengthens the programme: a broad involvement also makes it easier to intervene in situations that are normally not accessible to mental health workers.

Working as a broadly based, multi-sectoral team also brings people who are not directly concerned with mental illness into contact with mental health service personnel, with consumers, with their families, and with others who are concerned with mental illness. Narrowing the gap that exists between psychiatry and the rest of medicine and society is of great importance for the survival of the programme and for an improvement of mental health care.

Fifth, the programme should employ those who have had experience of schizophrenia, directly or in their family, in the day-to-day functions of the programme. As examples from the participating sites show, the active involvement of people who have the experience of suffering from the illness can reveal areas of need and remedial measures to which medical

---

[3] References to these publications are given in the report on the programme [2].

[4] To obtain this information a number of WPA programme sites have joined efforts in a new project, specifically designed to develop instruments for recording experiences of people with schizophrenia and their families (the INDIGO project). More information about this project can be obtained on request from the author.

professionals might not otherwise have given much priority. Just as important, their active involvement in the programme acts against the loss of self-esteem, a loss that increases stigmatization of those who are ill by themselves, and represents a great obstacle to any effort to rehabilitate a person who has suffered from a mental illness.

Sixth, it has been critical to develop a model that can be easily understood and used in both the planning and evaluation processes of the programme. The vicious circle model that was developed for the WPA programme is shown in Figure 3.1. One of the advantages of this model is that it can be used to counteract the reluctance of those involved in supporting a programme against stigma because its main message is that there are numerous entry points for action against stigmatization and its consequences and that therefore no one can be excused from helping. Potential partners in fighting stigma can be shown concrete areas where their expertise can apply in breaking the vicious cycle at different stages of development. Similar models of vicious circles have been constructed for the effects of stigma of the family of the person who is ill and on the mental health service [2].

Seventh, one of the many enemies of long-term projects is the fatigue and burnout that leaders of the programme experience. Every effort should therefore be made to add a component to the programme to prevent burnout.

The involvement of a large number of centres helped to fight burn-out in this programme. Working with others involved in the same area of work in other parts of the world is both encouraging and an opportunity to learn from others' experiences. In addition, the large number and the variety of those participating in the programme offered possibilities for small-scale collaboration among groups that would otherwise have had difficulty in identifying partners among professional groups, e.g. organizations of patients and their relatives. Such collaborative ventures proved to be very valuable in reducing the risk of burn-out and in making the participating sites feel that they belong to a group with similar ideals and goals.

Eighth, in addition to using modern technology and to linking sites electronically via a website, the WPA has also invested in organizing face-to-face encounters between participants in the programme. Heads of sites that had already completed work served as consultants for new sites. They were invited to report on their experiences at scientific meetings and at annual meetings of participating sites. Newsletters and annual reports were used to record and publicize the work done and to give recognition to the achievements of the participants. Exhibits were developed for scientific meetings where the progress of programmes could be displayed.

Ninth, a programme has to have tools to help newcomers to the programme and to facilitate the decision of those who might be hesitant to participate. Among the materials produced to help local Action groups in their work are:

- A volume giving guidelines and a detailed description of the different stages that should be followed and milestones that should be met (this volume can be downloaded from the website of the programme www.openthedoors.com);

- A description of the work done in different sites of the programme (published yearly and incorporated into the book by Sartorius and Schulze [2]);

- A bibliography of articles and books dealing with stigma, focusing on work over the past two decades (available from the Chairperson of the WPA Section dealing with Stigma and Mental Illness, Prof. Heather Stuart, e-mail: heather.stuart@queensu.ca;[5]

---

[5] Also published as [5] and [6].

- A list of papers produced by the programme sites;

- A volume summarizing knowledge about schizophrenia and indicating issues that are of particular importance in preventing or diminishing stigmatization (see www.openthedoors.com);

- An inventory of posters, videos and other materials used in different countries (see [2]);

- A manual for programme implementation (available from www.openthedoors.com);

- Standard curricula and syllabi for courses on how to start a programme (available from Prof. Heather Stuart – see above).

Tenth, the evaluation of a programme against stigma has to be done (i) in relation to improvements in target areas identified by people with schizophrenia and their families, and (ii) by measuring changes of behaviour and of situations rather than stop at measuring changes in attitudes or the amount of knowledge that have been the usual areas of programme evaluation in most projects to date.

Finally, the most important statement that can be made on the grounds of experience gained from this ten-year effort is that a successful programme against stigmatization and its consequences can be launched in any country – small or large, rich or poor, industrialized or developing – and that the success of this work is richly rewarding for all those involved because it gives them the certainty that they have done something that must be done in a civic society. To people who suffer from mental illness and to those who care for them the reduction of stigma and of its consequences gives a new lease on life and hope for a better future.

At present, work against stigma in the various centres involved in the WPA programme is monitored by the WPA Section on Stigma and Mental Disorders (Chairperson: Prof. Heather Stuart – e-mail: heather.stuart@queensu.ca). Regular courses (e.g. during congresses of the Association of European Psychiatrists and of the World Psychiatric Association) are held to facilitate the initiation of programmes in various countries. The WPA Programme against Stigma because of Schizophrenia is the largest anti-stigma programme concerning mental or other diseases ever undertaken. Its success is the result of selfless involvement of many people whose main reward has been the programme's success and the awareness that they have made a significant contribution to the fight against stigma which was and remains the main obstacle to mental health programmes and to a better quality of life of people with schizophrenia.

References

1. Sartorius, N. (2000) Breaking the vicious cycle. *Mental Health and Learning Disabilities Care* **4**(3), 80–82.
2. Sartorius, N. and Schulze, H. (2005) *Reducing the Stigma of Mental Illness. A Report from a Global Programme of the World Psychiatric Association.* Cambridge: Cambridge University Press. The website of the programme www.openthedoors.com contains a large set of materials produced by the programme.
3. Asociación Mundial de Psiquiatria, Juan J. López-Ibor, Olga Cuenca (2000) *La Esquizofrenia Abre Las Puertas. Programa de la Asociación Mundial de Psiquiatria para combatir el estigma y la discriminacion debidos a la esquizofrenia. Volume II,* Qué es y como se trata la esquizofrenia.

4. Sartorius, N. and Helmchen, H. (1981) Aims and implementation of multicentre studies. *Modern Problems of Pharmacopsychiatry*, **16**, 1–8. Basel, Munich, Paris, New York: Karger.
5. Pickenhagen, A. and Sartorius, N. (2002) *Annotated Bibliography of Selected Publications and Other Materials Related to Stigma and Discrimination because of Mental Illness and Intervention Programmes Fighting It*. World Psychiatric Association Global Programme to Reduce the Stigma and Discrimination because of Schizophrenia.
6. Aichberger, M. and Sartorius, N. (2006) *Annotated Bibliography of Selected Publications and Other Materials Related to Stigma and Discrimination. An Update for the Years 2002 to 2006*. WPA Global Programme to Reduce Stigma and Discrimination because of Schizophrenia.

4 'Fighting stigma and discrimination because of schizophrenia – Open the Doors': a collaborative review of the experience from the German project centres

A.E. Baumann, W. Gaebel *et al.*

Department of Psychiatry and Psychotherapy, Heinrich-Heine-University, Düsseldorf 40629, Germany

Introduction

Stigma associated with mental illness and psychiatric treatment, and the discrimination towards people with mental illnesses that frequently results from this, are the main obstacles preventing early and successful treatment. To reduce such stigma and discrimination towards mentally ill people and especially those with schizophrenia, the World Psychiatric Association's (WPA) anti stigma programme 'Open the Doors' [1] is currently being implemented in more than 20 countries. Since August 1999, the programme has been undertaken in seven project centres in Germany. Public information programmes and educative measures aimed at selected target groups are intended to improve the public's knowledge regarding symptomatology, causes and treatment options for schizophrenia. Improved knowledge should in turn reduce prejudice and negative perceptions and facilitate the social reintegration of those suffering from mental illness.

Education, protest and contact are the key elements of anti stigma strategies recommended by the WPA and various research groups [2, 3]. These anti stigma strategies include improving psychiatric care and psycho-education of patients and families, involving patients and family members in all anti stigma activities, including anti stigma education in the training of health care providers, initiating educational activities in the general public and specific target groups, and promoting social and legal action to reduce discrimination. In the following report, we describe how these strategies are employed in the German project centres participating in the WPA programme. We also describe the findings from the evaluation of selected interventions.

Understanding the Stigma of Mental Illness: Theory and Interventions   Edited by Julio Arboleda-Flórez and Norman Sartorius
© 2008 John Wiley & Sons, Ltd

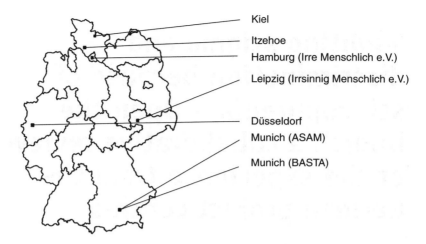

Kiel

Itzehoe

Hamburg (Irre Menschlich e.V.)

Leipzig (Irrsinnig Menschlich e.V.)

Düsseldorf

Munich (ASAM)

Munich (BASTA)

Figure 4.1   Open the Doors in Germany: project centres and associated initiatives

Open the Doors programme in Germany

In autumn 2000, the following seven German project centres joined to become the Open the Doors Society: Hamburg, Kiel, Itzehoe, Leipzig, Düsseldorf and Munich (two centres) (**Figure 4.1**). Each of the German project groups operates independently, assessing needs in a particular community and appropriate responses. Each centre has developed its own interventions; joint activities are coordinated from the Düsseldorf centre. Centres in Düsseldorf and Munich (Ludwig-Maximilians University [LMU]) are evaluating their measures within the framework of the German Research Network on Schizophrenia.

The interventions in Düsseldorf and Munich (LMU) target both the general public and specific groups having close contact with persons with schizophrenia. Such interventions are art exhibitions, film and theatre evenings as well as advanced training with staff in psychiatric hospitals. The second Munich project group – the Bavarian Anti-stigma Action (BASTA), located at the Technical University – is an action group of psychiatric patients, their relatives and psychiatric professionals who have combined to tackle discrimination toward people with mental illness in society. Various projects provide the public and specific target groups with information about mental illnesses, e.g. in workshops with the police faculty from the Bavarian training college for civil servants. Using the Australian Stigma Alarm Network (SANE) as a role model, this action group also initiated the Internet-based SANE, which facilitates reporting of discrimination against those with mental illness in advertisements or press reports. To tackle stigma and discrimination in rural areas, activities in Itzehoe and Kiel focus on establishing a network of individuals with mental illness and their relatives, professionals and decision makers within the political arena and society in general. The project groups in Hamburg and Leipzig provide information based on focus issues in schools. The school projects promote direct contact between young people and persons with mental illness during project days or weeks in which schoolchildren are first sensitized to the issue.

Open the Doors Düsseldorf

Anja Esther Baumann, Harald Zäske and Wolfgang Gaebel

The interventions at the Düsseldorf and Munich (LMU) centres are being carried out as part of a research project of the nationwide German Research Network on Schizophrenia

(GRNS), funded by the German Ministry of Education and Research (Grant No. 01 GI 9932). The GRNS is one of 17 'Competence Networks in Medicine' to bring together the leading research institutions and qualified routine care facilities [4]. With Düsseldorf as the Head Office, the network comprises several multi-centre treatment studies, biological and genetic research projects and general topics such as health care economy and training. High priority is given to public education [5]. Therefore, there is, besides an awareness-raising programme, a programme on the 'Reduction of stigma and discrimination because of schizophrenia – Open the Doors', which is evaluated within the framework of the GRNS. Including the general public relation activities of the GRNS Head Office, about 200 press reports have been released since the network was set up, and network members have been involved in nearly 40 radio transmissions and television broadcasts.

Surveys in the public and in patients

The centre in Düsseldorf conducted pre- and post-interventional surveys of knowledge and attitudes in Düsseldorf, Munich, Cologne, Bonn, Berlin and Essen [6]. Following the pre-test survey, the centres in Düsseldorf and Munich (LMU) conducted a variety of multi-level anti stigma interventions. More than 80% of those sampled stated that more positive media reports, more occasions for personal contact with mentally ill people and more public information about mental illnesses would be useful possibilities to improve the public acceptance of mentally ill patients. Eighty percent of those surveyed thought that patients suffering from schizophrenia suffer from a 'split personality'. Another survey was conducted with inpatients at the Department of Psychiatry and Psychotherapy. The patients reported that most of the discriminating situations they faced were in the workplace. Colleagues and employers were rated as supportive, but this group is also rated as the highest discrimination source.

Interventions in the general public, with journalists and at schools

Many interventions have been undertaken and evaluated in the target groups 'general public', 'schoolchildren' and 'journalists', e.g. the exhibitions 'Psyche and Art' and 'Ex neuron', readings with young patients and actors *Wenn die Seele überläuft* (When the mind overflows), film evening *Das weiße Rauschen* (The White Noise), panel discussion; theatre event *4.48 Psychose* (4.48 Psychosis), benefit concert 'Katja Riemann: Favorites', popular scientific lectures, open days in the psychiatric hospital in Düsseldorf, educational lectures and seminars at secondary schools and institutes for adult education, workshops with journalists and continuous press and media work.

Publications

The project team in Düsseldorf produced numerous publications on the research results and evaluation of the anti stigma activities in national and international journals. The group organized various symposia and panel discussions and reported about the progress of the Open the Doors programme in Germany in presentations and scientific posters as well as information booths at national and international congresses.

As members of the WPA Training Manual Task Force, the head and the programme coordinator of the team in Düsseldorf contributed to the development of the 'Training

Manual' [7], a handbook which gives practical information on the planning, conduction and evaluation of anti stigma programmes and target-group interventions.

A textbook, *Stigma – Discrimination – Coping Dealing with Social Exclusion of Persons with Mental Illness*, by Professors Gaebel, Möller and Rössler has been published (in German) [8]. It contains reports about the varied experiences of individuals suffering from mental illness and their relatives, multi-disciplinary scientific reflections on causes for stigma and discrimination, as well as strategies and programmes regarding how to overcome them.

Anti Stigma Prize

At one of the country-wide journalist workshops in Düsseldorf (June 2003), the society 'Open the doors' awarded for the first time the 'Anti stigma Prize', which will be awarded every year to a person or institution for special engagement with stigma. Since 2004 the prize (€ 6000) has been awarded jointly with the German Society for Psychiatry, Psychotherapy and Nervous Diseases (DGPPN) and Sanofi-Aventis.

International collaborations

The head and the programme coordinator in Düsseldorf are members of the WPA Section on Stigma and Mental Health. They represent the German anti stigma activities in the Section.

The results of the above-mentioned public opinion survey in six large cities in Germany [6] carried out by the Düsseldorf research group showed that less than 10% of the 7246 interviewees admitted being afraid of talking to someone with schizophrenia, while almost 16% said they would feel disturbed working alongside someone with schizophrenia. One third indicated concern if a group of 6–8 people suffering from schizophrenia moved into their neighbourhood, more than 40% would be opposed to sharing a room with a person with schizophrenia, e.g. in a hospital, and over 70% would not marry someone with schizophrenia. These results concerning social distance are similar to those of a study carried out by the Canadian research group which also conducted a public survey in the framework of the 'Open the doors' programme [9]. Both studies show that the extent of social distance increases with increasing intimacy of the relationship. That means the closer and more private the imagined situation is, the more rejection of people with schizophrenia is to be expected. An extensive comparison of the two studies can be found in [10]. The public opinion survey in Germany also showed that the amount of social distance is dependent on contact with people affected with mental illness. People who know someone with schizophrenia or are themselves affected, have lower social distance than people who have no such contact or are not affected themselves. The extent of social distance is likewise dependent on knowledge. People knowing less about the behaviour and symptoms associated with schizophrenia as well as the treatment options for schizophrenia have greater social distance.

A further international cooperation took place in the framework of a joint research project with a research team in Nürnberg, Germany, and the Macedonian Anti stigma Association in Skopje, (former Yugoslav Republic of) Macedonia. The team in Macedonia conducted an attitude survey among the Macedonian public with the same questionnaire which has been used to assess public attitudes in Germany. The results of the surveys have been compared [11], especially as regards potential coherences of attitudes and differences in the health care systems in the two countries. Based on the survey results, intervention strategies for the anti stigma work in Macedonia will be developed in close cooperation of both research teams. A further cooperation is in planning: a comparative study about attitudes of psychiatric professionals towards mentally ill patients in Macedonia and Germany. In October 2006, on the occasion of the III International Stigma Conference in Istanbul, Turkey, the Macedonian team became a member of the WPA Section on Stigma and Mental Health.

Anti-stigma training modules

On the basis of the gained experiences and data from evaluation of the conducted interventions, the development, production, evaluation and implementation of educational modules is the next step in the fight against stigma and discrimination in the project centre in Düsseldorf. So called 'Anti-stigma modules' will be produced, tested and implemented in the framework of the anti stigma project of the GRNS. The 'anti-stigma modules' include two parts comprising (a) methodological information about the conduction and evaluation of anti-stigma interventions with a target group and (b) information (e.g. 'Causes of schizophrenia', 'Treatment of schizophrenia') produced for the special needs of a target group. The 'anti-stigma modules' will enable interested persons and institutions to autonomously conduct anti-stigma interventions in a specified target group (for example, journalists, hospital ward staff) and furthermore will be integrated in education schedules. Implementation and evaluation will be conducted in cooperation with centres of the Open the Doors society. Focus interviews and patient surveys have shown that a substantial proportion of psychiatric patients feels discriminated against by health care staff. It is known that even mental health professionals tend to hold stereotyped images about mental illness and mentally ill persons. Modules for anti-stigma training with mental health professionals have not yet been developed and are therefore in the focus of the future work of the centre in Düsseldorf.

Competence Centre for Destigmatization of People with Schizophrenia

For long-term maintenance of these modules, a Competence Centre for the Destigmatization of People with Schizophrenia (CCDPS) will be established under the umbrella of the GRNS in Düsseldorf, providing for a fee services such as advice in implementation and evaluation of the modules, 'Train the trainers' seminars, evaluation services and continued updating and further development of the modules.

Post-initiative survey

In summer 2004, the project group in Düsseldorf conducted the post-initiative survey in the general public with almost 4700 interviewees (the same sample as in 2001). First results show positive effects of the anti-stigma work in Germany over recent years. The researchers found an increase of knowledge about causes, symptoms and treatment options for schizophrenia and a decrease of social distance towards individuals with schizophrenia. Social distance decreased significantly in those interviewees who knew at least one of the anti stigma initiatives, Open the Doors, ASAM (Anti-stigma Action Munich) or BASTA [12, 13].

Involvement in further national and regional anti stigma programmes

The project group in Düsseldorf has been invited to conceptualize the action plan and is actively involved in the 'Alliance for Mental Health' (Aktionsbündnis Seelische Gesundheit), which has been initiated by Open the Doors and the DGPPN, assisted by the Federal Health Ministry under the auspices of the Federal Health Minister.

The group is also significantly involved in the planning, conduction and evaluation of a regional campaign to raise the awareness of depressive disorders in the public, the Düsseldorf Alliance against Depression, which was initiated by the regional Medical Association in April 2005.

ASAM – Anti stigma Action Munich: Activities and experience

Petra Ursula Decker and Hans-Jürgen Möller

Improving public attitudes

Stigma attached to schizophrenia creates a vicious cycle of alienation and discrimination for those who suffer from it and often for their families. Stigma can become the main cause of social isolation, inability to find work, alcohol or drug abuse, homelessness, and excessive institutionalization, all of which decrease the chance of recovery. To counteract stigma and prevent discrimination the WPA programme aims to increase the awareness and knowledge of the nature of schizophrenia and treatment options and to improve public attitudes to those who have or have had schizophrenia and their families, as well as to generate action to prevent or eliminate discrimination and prejudice. Therefore from the beginning of the anti stigma programme the LMU group 'Anti-Stigma-Action Munich (ASAM)' organized events for the general public such as monthly lectures and readings with well-known authors, art exhibitions, cinema shows that include panel discussions, and poster actions such as 'Artists against Stigma'. At many of these activities surveys were conducted, measuring the knowledge and attitudes of the relevant target groups such as the public, patients, and psychology and medical students. For this work ASAM received the 'Lilly Schizophrenia Awards 2002 – Innovative concepts for new perspectives'. Furthermore, training for hospital staff will be implemented to reduce stigma and discrimination because of schizophrenia. In the following section the problems and success of some of these activities will be discussed.

Public relations in psychiatry demand a qualified contact with the media. A good personal contact between psychiatry and media is important, as journalists are mediators for the public. Well-prepared press portfolios for the media are an absolute must. ASAM started with press conferences in April 2001 and April 2002 and created media workshops in March 2003 and November 2004. Readers from both sides – the media and psychiatry – discussed particular topics and problems, e.g. negative headlines and reports in the news concerning the mentally ill, their negative portrayal in movies or misunderstandings between the writer or interviewer and the interviewee in printed articles. The main topic for 2004 was the article 'Life with the delusion', a sensitive portrayal of a women who suffers from schizophrenia, in the German magazine *Stern* No. 42, 7 October 2004. The author and the subject attended the workshop and discussed the article with the journalists.

Important for the media is to have an opportunity to talk to the mentally ill, their relatives and the professionals together, but also to respect the person and their privacy. Moreover, diverse positions increase the authenticity to the public. A life story heard from a mentally ill person affects people more than hearing statements about their medical reports. Afterwards people feel more empathetic and their sympathy for the mentally ill increased, as was measured with questionnaires at the cinema shows in Munich.

In August 2002, 2003 and 2004 ASAM and BASTA participated at the Munich International Film Festival. With the topic 'Psychiatry in movies' several films such as *A Beautiful Mind*, *I Never Promised You a Rose Garden*, *Open Your Eyes* and *Elling*, were shown and discussed with the audience afterwards. All films were evaluated with pre-post questionnaires.

As one important aspect in anti-stigma work is to ameliorate knowledge about schizophrenia, in April 2001 four brochures were created and designed concerning the illness of schizophrenia, the therapy methods of schizophrenia, the causes of schizophrenia and the stigmatization of schizophrenia. Ten thousand copies of each brochure were produced in 2004 and circulated to the public, health institutions and doctors and psychologists throughout Germany.

Since the project started, ASAM has been able to inform the public about stigma and discrimination because of schizophrenia in the daily national press, regional press and tabloids. Furthermore, face-to-face interviews and special articles were given to the regional press and medical journals.

A unique activity was the poster session 'Artists against Stigma' in 2003: 80 artists from literature, movies, theatre and arts, such as the Nobel prize winner for literature Günter Grass, supported this project.

In February 2002 ASAM created a web site to reach more people for fighting against stigma and discrimination because of schizophrenia: http://psywifo.klinikum. uni-muenchen.de/open. Since then, 82,156 people have visited the homepage. Mean daily number of visits has been 245.58 with a maximum of 500 people per day and an increasing rate. At the homepage we mentioned links to other important institutions. The homepage, the poster, the press portfolios and the folders have the same design in order to reach a high recall value in the population.

Not just mentally ill people are stigmatized but also psychiatry as an institution is stigmatized. Nearly 50 per cent of the German population associate psychiatry with padded cells. This stereotype is hard to break. Therefore the clinic offers 'open days', workshops and guided tours in the clinic for the public, the police and pupils as well as face-to-face discussions with patients, psychologists and psychiatrists.

Survey results

Anti-stigma surveys, as mentioned before, were performed with self-assessment questionnaires for the public, for medical and psychological students and for patients. Some details from the Munich surveys: 85.2% of the Munich public ($n = 1278$) demanded more face-to-face meetings with the mentally ill, such as art exhibitions or theatre events; so did the psychological (58.7%) and medical (53.3%) students of the Ludwig-Maximilians University Munich. Of the Munich public ($n = 1092$) 77.3% considered face-to-face contact with the mentally ill during open-day activities as important or very important. Of the Munich patients ($n = 37$) with schizophrenic disorders (ICD 10) from the BKH Haar in 2001, 83.8% required more positive portrayals and reports in the media: 88.2% from the public of Munich ($n = 1092$) wished the same. Of the psychological students 79.4% and of the medical students 79% had similar requirements. The patients were asked: from which of the following groups did they feel discriminated against or supported. Mostly they were stigmatized in the workplace (40.5%), followed by in their families (40.5%), by doctors or therapists (29.7%), by the police (24.3%) and by their friends (18.9%). At the same time they found support from doctors or therapists (54%), their friends (51.4%) and their families (51.4%), followed by the police (45.9%) and their colleagues or boss (37.8%). Of interest was also the result of the medical students among whom 42.9% felt afraid by just having a conversation with mentally ill patients, even after they have had their psychiatric course. More education and studies are necessary in this respect.

BASTA – The alliance for mentally ill people

Kerstin Wundsam, Romain Beitinger and Werner Kissling

BASTA is an organization consisting of consumers, caregivers, psychiatric professionals, and other interested persons (e.g. journalists, teachers and students) with its main office located in Munich and project centres throughout southern Germany. Since the year 2001, approximately 25–35 members have been developing various project groups with special anti-stigma activities. Within these interventions, BASTA aims to counteract stereotypes about mental illnesses (mainly schizophrenia), diminish established prejudices towards inflicted people and generally work for a greater interest in and better knowledge about psychiatric and mental health topics. To meet these goals, BASTA informs the general public and specially chosen target groups (e.g. students and police officers) about symptoms and treatment opportunities for mental illnesses, about stigma and its consequences. In addition, the demystification of the psychiatric profession, psychiatric treatment and associated institutions are further areas of interest. In order to improve compassion for and understanding of a particular group of people, we know from previous research [2, 14, 15, 16] that personal contact is extremely important and can positively influence attitudes, prejudices and future behaviour. Therefore, the core of all BASTA projects is to offer facilities for more communication and contact between the respective target group and people living with mental illness, care givers and/or psychiatric professionals. To estimate the efficacy of these anti-stigma interventions and to identify possible misleading or harmful effects, the main projects were evaluated via surveys.

The anti-stigma project for students

To offer a school project that meets the needs of teachers while simultaneously 'playfully' informing the students about mental illnesses and raise their interest, BASTA developed the 'Learning Kit: Mentally ill people', consisting of four units. The first three units familiarize the students with the topic 'mentally ill people' and 'stereotypes and prejudices towards psychiatric diseases". The materials of this Learning Kit can be easily modified, depending on the age of the students and varying levels of proficiency – and can be easily integrated into the normal curriculum of the class. Meeting a 'real patient' together with a psychiatric professional in unit 4 represents the core of the Learning Kit. The team visits the class for a minimum of 90 minutes. The students are encouraged to ask questions or speak openly about any topic of interest to them in regard to psychiatric conditions, personal experiences within the family of the consumer of mental health services as well as prejudices and discriminating behaviour due to mental illness. We found that the interventional programme significantly increased the students' knowledge about schizophrenia and improved 'negative stereotypes' and their 'social distance', i.e. the students readiness to enter into different types of social relationships with someone who has had schizophrenia. All participating students and teachers enthusiastically accepted the project.

An awareness training programme for police officers

Police officers frequently become involved with acutely mentally ill people and often feel neither sufficiently prepared nor supported. Little knowledge regarding psychiatric diseases, like schizophrenia, and the anticipation of increased violence and threat posed by psychiatric patients can end up in 'tense' and difficult situations. The contact between officers and patients with schizophrenia is commonly associated with conflict situations, e.g. when patients require clinical admission because of 'danger to self or others'. These interactions are often sources of stigmatization and discriminating behaviour.

The training programme was planned and realized by BASTA in cooperation with psychiatric patients, care givers, psychiatric professionals and sociology teachers at a police academy near Munich, Germany. Police officers participate in a one-day seminar, which consists of three teaching units and lasts 4.5 hours in total. The core of the seminar is the personal contact between officers and people who have experienced mental illnesses, and aims for better understanding and knowledge as well as improved compassion and empathy with psychiatric patients and their families. Approximately 200 police officers were enrolled into an evaluation during the pilot project. We found that the need for special training of police officers regarding psychiatric patients and their problems was generally acknowledged. The project was enthusiastically welcomed by the officers and teachers at the police academy. Participants embraced the seminar presented and rated it highly. The personal conversations with people who had previously experienced mental illness offered the police officers an opportunity for interesting discussions and new information to integrate in their everyday professional life. Officers emphasized that most of them had never had contact with 'healthy patients' before. This personal contact seems to be very important and positively influences the empathy and understanding of police officers with the mentally ill and their families.

Anti-stigma projects for the general public

Readings (including poetry), theatre performances, lectures, diverse arts exhibitions and further screening of movies (e.g. *Elling*, *Iris*, *The White Noise*, *A Beautiful Mind* and *Open Your Eyes*) were conducted. To examine the impact of these films, BASTA surveyed the audiences' ($n = 311$) beliefs and social distance before and after three films. *A Beautiful Mind* and *Open Your Eyes* had no negative influences, but did not improve the audiences' attitudes or social distance. On the other hand, *The White Noise* did increase social distance and seemed to be, all in all inappropriate for anti-stigma projects. These findings confirm the results of Baumann *et al.* [17].

Working with the media

Regional and national newspapers and magazines printed many articles and interviews with anti-stigma messages, and documentaries have appeared on radio stations in Munich. Working closely with the media and supporting journalists, as well as the care for a positive and benevolent cooperation with representatives of the media, are very important components within the anti-stigma campaigns. Furthermore, projects with the media also empower consumers and caregivers involved by acknowledging their expert role.

Fighting against acute stigmatization

In order to protest against discrimination within advertisements, TV series, movies and press reports, BASTA has founded 'SANE', a web-based 'Stigma-Alarm NEtwork'. The idea for 'stigma-busting' networks was originally realized in the USA (NAMI) and Australia (SANE) and both have had an impressive number of successes since their establishment. At the German SANE, those interested can participate in the network at no cost and enrol simply by registering personal e-mail addresses at the BASTA website (www.openthedoors.de). Via Internet-based communication, the members can inform BASTA of discriminating cases and vice versa, get information in the case of an official action of BASTA to stop stigmatization or discrimination (including contact information of the originator). Everyone can voluntarily participate in these protest actions (through personal letters, e-mails, telephone calls, etc.) and follow the ongoing progress in the category 'SANE' at the BASTA homepage.

A change of views about mentally ill persons among those who stigmatize can be brought about and discrimination in many cases can be stopped. The power of SANE is of course dependent on its members and their activities in a stigma-case. At the moment there are 700 SANE members registered and enrolment is steadily increasing (following various public relation actions). One future plan is the establishment of SANE Europe, with different countries participating in the network for strong and powerful actions throughout Europe. Financial sponsors and a well-planned language network would be necessary to mount such an ambitious project.

General services and support

BASTA provides support for referenced papers, as well as diploma or doctoral theses for university students who wish to collaborate on and deal with anti-stigma issues. Additionally, BASTA releases monthly newsletters (free of charge), where members get information regarding different activities, event notes and general news. Registration is quick and simple at the website www.openthedoors.de.

Changing people's views – Building bridges: For more normality in dealing with mental health problems
Irrsinnig Menschlich e.V. Leipzig

Manuela Richter-Werling and Matthias Angermeyer

Irrsinnig Menschlich e.V. (www.irrsinnig-menschlich.de) is the first German association committed to Public Relations in Psychiatry. The aim of Irrsinnig Menschlich e.V., which was founded in 2000, is to promote dealing with mental disorders in an open and enlightened way. That is why the association considers itself as a contact pool for all people who want to learn more about mental health, mental disorders and available treatment. One of the most important intentions of Irrsinnig Menschlich e.V. is to promote personal contact with persons with mental health problems, to make the seemingly incomprehensible understandable, to reduce prejudices and fears and to promote integration. The association takes advantage of the many different points of views of its members: patients, relatives of persons with mental disorders and professional helpers, journalists, politicians, artists and committed citizens; they all work together for the common cause with their individual experiences and resources.

First and foremost, however, the work of Irrsinnig Menschlich e.V. benefits from the activity of those who are affected by stigmatization: people with mental disorders and their relatives. Their motivation to fight against stigma and discrimination is very strong. Breaking the spiral of discrimination based on stigma can only be successful by joint efforts of patients, relatives, professionals and the public. That is why Irrsinnig Menschlich e.V. considers itself as an association that 'builds bridges' between psychiatry and the public. The projects of the association are based on results of up-to-date stigma research. In particular personal encounter with people with mental disorders results in a reduction of stereotypes, fears and distance. The goals of Irrsinnig Menschlich e.V. are:

- To facilitate encounters with people with mental disorders.

- To promote the sharing of experiences of those affected, relatives of people with mental disorders and the public.

- To consider itself as the contact pool for the media and to contribute to setting the agenda.

- To cooperate with international initiatives which are engaged in promoting tolerance for and understanding of people with mental disorders.

The following components have been developed to accomplish these ambitious goals.

The school project 'Crazy? So What!'

According to the WHO European Ministerial Conference on Mental Health held in Helsinki in 2005, prevention and promotion are of the greatest importance when it comes to the mental health of children and adolescents. The school project 'Crazy? So What!' – developed, tested and positively evaluated by Irrsinnig Menschlich – aims in this direction. Since 2001, more than 2500 students from all over Germany have participated in the school project.

The *uniqueness* of 'Crazy? So What!' is manifested in the combination of prevention and de-stigmatization – in this way Irrsinnig Menschlich has created a new field of health education. The project, which is designed for students starting at year 9 raises awareness about good mental health and contributes to prevention and promotes openness, understanding and tolerance in interpersonal relationships. At the same time it encourages people who have experienced mental health problems to participate in society with more self-confidence. The core aspect of the school project is the direct contact between students and people with a mental disorder. The project takes place for one day or longer in school and is conducted by a moderator and a person who has experienced a mental disorder. Because of the growing national interest in the project which has been expressed by students and teachers, the association has filed a grant application to the Aktion Mensch in 2005 for the nationwide implementation of 'Crazy? So What!' The aim is to establish regional groups in all 16 federal states to offer and conduct the project independently at schools in their region and in the future also train and instruct new regional groups. At the same time a network is being established to secure the school project in the long term. Among the partners are the Ministries of Culture and Ministries of Health of each federal state, people affected and relatives' associations, the central associations of social welfare, the institutes for the further education of teachers in each federal state and the local education authorities.

Organizations from Slovakia and the Czech Republic are planning to adopt the school project in their countries and are undertaking special courses to be trained in the implementation of the project. The association has been successful in collecting promotional funds from the European Union for the implementation of the project in these two countries.

MUT 2005 (Courage 2005) – prize for political action for the benefit of people with mental disorders

Society is paying a high price for mental disorders, in the form of both human suffering and economic costs. Realizing that the maintenance and promotion of mental health is in the end a political task, is only slowly becoming accepted. To accelerate this process, Irrsinnig Menschlich has been awarding the MUT Prize since 2003. The immense interest in the prize indicates that the association actually motivates politicians to become more committed to people with mental health problems. At the same time it shows that mental health and mental illness are topics of major interest to the public.

Irrsinnig Menschlich e.V. wants to:

- acknowledge the courageous commitment of politicians to the disadvantaged group of people with mental disorders;
- promote the establishment of a network made up of politicians, prominent advocates, the media, institutions and organizations;
- call upon politicians to act in favour of a lasting improvement of the situation of people who have experienced and are experiencing mental health problems;
- encourage the public, the media and politicians to pass on information about mental disorders and to reduce prejudices against people with mental disorders;
- accomplish that maintaining and promoting mental health as well as preventing mental disorders become a part of the social agenda.

Irrsinnig Menschlich decided to name the prize 'MUT' (courage) because being active on behalf of people with mental disorders cannot be taken for granted. In times of cuts in the social sector and the reorganization of social security systems politicians can and must set an example!

Against the images in our heads – media work for people with mental health problems

The mass media have the strongest impact on people's attitudes and opinions. The media constitute an indispensable partner when it comes to reducing the stigmatization of and discrimination against people with mental disorders. However, media reports can only be accurate when journalists receive accurate information. That is why Irrsinnig Menschlich encourages people with mental disorders to do public relations on their own behalf and supports journalists and also initiates media projects. These include the establishment of the first international media workshop for people with schizophrenia in Michalovce, a joint project of the Slovakian anti-stigma initiative ODOS and Irrsinnig Menschlich e.V. In cooperation with German public service broadcasting, Irrsinnig Menschlich e.V. has initiated theme nights on mental health problems. At the moment the association is working on a cinema ad about mental disorders in co-operation with the MDR (broadcasting station in central Germany).

Future prospects

Initiatives like Irrsinnig Menschlich e.V., which are committed to maintaining and promoting mental health and to preventing mental disorders, are experiencing a growing interest from the public. In the future their role will be increasingly that of mediator between politicians, people affected and their relatives, the care system and the public. This has been emphasized by the WHO European Ministerial Conference on Mental Health held in Helsinki in January 2005. The association Irrsinnig Menschlich is prepared to face this challenge. However, in order to do so, a financial basic coverage with public funds is necessary to secure the work of the association.

Psychiatry goes to school-Special open days for schoolchildren and students – a 'trialogic' campaign in Hamburg

Thomas Bock and Dieter Naber

'Irre menschlich Hamburg' (madly human) has been in existence for many years; it emerged from a Psychosis Seminar in Hamburg, independently from 'Open the Doors' and has a tripartite organization consisting of persons who had experienced psychosis, relatives and professional experts [18]. First, they try to reduce all mutual prejudices and then join forces to meet the prejudices held by the public. Their motto is to endeavour to set an example for the more than 100 psychosis seminars in German speaking countries, to summon up courage and confidence to come into the open and exercise influence on the public opinion – it is an anti stigma campaign from below. With this triad concept, this organization aims also at trying to achieve cooperation with other programmes such as 'Open the Doors'.

Tasks of Irre menschlich Hamburg

- Providing 'first-hand information' to journalists (participation in major talk shows, short reports on national TV, special radio spots, journal articles);

- Information at schools (a total of 120 projects for all grades, integrated into the lessons), PR work at universities, further training for teachers, mentors etc. with the focus on 'mental illness as a teaching subject' and 'mental illness in schoolchildren';

- Information projects in companies (e.g. regular presentations at police academies);

- Support of theatre and movie projects and operation of its own website (www.irremenschlich.de);

- Organization of special open days for schoolchildren: 'Psychiatrie macht Schule' (Psychiatry goes to school);

- Research activities (e.g. an award-winning paper on the 'The image of mentally ill persons in the children's and adolescents' literature of the German language').

Principles

Trialogue: Psychiatry has not been innocent with respect to stigmatization, historically or in the present day. Therefore, psychiatrists have to assume responsibility in the process of exercising positive influence not only on public awareness of psychiatry but also with respect to the public image of mentally ill persons. They can only be credible in cooperation with these persons and their relatives.

Encounter: Direct contacts with mentally ill persons are the only convincing encounters. Therefore, information projects in schools and in companies include direct contacts.

Rehabilitation and prevention: Meeting persons who have experienced psychosis helps to reduce fears, acts against prejudices and contributes to an attitude that does not leave unchallenged certain cultural and media-shaped norms. Thus, anti stigma activities reduce not only fear but also pressure. Tolerance of others leads to greater generosity and sensitivity towards the self and thus acts preventively. The projects in schools and in some business organizations therefore fulfil political purposes concerning both health *and* education.

Identity of school: The school is involved in its very own identity as school, and not as a place of early intervention, and teachers are involved as teachers and not as amateur psychologists. The educational projects intentionally do *not* have the aim of performing early diagnosis. The danger of stigmatization would be too great. The effect is to reduce the fear of psychiatry in an indirect but effective way, thus smoothing the way to seek help in case of need. The open encounter inspires confidence and seems to be a good alternative to symptom-related measures of early diagnosis.

Methods of anti stigma activities at schools

Unlike the Austrian anti stigma campaign, 'Irre menschlich' does not work for or instead of teachers, but closely cooperates with them. In contrast to the sister project 'Irrsinnig menschlich' in Leipzig, the Hamburg project not only organizes special project weeks, which are not rooted in educational legislation, but organizes educational units of various lengths, according to the needs and possibilities, the teacher's specialization and the age of the children. Minimum duration is six double periods for authentic information, encounters and evaluation or own references.

The teachers will be advised and receive 'media boxes' with material put together according to the class's needs, containing books, movies, background information etc. The central element of each teaching unit is the direct encounter, the personal meeting of schoolchildren and crisis-experienced persons, who act as 'teachers of life'. The educational goals differ according to the available time, the teacher's specialization and, above all, the children's age.

In lower grades, the goal is to reinforce in a casual way children's openness and awareness by introducing certain children's books, e.g. *Die Bettelkönigin* (The Beggar Queen) [19], and by the encounter with an exceptional person, e.g. the central person of the book, the artist Hildegard Wohlgemuth. In middle grades, the development of prejudices and their effects is the central theme. In upper grades, it is possible to reflect also the child's own life, own goals, possible crises and available resources.

So far, class teachers of lower grades and teachers of religion and ethics (9th grade), biology (10th grade), German, history, art, philosophy and psychology (upper grades) have been involved, often organizing cross-subject teaching. The projects are almost equally distributed among lower, middle and upper grades. So far, a total of 1400 children have been reached, about 600 of them by projects offered at the local psychiatric hospital.

Speakers are available on a variety of subjects such as psychosis, drugs and psychosis, mania, eating disorders, self-injuring behaviour and borderline disorders.

'Psychiatrie macht Schule' – special open days for schoolchildren

Open days are most often meant for neighbours and former patients, relatives and colleagues. For the past three years, the target groups have been expanded with the aim of inviting the schools of the neighbourhood. The *school panels*' motto of the first year was: 'It is normal to be different'; in the second and third years, the main theme was 'Psychiatrie macht Schule' which is, in German, a play on words and might be translated by 'Psychiatry goes to school', but also meaning 'Psychiatry is the accepted thing'. Inviting schoolchildren is part of an overall strategy – it is, in a way, a return invitation with respect to projects at schools all the year round. The programme includes documentary films, an art exhibition, music contributions, food and drink, information booths, book displays, presentations and special workshops for schoolchildren.

The short presentations on various disorders in the lecture hall are intentionally presented in pairs: professional experts and persons who have experienced mental illness jointly present the subject. But the main focus is on workshops, which are adjusted to pupils of different ages and are organized in cooperation. The workshops for school children are similar to the teaching projects at schools; i.e. the personal encounter is most important: one or more persons who have had contact with psychiatry speak about a more or less youth-specific subject and their own personal experience, their presentation being supported by professionals. Most coordinators have now gained experience in talking about themselves in the psychosis seminar. Some of them were already involved in school projects. A small remuneration rewards their participation. This is meant to underline their position as coordinators.

Overview of dialogical workshops for pupils on open days

Coordinators make presentations and distribute materials that have been devised specifically for children on many different areas of importance for mental health and for the understanding of mental conditions.

Extreme sensitivity – thin-skinned psychosis

(1) *Die Bettelkönigin* – The Beggar Queen – by artist Hildegard Wohlgemuth. Model of a book for children – reading, film, pictures (10 years and older).

(2) *Pias lebt . . . gefährlich* – Pias lives . . . dangerously – an outsider talks about his life on the street (12 years and older).

(3) *Die erste Psychose* – First episode psychosis. Extreme obstinacy – how can it start? Are there typical crises? What happens to the soul, to the family? (14 years and older).

(4) *Stimmenhören* – Hearing voices – messages from the inner world? (12 years and older, parents, teachers).

(5) *Durch Drogen psychotisch* – Drug-induced psychosis. How great is the danger? Report from own experience with cannabis (14 years and older).

Extreme moods – mania and depression

(6) *Gute Zeiten, schlechte Zeiten* – Good times, bad times. Depression and mania – extreme fluctuations of mood and energy. How is the dynamism perceived? What is helpful, what isn't? (14 years and older).

Grenzgänger – borderline

(7) *Auf der Grenze der Realität* – At the borderline of reality. What does it mean, if the personality is easily 'disturbed'? Which questions and conflicts are typical? What is helpful to achieve greater stability?

(8) *So rot wie Blut* – As red as blood. Sniping, self-injuring behaviour. What is the message? Own experience, speaking through clay figures (14 years and older, parents, teachers).

Dependence and addiction

(9) *Is(s) was? – Magersucht und Bulimie?* – Eating disorders – starving, throwing up or both – for an ideal of beauty? (12 years and older).

(10) *Bekifft in der Schule?* – Stoned in the school? How dangerous is cannabis? (14 years and older, parents, teachers).

(11) *Hell-Blau* – Light drunk. Alcohol problems already at 12? Information, prevention (12 years and older, parents, teachers).

Anxiety

(12) *Angst und Zwang – normal oder verrückt?* – Anxiety and compulsion. Normal or mad? Aren't certain fears and compulsions part of life? Where is the borderline? (12 years and older).

The selection of titles intends to appeal to adolescents and introduce the subject effortlessly but without triviality. The aim is to put right the clichés one might entertain about the coordinator and his or her history and to raise interest in further information.

Experiences and results

In the first year, 500 schoolchildren were reached, and 800 in each of the following two years, coming from about 40 schools, mostly high schools, comprehensive schools and vocational schools. The most interesting ones were workshops that were organized jointly by patients and professionals. Most panels had to be offered two and three times over, due to the great interest. For many teachers, the open day is the beginning of further cooperation with 'Irre menschlich Hamburg', but at the same time they value the visit to the hospital as having educational importance of its own.

The benefit of this project is emphasized by a first evaluation. The schoolchildren assess the workshops with psychiatry-experienced persons with marks of 1 or 2, but give significantly lower marks for only professional workshops. About one third of students reported having been affected personally by the subject – either because of their own unusual experiences or those of relatives and friends. The patients who participate benefit from increased empowerment.

Own affectedness

An amazingly high number of schoolchildren report in an anonymous questionnaire that they recognize the various experiences of the patients in their own experience: 18.5% from their own experience, 17% from the family and 38.3% from friends. With respect to their own experience, the percentage of male adolescents (20.9 vs. 17.3%) is slightly higher than that of female adolescents, with respect to family experience (14.4 vs. 18.3%) and experience among friends (33.7 vs. 40.4%) it is slightly lower. It must be kept in mind that these figures refer to all disorders and cannot be differentiated.

Assessment and marking

The pupils were asked to assess and mark the workshops. The return rate was more than 80%. The analysis of the differentiated assessments has not yet been done. The marking according to school marks (1–6) is encouraging. A total of $n = 555$ (81.4%) marks have been given: the mean value was 2.1, the standard deviation 0.8. Workshops in cooperation with (former) patients received highly significantly better marks. The assessment by male adolescents is slightly better than that by female adolescents. Adolescents with own or family experiences confer better marks than those without own experience. Although these differences are not statistically significant, they are remarkable because they are rather unexpected: Boys also respond to the subject. Moreover, adolescents, directly or indirectly affected, can be reached by this kind of workshop, without feeling unsettled or shamed!

In regard to the coordinators, their task usually starts an amazing process of empowerment for persons who have experienced psychosis. The schoolchildren impress by the high level of openness and tolerance in their discussions. For younger children, unusual perceptions are still relatively natural, the encounter with unusual persons falling on fertile ground. As for adolescents of upper grades, the focus is often on self-awareness, on their own vulnerability to crisis, on their own image of human beings and on tolerance within the class. Thus, education and information on 'being different, madness, mental illness' is not only relevant for health policy but also in the context of education. In a world with ever increasing pressures, it is important to prepare schoolchildren for life and discuss with them their own life plans and possible crises.

Conclusion

One of the main obstacles to successful treatment of schizophrenia is the stigma frequently associated with the disorder. The diagnosis of schizophrenia and the disorder's perceptible characteristics can mean that the heterogeneity of behaviour attributable to the illness is negatively judged and leads to social exclusion and disadvantage. Educative and training programmes such as Open the Doors can improve knowledge of mental illness and modify negative attitudes in the general population as well as in specific target groups, such as those employed in mental health care. In addition to providing information about the nature, causes and treatment of mental disorders, interventions should place special emphasis on achieving a more positive media portrayal of people with mental illness and on promoting personal contact with them. Information on the disorder and on the factors underlying its stigmatization should reach relatives, friends, colleagues and supervisors, as well as physicians, therapists, and nursing staff. The frequently expressed desire for more encounters with people having mental illness – for instance, during open days at psychiatric institutions – and for more art exhibitions or theatrical productions involving those with mental illness are in line with the German anti stigma programme interventions. Interventions against stigma and discrimination toward those with mental illness can be effective, not only in specific target groups, but also for the general public. In addition to disseminating information about mental illness, special emphasis should be placed on achieving a more positive media portrayal of people with mental illness and on promoting personal contact with them.

Open the Doors Germany initiated the 'Alliance for Mental Health' together with the DGPPN, assisted by the Federal Health Ministry under the auspices of the Federal Health Minister. With the introduction of the 'Alliance for Mental Health' at the Annual Congress of the DGPPN in Berlin in November 2004 a trend-setting emphasis was placed on future engagement in the provision of psychiatric care and in German society generally. The participants in this programme, among them representatives of all project centres of Open the Doors Germany, want to devote their combined strength in the coming years to the de-stigmatization of mental illnesses by informing the public and specific target groups on various social levels throughout Germany.

Acknowledgements

The following persons contributed to this chapter: Josef Aldenhoff, Matthias Angermeyer, Anja Esther Baumann, Romain Beitinger, Thomas Bock, Petra Ursula Decker, Arno Deister, Wolfgang Gaebel, Werner Kissling, Hans-Jürgen Möller, Dieter Naber, Manuela Richter-Werling, Kerstin Wundsam and Harald Zäske.

References

1. World Psychiatric Association (1998) *Fighting Stigma and Discrimination because of Schizophrenia*. New York: World Psychiatric Association.
2. Corrigan, P.W., River, L.P., Lundin, R.K., Penn, D.L., Uphoff-Wasowski, K., Campion, J., Mathisen, J., Gagnon, C., Bergman, M., Goldstein, H. and Kubiak, M.A. (2001) Three strategies for changing attributions about severe mental illness. *Schizophrenia Bulletin* **27**, 187–195.
3. Penn, D.L. and Shannon, M.C. (2002) Strategies for reducing stigma towards persons with mental illness. *World Psychiatry* **1**, 20–1.
4. Wölwer, W., Buchkremer, G., Häfner, H., Klosterkötter, J., Maier, W., Möller, H.J. and Gaebel, W. (eds) (2003) German Research Network on Schizophrenia. Bridging the gap between research and care. *European Archives of Psychiatry and Clinical Neuroscience* **253**, 321–329.
5. Gaebel, W., Klosterkötter, J., Weßling, A., Baumann, A., Köhn, D. and Zäske, H. (2004) German Research Network on Schizophrenia. Public education programmes in Düsseldorf and Cologne, Germany. In: S. Saxena and P.J. Garrison (eds) *Mental Health Promotion. Case Studies from Countries*, pp. 38–40. A joint publication of the World Federation for Mental Health and the World Health Organization. Geneva: World Health Organization.

6. Gaebel, W., Baumann, A., Witte, M. and Zäske, H. (2002) Public attitudes towards people with mental illness in six German cities. Results of a public survey under special consideration of schizophrenia. *European Archives of Psychiatry and Clinical Neuroscience* **252**, 278–287.

7. World Psychiatric Association (2005) *Fighting Stigma and Discrimination because of Schizophrenia. Anti stigma Training Manual.* New York: World Psychiatric Association.

8. Gaebel, W., Möller, H.J. and Rössler, W. (eds) (2004) *Stigma – Diskriminierung – Bewältigung. Der Umgang mit sozialer Ausgrenzung psychisch Kranker.* Stuttgart: Kohlhammer Verlag.

9. Stuart, H. and Arboleda-Flórez, J. (2001) Community attitudes towards people with schizophrenia. *Canadian Journal of Psychiatry* **46**, 245–252.

10. Gaebel, W. and Baumann, A. (2003) Interventions to reduce the stigma associated with severe mental illness: experiences from the Open the Doors programme in Germany. *Canadian Journal of Psychiatry* **48**, 657–662.

11. Baumann, A.E., Richter, K., Belevska, D., Zaeske, H., Gaebel, W., Niklewski, G., Ortakov, V., Bajraktarov, S., Pesevska, J. and Wahlberg, H. (2005) Public attitudes towards people with schizophrenia: a comparison between Macedonia and Germany. *World Psychiatry* **4**(1), 53–55.

12. Baumann, A., Zäske, H., Decker, P., Klosterkötter, J., Maier, W., Möller, H.J. and Gaebel, W. (2007) Veränderungen in der sozialen Distanz der Bevölkerung gegenüber schizophren Erkrankten in sechs bundesdeutschen Großstädten: Ergebnisse einer repräsentativen Telefonbefragung 2001 und 2004. *Nervenarzt* **78**: 787–795.

13. Gaebel, W., Zäske, H., Baumann, A.E., Klosterkötter, J., Maier, W., Decker, P. and Möller, H.J. (2008) Evaluation of the German WPA 'Program against stigma and discrimination because of schizophrenia – Open the Doors': Results from representative telephone surveys before and after three years of antistigma interventions. *Schizophrenia Research* **98**, 184–193.

14. Desforges, D.M., Lord, C.G., Ramsey, S.L., Mason, J.A., Van Leeuwen, M.D., West, S.C. and Lepper, M.R. (1991) Effects of structured cooperative contact on changing negative attitudes toward stigmatized social groups. *Journal of Personality and Social Psychology* **60**, 531–544.

15. Pinfold, V., Huxley, P., Thornicroft, G., Farmer, P., Toulmin, H. and Graham, T. (2003) Reducing psychiatric stigma and discrimination. Evaluating an educational intervention with the police force in England. *Social Psychiatry and Psychiatric Epidemiology* **38**, 337–344.

16. Corrigan, P.W., Rowan, D., Green, A., Lundin, R., River, P., Uphoff-Wasowski, K., White, K. and Kubiak, M.A. (2002) Challenging two mental illness stigmas: Personal responsibility and dangerousness. *Schizophrenia Bulletin* **28**, 293–309.

17. Baumann, A., Zäske, H. and Gaebel, W. (2003) The image of people with mental illness in movies: Effects on beliefs, attitudes and social distance, considering as example the movie 'The White Noise'. *Psychiatrische Praxis* **30**, 372–378.

18. Bock, T. and Naber, D. (2003) 'Anti stigmakampagne von unten' in Schulen – Erfahrungen der Initiative 'Irre Menschlich Hamburg e.V.'. *Psychiatrische Praxis*, **30**(7), 402–8.

19. Strathenwerth, I. and Bock, T. (1998) Die Bettelkönigin. *Freiburg i. Br.*, Kore Edition.

5 Stigma and health care staff

Juan J. López-Ibor Jr.[1,3], Olga Cuenca[2] and María-Inés López-Ibor[3]

[1]Past-President, World Psychiatric Association
[2]Psychiatrist and President of Llorente & Cuenca Communications, Spain
[3]Department for Psychiatry and Medical Psychology, Faculty of Medicine, Complutense University of Madrid, Spain

Introduction

The World Psychiatric Association *Schizophrenia Open the Doors* programme in Spain was conceived as a nationwide activity in contrast to other countries where the implementation was local or oriented to selected populations. Being the first to adopt such a perspective, and having started shortly after the programme in Calgary, Canada, we had to decide to carry it out in the whole of the country ("*La Esquizofrenia Abre las Puertas*", Figure 5.1). As the second location to carry out such a scheme, we had to improvise some new strategies and to learn by experience. On the whole the experience was very successful and led to a better knowledge of the nature of stigma and the actions to take to fight it.

What is stigma?

Stigma is a Greek word meaning 'mark', and is derived from the verb *stizein* 'to tattoo', 'to prick', 'to puncture'. Stigma is usually a mark of disgrace or infamy, which leads to action: discrimination against the stigmatised person. To discriminate is to make distinctions prejudicial to people different from oneself (in race, colour or sanity). Discrimination leads to prejudice.

The stigma is a mark embedded on the subject, where it stays, often for ever. Even the stigmatising person loses the control of the stigma once it is imposed, and efforts to remove the mark make it more prominent. Stigma is a primitive but powerful coping strategy on occasions very efficient for survival because it identifies for ever a danger. By stigmatizing, a characteristic of the danger becomes an indelible distinctive mark, impressed on the memory of the stigmatiser.

The WPA programme has described the vicious cycle of stigma (Figure 5.2) which has to be attacked simultaneously at different levels.

Stigma on schizophrenia is so prominent and so much related to the nature of the disease that it could be also named 'stigmophrenia' and it is the main barrier for the appropriate treatment and rehabilitation of those who suffer from mental illness. The response to stigma is more stigma. The behaviour of stigmatising normal persons towards patients with schizophrenia is the same that patients have with their delusions. It is an imposed experience, self-evident, full in certainty, irrefutable by a logical line of argument because when

Figure 5.1   *La Esquizofrenia Abre las Puertas* logo

confronted with madness (one's own or others'), the answers are the same. Madness is perceived as losing one's own mind.

Mental health care in Spain

Spain is a country of about 550,000 km^2 inhabited by about 40 million persons, highly decentralized in 17 Autonomous Communities which, among other things, are responsible for providing health care. Health care is financed through the general budget of the administration, that is, by income taxes. It covers 100% of the population and takes care of almost every need. In mental health only formal psychoanalysis and hypnosis are excluded. When the WPA programme started there were in Spain 5 psychiatrists per 100,000, 0.9 psychiatric

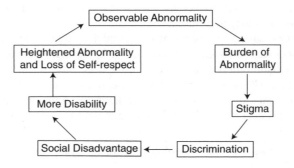

Figure 5.2   WPA programme: vicious cycle of stigma

beds per 100,000, no psychiatric hospitals with more than 1000 beds and 80% of people with schizophrenia were living with their own family.

Basic design

The programme was initiated by defining its goals and the actions to be carried out to reach them, according to the following schemes.

Objectives

(1) To enhance public attitudes of the target population groups selected by the programme in order to reduce the stigma, discrimination and prejudices towards people who suffer from schizophrenia; (2) empowerment of people close to those who suffer from schizophrenia and to the patients themselves to become leaders in fighting the stigma.

Strategy

The initial strategy was to carry out a nationwide publicity, campaign to increase awareness of schizophrenia, knowledge about the disease, its treatment and consequences, and to create a more positive attitude of the general public towards those who suffer from the disease. In order to test the feasibility of the project, a pilot programme in the Region of Madrid was to be followed by nationwide implementation. As will be described later the outcome of the pilot programme changed the strategy.

Working groups

Several committees were created in order to carry out the different tasks.

Steering Committee

Responsible for the overall implementation of the programme. The members were Juan José López-Ibor, Maria Dolores Crespo, Olga Cuenca and Blanca Reneses.

Programme Committee

Consisting of psychiatrists and other professionals interested in the programme, responsible for the translation and adaptation of the WPA programme to local needs.

Coordination Committees

Consisting of representatives of all the organizations, public or private, involved in the care of patients with schizophrenia at national and local administration levels. Health care in Spain has been decentralized and is under the responsibility of the governments of the 17 Autonomous Communities.

Teaching Committees

Consisting of psychiatrists and other mental health professionals who had shown interest in the programme.

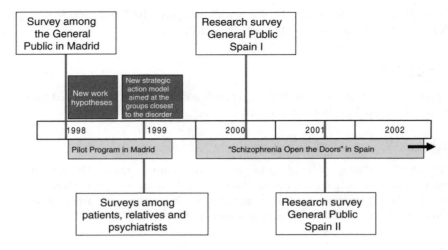

Figure 5.3   Research in Spain

Sponsors

The Ministry of Health and Consumer Affairs, the Ministry of Social Affairs, the Departments of Health and Social Services of the different Communities of Spain, the Spanish Anti-Drugs Agency, the Agencies of Health and Consumers of the different city councils involved, the National Association of Relatives of People with Schizophrenia (FEAFES) and their local organizations and others (e.g. universities).

The Lilly Company (Spain) provided full financial support for the period 1998 to 2006.

Headquarters

The headquarters of the project was located at Llorente and Cuenca,[1] a communication company, in order to make the functioning more efficient.

Pilot programme in the Madrid Region

An essential aspect of the WPA programme is that its strategy and activities are based on local data about knowledge on attitudes towards schizophrenia in the target populations and other data concerning health care. Three surveys at the general population level plus others on patients, relatives, psychiatrists and other health care personnel were carried out with the help of appropriate communication experts in the field together with research on stigma in the mass media and the impact of the programme (Figure 5.3).

Survey among the general public (Madrid Region, October-November 1998)

An independent public opinion poll was comprised of 518 random telephone interviews with people aged between 18 and 65 in urban and rural areas of the Community of Madrid.

---

[1] Hermanos Bécquer, 4 28006 Madrid (Spain). Tel: +34 91 563 77 22; fax: +34 91 563 24 66: e-mail: ocuenca@ llorenteycuenca.com; www.openthedoors.com.

Main results

Only 17% had seen, heard or read some of the advertisement campaign about schizophrenia or about persons that suffer this illness in the part six months: 73% through TV, 12% in newspapers, 11% in magazines, 5% on radio, 6% in books, 2% in pamphlets and 1% on billboards.

The typical patient suffering from schizophrenia is described as: mentally disturbed (19%), aggressive (18%), someone with strange behaviour (15%), a nervous (14%) or unstable (10%) individual, or as somebody who feels persecuted (7%) or who hears voices (4%). Of those surveyed 8% knew somebody who has been treated for schizophrenia.

Causes of schizophrenia were 24% mental disturbance, 19% genetic problems, 13% stress, 12% social problems, 6% childhood problems, 5% family problems and 4% drugs.

Of the interviewed persons 79% reported that schizophrenia is a problem that does no affect in any way their own life.

Of the sample 84% were in favour of the creation of a place to house 6 to 8 persons with schizophrenia in his or her neighbourhood

Sixty per cent thought that there is some kind of pharmaceutical treatment available at this time to treat the illness, but 96% did not know any names of relevant drugs.

Forty per cent believed that schizophrenia is an illness that can be defeated, whereas 44% said that it was not.

A cluster analysis of all the answers identified five main types of individuals:

1. **Those who accept schizophrenia** (38%): they consider schizophrenia a mental illness with possibilities of social rehabilitation. They are mainly women over 55 years of age with primary education and medium-lower class.

2. **The rationalizers** (31%): they believe that schizophrenia is a mental illness without many possibilities of social rehabilitation. They are mainly men 18–34 years of age with university degrees and medium-medium class.

3. **The anti-schizophrenics** (5%): do not want to know anything about the illness. They are mainly men over 55 years of age with elementary education and medium-lower class.

4. **The hesitants** (16%): they doubt that recovering through medication is possible and do not believe in rehabilitation. They are either men or women, 45–54 years of age, with secondary education and medium-medium class.

5. **The complacents** (9%): they consider that recovering through medication is possible but do not believe in social rehabilitation. They are either men or women, 35–44 years of age, with secondary education and medium-medium class.

Conclusions

There is little stigmatizing of people with schizophrenia amongst the Madrid population, probably because of a lack of knowledge about the illness and a high level of tolerance. Therefore, the results do not allow the design of specific messages, selecting a general audience or selecting mass media activities. Furthermore, the results suggest that an open public campaign would have the risk of increasing the stigma while increasing the knowledge about the disease.

Therefore, the strategic model of the programme was altered to cover different key audiences from inside out instead of from outside in (Figure 5.4).

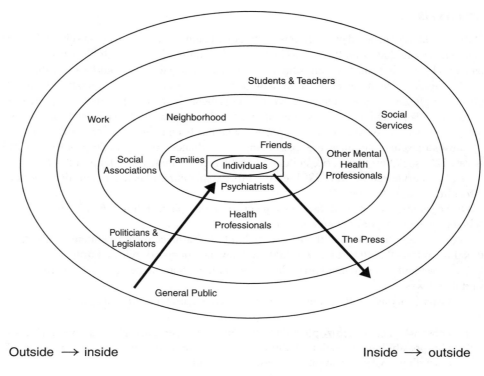

Outside →→ inside   Inside →→ outside

Figure 5.4

Surveys among patients, relatives and psychiatrists (Madrid, March 1999)

They were carried out to know the opinions and experiences of these population groups and identify specific situations of rejection and the origin of this rejection.

Anonymous questionnaires about the diagnosis, treatment, causes and origin of the illness, motives of rejection, etc. were collected from 60 persons with schizophrenia, 40 family members and 42 psychiatrists.

Main results

Seventy-one per cent of the patients know that they suffer from schizophrenia, but do not know its cause or origin, two-thirds believe that schizophrenia can be overcome, more than half have felt rejected due to aggressiveness secondary to the illness, 60% have experienced rejection sometime when visiting the psychiatrist, but 60% consider that the nursing staff treats them well. Only 17% say that their illness does not bother them and the most bothering thing for those that suffer the illness is isolation. Furthermore, patients believe that their illness does not allow them to drink alcoholic beverages, study or drink coffee.

Most of the relatives believe that schizophrenia is not curable (77%), and the worst features of the illness are the 'laziness' and, to a lesser extent, isolation, aggressiveness, lack of personal hygiene and not being able to lead a 'normal' life. They also believe that patients cannot drink alcohol or coffee, and cannot study, drive, live alone or have children.

Psychiatrists were interviewed with a questionnaire specifically prepared for the purpose by Dolores Crespo, Olga Cuenca and Juan Carlos Gómez. Sixty-two per cent of the

psychiatrists have felt rejected by their patients on some occasion because 'they do not accept the treatment', 'they do not have insight about their illness' and because they consider
the doctor to be a 'controller'. Fifty-two per cent have felt rejected by the patients' families
because they 'see no improvement' in the patient and 'do not accept the illness'. Forty-one
per cent consider that schizophrenics are chronic patients who cannot be helped much.
These results shocked us a little, because all the burdens experienced are really responsibilities of the psychiatrists who have to take care of compliance, to enhance insight and to
establish a mutually trustful relationship with patients and relatives. Furthermore, 30% of
the psychiatrists have felt rejected by other health professionals because 'they solve little'
and their 'specialty is not very useful'; only 12% believe that the patient feels rejected due
to the illness and 33% believe that the family members see the patient as a 'problem and
a burden'. Forty-six per cent of the psychiatrists believe that the neighbours of the persons
with schizophrenia see them as strange people that cause fear.

The main conclusion of these surveys is that rejection is concentrated among the groups
closest to the disorder, and that it is there where action should be prioritized, hoping that the
groups closer to the illness will also be better able to modify their perception and behaviour.

Activities undertaken

The first task was to elaborate the informative and educative material, translating the first
two volumes of the WPA programme and preparing other leaflets and texts. The logo, name
and stationery were also created during this initial period (May–December 1998).

The programme was then presented to the Local Action Committee for discussion and
approval.

The next step was seminaries to train the Teaching Committee members on schizophrenia,
the stigma and the discrimination (March–April 1999). They concentrated on aspects not
always well considered in everyday practice such as what are the burdens of the disease
on patients and their families, who were affected in their lifestyles, awareness of rejection
and the ways to fight it, on how to use the materials provided and skills to communicate
to the general public and to the mass media. A theoretical module updated knowledge
on the illness, the stigma and the discrimination, and a practical module consisting of
communications techniques allowed the putting into practice of the acquired knowledge.
Two such seminars took place; these were attended by 48 psychiatrists and were evaluated
as 'very interesting' by 96% of the participants.

The next step was to organize lectures, seminars or talks to patients, family members and
other audiences involved with the illness (health professionals, neighbourhood associations,
etc.), aimed at spreading knowledge and achieving social sensitization. The objectives were
to transmit to the patients and their families a message of hope with regard to therapeutic
alternatives, to provide the patients and their families with the necessary tools to learn to
live with the illness and to present the Madrid Programme and its results. The speakers were
a psychiatrist as representative of the local professional association and a representative of
the local association of patients and relatives. Twenty-nine teachers presented a total of 49
conferences to associations of patients and their families, professionals of mental health
centres, hospitals, clinics, residences, etc., as well as other groups ('cultural houses') of
the Autonomous Community of Madrid. Nine hundred and ninety persons assisted in these
presentations and 354 anonymous evaluations were gathered from the persons present that,
in more than half the cases, qualified the conferences as 'very positive'.

Nationwide campaign

During the initial period meetings of the different committees at a national level were convened and training seminars of the National Action Committee were organized. At the same time there were presentations of the programme at special sessions in national congresses of the discipline, always accompanied by press conferences in which national and local leaders appeared with representatives of users' associations and often responsible persons of the mental health administration.

After the pilot programme was held in the Regional Community of Madrid, and after analysing the results of the research conducted among the general population in Spain, the programme was extended to cover most of the country. In the period 2001–6 it covered the whole mainland plus the Balearic and Canary Islands.

On the basis of the guidelines established in the 1998 experience, a programme of activities was drawn up on the basis of the strategic model and aimed chiefly at the groups in closest proximity to the disorder. (Talks were held for patients and relatives, and there were seminars with psychiatrists and press conferences.)

Nationwide General Population Survey I (April–March 2000)

The main objectives of this survey were to ascertain the knowledge, perception and attitudes of the Spanish adult population with regard to schizophrenia and the people that suffer this illness and to evaluate if there are differences with respect to the survey carried out in Madrid in 1998.

The characteristics of the survey were: **Universe**: adult general population living in centres with over 2000 inhabitants; **Sample**: 1028 interviews distributed in a proportional way to the stratified universe, according to Autonomous Communities and inhabitants; **Method**: telephone interviews; **Sample error**: ±3.1%; **Content**: a structured questionnaire with a content similar to that carried out in Madrid in 1998.

Main results

Twenty-one percent had seen, heard or read some advertisement or campaign on schizophrenia in the last two months (compared with 27% in Madrid and 17% in 1998), mainly on TV or in the press. Twenty-seven percent remembered having seen, heard or read some news (compared with 39% in Madrid and 17% in 1998). The recall is higher in Madrid and its surroundings and it increases with the population of the area, the standard of general education and social class; it is also higher in women and in people of 35–54 years old. Eighteen percent of those interviewed knew a person treated because of schizophrenia, and 3% of them, in the close family. In Madrid, this knowledge reaches 22%, a higher number than the one recorded in 1998. Forty-one percent of the interviewed population consider that schizophrenia is a curable illness but the great majority are unaware of its treatment. Fifty-one percent of the general public believe that schizophrenia is not a curable illness. Only 16% believe that the illness can be cured.

With regard to the attitudes created by the people with schizophrenia, the idea that they are a public nuisance is mainly rejected, and more than half of the population does not think that they tend to live at the expense of the state-run health care. They think that patients can work normally; however, approximately half of the general public shares the idea that it is frequent to see these people talking to themselves and/or shouting in the streets. The idea that people with schizophrenia are not intelligent is mainly rejected. Around a half of the population believes that patients with schizophrenia suffer from double or multiple personality, hear voices telling them what to do or need to be admitted into hospital. The attribution of a violent personality and the menace it could be, split the general public into two quantitatively similar groups and, in general, they consider that people with schizophrenia need medication, although around a half of the population believe that there are alternative treatments (psychotherapy and/or social support).

In general, the surveyed population expressed integrative behaviours, such as willingness to talk, work, start a friendship or sleep in the same room with someone suffering from schizophrenia, an attitude which decreases when the relationship gets closer.

Clusters

Five clusters were identified with regard to the attitudes toward the patients and the behaviours they manifest:

1. **The integrators** (30%).

2. **The distant/excluders** (24%).

3. **An integrated social/exclusive familiar group** (34%).

4. **Two stigmatizing profiles** (stigma understood as rejection without a clear knowledge about the illness and the people who suffer from it and those who would be ashamed if they or a relative suffered from schizophrenia) (5%).

5. Those who consider these patients as **mentally handicapped** (7%).

In summary, the results for the whole of Spain show a similar degree of information and attitudes as in Madrid, with some different clusters appearing. What is more important is that in Madrid the knowledge had increased, the attitude improved (more people were willing to recognize that there are more persons with schizophrenia among their relatives or acquaintances) and the stigma decreased.

Nationwide General Population Survey II (July–August 2001)

After the pilot programme was held in the Regional Community of Madrid, and after analysing the results of the research conducted among the general population in Spain, the programme was extended to cover most of the country.

On the basis of the guidelines established in the 1998 experience, a programme of activities was drawn up on the basis of the strategic model and aimed chiefly at the groups in closest proximity to the disorder (talks held for patients and relatives, seminars with psychiatrists and press conferences).

Once the main activities of the national campaign were completed, the same survey was conducted again among the Spanish population in order to evaluate the impact.

The characteristics of the survey were: **Universe**: adult general population living in centres of over 2000 inhabitants; **Sample**: 988 interviews distributed in a proportional way to the stratified universe, according to Autonomous Communities and their inhabitants; **Method**: telephone interviews; **Sample error**: ±3.1%; **Content**: the structured questionnaire used in 2000.

Main results

The number of people who say they remember news of advertisements about schizophrenia hasn't changed (+1%); nevertheless, the recall of the content of these has changed, since just 15% remember aggressive or violent behaviours, compared with 23% one year before. 'Mentally ill people' is the way most often used to describe people affected with schizophrenia as portrayed in this information (16%) and a new category appears, showing a greater knowledge of the disorder: 'persons with loss of reality' (6% of those surveyed). The knowledge of someone affected by a serious emotional problem increases from 26% to 34%, and when asked who those were, 10% place them at the nuclear family (self, spouse, children) versus 7% in 2000; furthermore, schizophrenia is the most quoted illness (49% in 2001 versus 44% in 2000).

The knowledge of specific aspects of schizophrenia (symptoms, behaviours) grows from 16% to 30%. When a definition of schizophrenia is provided, the acknowledgement of someone affected by the disorder also grows compared with the 2000 survey (18% vs. 25%) and also grows as regards those who had acknowledged knowing someone before a definition was provided (17% vs. 25%). There is an improvement in the knowledge of treatments available, the answers becoming more medical and more specific. The percentage of people who believe the illness can be defeated almost doubles: 30% in 2001 versus 16% in 2000, and 25% believing the main cause of the illness is genetic (7% more than in the previous survey).

Cluster analysis

The attitudes towards persons with schizophrenia and the behaviour developed clusters in five groups:

1. **Those who accept them** (38%): consider schizophrenia as a mental illness but with possibilities of social rehabilitation. Female over 55 years of age with primary education and medium-lower class.

2. **The anti-schizophrenic** (5%): does not want to know anything about the illness. Male over 55 years of age with elementary education belonging to a medium-lower class.

3. **The realist** (31%): schizophrenia is a mental illness without many possibilities of social rehabilitation. Male 18–34 years of age with university degree and medium-medium class.

4. **The indecisive** (16%): doubts that recovering with medication is possible and does not believe in social rehabilitation. Either male or female, 45–54 years of age, with secondary education and medium-medium class.

5. **The complacent** (9%): considers that recovering with medication is possible but does not believe in rehabilitation. Either male or female, 35–44 years of age with secondary education and medium-medium class.

The clusters show some interesting changes (Figure 5.5). The extreme groups remain almost the same: who accepts it, not knowing much about it (2000: 30%; 2001: 28%); the anti-schizophrenic (2000: 24%; 2001: 22%). The group who stigmatizes because of shame increases slightly (2000: 5%; 2001: 8%). The social integrator group/familiar excluders

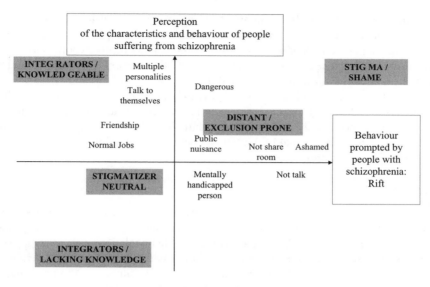

Figure 5.5 Evolution of the categories

evolves to a new typology: the integrator/knowledgeable (27%), with a less discriminatory attitude towards the illness and the socially stigmatizing group, who consider these patients mentally retarded (2000: 7%), evolves to a more neutral stigmatization (15%), less conditioned by wrong beliefs about the illness.

Overall summary of activities

One hundred and eighty psychiatrists took part in the programme by sitting on committees or taking an active part in organizing activities, 50 more mental health professionals received information or contacted the programme's Technical Secretariat, 65 talks and lectures were held and were attended by more than 1800 people (lay public, patients, relatives and mental health professionals), over 1200 copies of Volume II and News Dossiers were handed out and altogether 223 news items about the programme were either published or aired by the news media all over Spain.

National, regional and local media campaigns

Although the mass media have been used as the basic vehicle to reach patients, relatives and health professionals, it has also been taken into consideration that they are the main information source for the general public (the main information source for 90% of the population, according to the survey made by the Robert W. Johnson Foundation in 1990). When we started the programme, the most prevalent and stigmatising news items in Spain were related to violent behaviour or to 'chronicles of crime', because media can contribute to, create and perpetuate stigma. The factors increasing this type of media coverage are, among others: the evolution of mass media towards a sensationalistic approach in order to generate higher audience ratings; these types of stories are usually provided by journalists with a generalist background, not by those specialized in health, who have a certain knowledge of mental health and how to use the terminology properly; barriers between entertainment and information are falling, from sitcoms to soap operas, mental health issues are also portrayed in fiction; a wrong choice of words reinforces wrong beliefs (e.g. describing changing weather as 'schizophrenic'), bad news is good news (crime reports, unsuccessful treatment stories), good news is no news (social integration means a 'normal life', and there seems to be nothing newsworthy in a normal life).

Media professionals can diminish the stigma by working together with mental health professionals to reduce this sort of coverage and to achieve balance and fairness in media coverage. This is more easily achieved when journalists choose the right language when covering issues and using mental health terms, double-check the information with experts and get rid of their own prejudices.

Basic strategy

It was decided to use the media to make public perception more balanced by two means: stigmatising information items should be decreased gradually and positive coverage should neutralize as much as possible the negative coverage. Media relations were managed so that the coverage focused mainly on informing the public about schizophrenia's symptoms and treatments, rather than just on the institutional aspects of the initiative. The press materials have been carefully elaborated in order to ensure that the main messages were about the disorder: clear and specific information about the causes, treatment, stigma, social burden; a few messages were selected to repeat and explain in depth. In order to maximize the impact of the information spread, media activities were initially focused on regional journalists instead of acting at a national level, adapting press releases to regional data and taking into consideration the regional media characteristics, involving spokespersons from the region.

In order to deal effectively with the media it is important to understand the role of the media in fighting stigma, to knowing the media and how journalists work, to be aware of the barriers and fears on both sides and to be able to build messages for each type of media and to get them through.

Materials developed specifically for journalists

A 'Useful guide for mass media about schizophrenia' was distributed to journalists. This is an information source to treat correctly the contents related to schizophrenia.

Spreading extended information about the disorder: translation, adaptation and publication of the book *What Is Schizophrenia, How Can it Be Treated and How to Combat the Stigma* (Vol. II).

Monitoring the press, in order to be able to react when negative messages appear (e.g. an informative letter was sent to the media regarding a violent incident that occurred in Madrid, 'Schizophrenic doctor kills some of her colleagues'. It explained how violence and schizophrenia are related.[2])

Analysing the information pieces published quantitatively and qualitatively, in both national and regional press.

Opening a specific area for journalists in the webpage www.openthedoors.com and in future www.fundcionlopezibor.es.

---

[2] Interestingly enough, the Minister of Health and Consumer Affairs sent the programme a letter of congratulations for the initiative, commenting how useful it was to her to better understand the disease and the stigma attached to it.

Selective media campaign

Following the survey of the general public in Madrid (1999) the programme decided to carry out a selective media campaign. A press release on the programme and on schizophrenia was prepared and press conferences were organized with the participation of psychiatrists who had attended training seminars. It was considered that the same messages put out by many different people would be most effective. One of the stigmas of psychiatry is that professionals never agree on anything.

The information was covered by local (16 news items) and national press (2 items), radio broadcasting (11 local and 7 national) and TV (2 local and 1 national, this in a maximum audience news programme with a total audience of 6.5 million people[3]).

On the whole the campaign was covered 39 times by information in newspapers, radio or TV in the Autonomous Community of Madrid. The total accumulated audience was more than 34 millions persons and the information about the disease not only increased but changed its format. It appeared now in pages or spaces devoted to health or social issues and not linked to crime and more often than not the news was about the disease ("schizophrenia") and not about the patient ("the schizophrenic") and putting emphasis on more positive aspects of treatment and management.

The launching of the programme in the press

The programme was presented to the media in Madrid on 16 July 2001, leading to 184 information items being published or aired on 130 different media outlets with an estimated audience of 23.7 million people. The contents focused on the characteristics of the schizophrenia Open the Doors programme, on schizophrenia having the highest level of stigma, on the specificity of the stigma of different diseases, mental and physical, on collaboration with many partners and on the fact of being a programme and not only a once-in-a-lifetime campaign.

Information about the programme has been spread through presentations and interviews with the mental health professionals involved (in total there have been 14 press conferences and 223 information pieces published or broadcast about the program in the Spanish media).

Reports

In order to find out how the media present news and topics about schizophrenia, the programme in Spain has developed different periodical reports for analysing the news in the written media. 'Periodical study on the informative treatment of schizophrenia in Spanish written media' has been carried out every three months since June 2005 by Llorente & Cuenca, and covered news published in the written press in the principal media of Spain, national, regional and specialist. A more extensive study was made on 2005: 'Report on the presence and projection of the image of schizophrenia in the written print media in Spain in the years 2003–2004', carried out by the Institute of Official and Business Communications of the Complutense University of Madrid.

---

[3] The interview was broadcast on 19 October 2000, and it gave the chance to spread live the key messages about schizophrenia for more than 6 minutes.

Other activities with the media

Every time a set of actions was carried out a press conference was convened where a press release was distributed and interviews with professionals, users and responsible persons of the mental health administration and other opinion leaders were held.

The programme also organized a three-day course at the Universidad Complutense summer school for mental health professionals and journalists, in collaboration with the Spanish Press Association and the Asociación Nacional de Informadores de la Salud (ANIS, National Association of Health Informers), including among the speakers the main journalists covering health issues. A similar approach was taken to organizing symposia and workshops at national and international psychiatric meetings.

Another activity has been the preparation of a dossier for psychiatrists to be able to convene appropriate and consistent messages to the press on the occasion of important news about mental disorders such as when a patient commits a sensational crime or when the film *A Beautiful Mind* was first shown in Spain.

Conferences and participation in scientific meetings

Over recent years, several events have been organized with the objective of increasing the awareness about stigma among different audiences, such as university students and health and other professionals who work with patients.

The main activities were:

Participation in the 2nd International Congress 'Together against Stigma' held in Kingston, Canada, in October 2003. Creation of abstracts and later lectures 'Evolution of knowledge of and attitudes towards schizophrenia among the Spanish population after the implementation of Schizophrenia Open the Doors on a national level', and 'Fighting the stigma in the media: the experience of the Spanish "Schizophrenia Open the Doors" Programme'. Both lectures were presented by Juan J. López-Ibor.

Presentation of two posters of the programme for the 'XII Biennial Winter Workshop on Schizophrenia' held in Davos, Switzerland in February 2004: 'Fighting stigma in the media. The Spanish experience' and 'Changes in knowledge and attitudes towards schizophrenia in Spain'.

Workshop on the stigma of schizophrenia for psychiatrists and students, presided by Juan J. López-Ibor at the conference 'Value-based psychiatry and the stigma of schizophrenia' (13–14 December 2004, San Carlos Clinical Hospital) The participants were Professor Juan J. López-Ibor, Norman Sartorius (Switzerland), Ahmed Okasha (Egypt), María Inés López-Ibor, Blanca Reneses, Olga Cuenca.

Organization of the conference 'Psychiatric morbidity in prisons' and the workshops 'Schizophrenia in 21st century society' held in Alicante on 1 December 2004. The proposed initiatives had the goal of reaching the key audiences: professionals and families.

A remarkable activity took place on July 2005, with the organization of a session on 'The stigma of mental illnesses in the media', within the Summer Courses of the Complutense University of Madrid. The course attempted to gather the opinions of everyone involved in mental illnesses and communications, hence opinions were sought from experts representing a variety of interests: psychiatry (with national and international representatives), families of patients, public institutions and the media.

During 2006, the 'WPA Centennial Congress', Madrid, 19–22 April 2006 was the scenario for a special seminar about 'Thresholds and limits of mental illness in the media'.

Website

The programme in Spain www.esquizofreniabrelaspuertas.com/ developed the Spanish version of the programme website www.openthedoors.com. The website has been updated recently to make it more dynamic and increase traffic with links to internal pages and an information service of news related to schizophrenia and general mental health news.

Epilogue

The World Psychiatric Association Executive Committee while presenting the activities of Schizophrenia Opens the Doors at the General Assembly in Cairo in September 2005 proposed that after nine years the programme had achieved its goals and should be halted, recommending member societies and professional pursue anti stigma activities on their own, based on the experience and the materials of the WPA programme.

In Spain, after six years of generous and unrestricted support the Lilly Company concluded that the purposes of the programme had been achieved.

We have shown that it is possible to change the stigma of schizophrenia at both general public and mass media levels nationwide, which was the first objective of the programme in Spain.

In 2006 the Confederación Española de Agrupaciones de Familiares y Enfermos Mentales (FEAFES, Spanish Confederation of Groups of Families and Patients of Mental Illnesses), who strongly collaborated with 'La Esquizofrenia Abre las Puertas', decided to launch its own anti-stigma campaign. This means that our second objective, empowerment, has also been achieved.

In the future we will follow anti-stigma activities in collaboration with other organizations under the patronage of the Juan José López-Ibor Foundation (http://fundacion@lopez-ibor.com). On 17 December 2007, it is foreseen to re-launch the contents of the programme through the celebration in Madrid of a conference regarding the integration of mental patients in society, together with an exhibition of work realized by social associations and other institutions.

Acknowledgements

Ministerio de Sanidad y Consumo (Heath and Consumers Affairs Ministry), Ministerio de Trabajo y Asuntos Sociales (Labor and Social Affairs Ministry), Plan Nacional sobre Drogas (National Anti-Drug Plan), FEAFES – Confederación Española de Agrupaciones de Familiares y Enfermos Mentales (Spanish Confederation of Groups of Families and Patients of Mental Illnesses), ANIS – Asociación Nacional de Informadores de la Salud (National Association of Health Informers), Fundación Sanitas, Fundación Areces.

6 Evaluating programmatic needs concerning the stigma of mental illness

Beate Schulze

University of Zurich, Department of General and Social Psychiatry, Zurich, Switzerland

Introduction

Stigma has been described as the single most important obstacle to the recovery, social integration and quality of life of people with mental illness [1–5], as well as to the provision of timely and adequate mental health services. [6]. Hence those suffering from mental illness are disadvantaged on two levels: (1) adverse societal reactions leading to social exclusion and causing help-seeking barriers due to fear of the negative consequences of being diagnosed with a mental illness, and (2) the rather marginal position of mental health care within medicine when it comes to health care funding as well as financial support for research [6].

A large number of programmes to fight stigma and discrimination due to mental illness have been initiated – on the local, national and international levels. The largest global effort has been undertaken by the World Psychiatric Association's 'Open the Doors' Programme against Stigma and Discrimination because of Schizophrenia [7], aiming to:

- Increase the awareness and knowledge of the nature of schizophrenia and treatment options.

- Improve public attitudes about those who have or have had schizophrenia and their families.

- Generate action to eliminate discrimination and prejudice. (p. 1)

How, then, are these objectives to be realized? How are they understood from the point of view of those who should be the main beneficiaries of anti-stigma initiatives – those with mental illness and their families? Which strategies should be pursued to obtain programme goals? Who should be addressed by the programme, which groups should be involved in anti-stigma activities?

It becomes apparent that programme planning requires many decisions. For them to be informed choices, a thorough knowledge of stigma and its consequences is needed.

Research on stigma has attempted to throw light on the various components of the stigma process. Both enquiries into attitudes and beliefs about mental illness among the public

Understanding the Stigma of Mental Illness: Theory and Interventions   Edited by Julio Arboleda-Flórez and Norman Sartorius
© 2008 John Wiley & Sons, Ltd

and analogous behaviour experiments measuring stigmatising behaviours have produced a predominantly negative picture. People with a mental illness are perceived to be unpredictable, aggressive, dangerous, unreasonable, unintelligent, lacking in self-control and frightening [8], and a large share of the general population would reject entering social relationships such as sharing a flat with someone with schizophrenia, recommending a person with schizophrenia for a job, or having him or her looking after their children [9, 10]. Likewise, experimental studies revealed that if a person mentioned a mental health problem, she or he faced greater difficulty in finding a job, renting an apartment or being accepted in a neighbourhood [11–13].

Why assessing need?

Does the clear picture emerging from stigma research imply that we already know what we need from an anti-stigma programme? While there is a wealth of information from scientific inquiry, clinical experience and the media as well as experience from previous efforts to challenge stigma and discrimination, specific needs for efforts against stigma and discrimination typically arise from a concrete local context. Populations that seem quite similar demographically, or face a common problem such as a mental illness, may perceive their needs as being very different from each other. So while most programmes against mental-health-related stigma will share the global aims spelt out above, the paths to achieve these goals may vary considerably between programme sites. Factors affecting choices on the most effective strategies to combat stigma in a particular local setting include the perception of concrete concerns among the programme's target groups, specific cultural meanings ascribed to mental health and illness, the organisation of mental health care, relevant policy choices and legal regulations, as well as the resources available for designing and implementing anti-stigma interventions. A thorough evaluation of specific programmatic needs is therefore a crucial prerequisite for the effectiveness and sustainability of an anti-stigma intervention.

Although vital for programme success, a decided focus on identifying needs and problems will leave us with an incomplete picture. It is equally important to include in the planning process an analysis of *capacities, skills and resources* that can be brought forward by both individuals and communities in combating stigma. In fact, paying attention to the resources and skills of people with mental illness and their families seems inherent in the very cause of anti-stigma efforts. Not only is a thorough understanding of the resources and skills available to put programmatic goals into practice essential for a sustainable implementation of anti-stigma strategies, but it simultaneously counteracts stigmatising notions of people with mental illness as being incompetent, lazy, unintelligent, and, above all, primarily in need of help and protection. In addition, conducting a capacity assessment can contribute to enhancing service users' self-esteem, combating internalized stigma, and to developing coping skills to successfully deal with adverse environmental reactions. In this chapter, programmatic needs will therefore be understood to include both the needs and the resources of relevant stakeholders in anti-stigma efforts.

Needs assessment – concepts and definitions

To set the scene for introducing assessment methods and practical steps in assessing programme needs, the reader will be made familiar with relevant concepts and definitions. What is the purpose of a needs assessment? How do we conceive of needs and capacities?

What is the purpose of assessing need?

In general terms, a needs assessment is conducted to derive *information* and *perceptions of values* as a *guide* to making *policy and programme decisions* that will *benefit specific groups* of people [14]. In other words, it is the first step in making the central programme decisions. By deciding which groups to include in a needs and capacity assessment, one already defines the programme's beneficiaries. Hence a needs assessment can also provide baseline data against which programme results can be judged as part of programme evaluation (see Stuart, Chapter 8 in this book).

What is a needs assessment?

Needs assessment is the process of identifying and evaluating needs in a community or other defined target population. In the process, 'problems' of a target population are being described and possible solutions discussed. A needs assessment applies

> a systematic set of procedures undertaken for the purpose of making decisions about program or organizational improvement and allocation of resources, setting priorities for later action on the basis of identified needs. [14, p. 4]

Needs assessment starts from the assumption that groups of people have needs that are not being met and not being addressed adequately. It seeks to uncover unmet needs, both recognized (e.g., expressed as demands) and latent. In addition, it involves identifying individual, group and community resources that can be brought forward to increase mental health awareness and fight stigma. A summary of the central characteristics of a needs assessment is given in Figure 6.1.

What are needs and capacities?

A *need* is generally considered to be

- A discrepancy or gap between 'what is', or the present state of affairs, and 'what should be', or a desired state of affairs. [14]

- A gap between real and ideal that is both acknowledged by community values and potentially amenable to change. [15]

A needs assessment

- is a *systematic* approach that progresses through a defined series of phases

- gathers data by means of *established procedures and methods* designed for specific purposes

- sets *priorities* and determines *criteria for solutions* so that planners can make informed decisions

- leads to *action* that will *improve* programmes, services, organisational structures and operations as well as values, or a combination of these elements

- sets *criteria* for how to best *allocate* available money, people, facilities and other *resources*

(Adapted from [14])

Figure 6.1 Defining needs assessment

Capacity refers to

- Both collective and individual resources that can be mobilised to bridge the gap identified in the needs assessment process.

Three elements are common to the concept of needs. First, a need is neither the present (e.g., young people's unawareness of help-seeking options) nor the future state (e.g., better access to mental health services, including improved outcomes for those experiencing mental distress) – it is the *gap* between them. A need is therefore an *inference* drawn from *examining a present state* and *comparing it with a vision of a future (better) state*. Second, this gap should lend itself to *consensus* and *change*. Third, adequate *skills* and *resources* must be available to affect the desired change. These three elements are crucial in creating buy-in into anti-stigma programmes and enhancing the motivation of project participants.

As Witkin and Altschuld [14] point out, needs should not be confused with *something* we need – like more health care funds for innovative treatments, more positive reporting about mental health issues in the press, crisis consultation for family members, money to hire an extra social worker, or school programmes for mental health promotion. All of these are provisions required or desired to fill a discrepancy – they are solutions, means to an end. There is a risk in conducting a needs evaluation to confuse these two meanings of 'need'.

To relate these definitions to their concrete application in developing anti-stigma interventions, Figure 6.2 gives an overview of relevant needs and capacities to be identified in defining programme priorities and pathways of action in fighting mental-health-related stigma.

Whose needs and capacities? Target groups and levels of need

Successful anti-stigma interventions will be targeted to specific groups and communities. In this, two aspects can be distinguished:

1) Those who are to ultimately benefit from the programme.

2) Groups whose attitudes and behaviour should change to relieve stigma-related burden or who are in the position to affect change at community or societal levels.

Planning a needs assessment must start with drawing up a first list of potential target groups [16]. Experience shows that it takes multiple avenues of action to make a sustained impact on public perceptions and social provisions for people suffering from mental health problems. This requires analysis of needs pertinent to each specific direction a programme intends to be going. For example, a programme in a rural community that hosts a housing project for mentally ill people identifies three main target groups to reduce the social distance between residents of the project and the local community: house owners who fear that the value of their property will decrease with mentally ill people present in the community, the clergy who exert a strong influence on public opinion and could be a multiplier in promoting tolerance and acceptance, and bus drivers and officials of the public transport company connecting the village to a nearby town that hosts important facilities for daily life. Consequently, the perceptions of these groups must be obtained in order to define programme needs.

NEEDS

Subjective stigma experiences. The perspective of people with mental health problems and their families is essential in deciding on the type of anti-stigma interventions. Their experience of mental illness and its social consequences makes them experts in identifying the most pressing issues.

Public attitudes. What does the general public know and think about mental illness? What are the central ingredients of the stereotype of mental illness? How would people behave towards someone with a mental health problem? Are they able to recognize mental illness, and what treatment recommendations would they make?

Policies. What is the legal situation of people with mental illness? Do mental health services get an appropriate share of resources in the healthcare system? Which laws are in place that protect the rights of those with a mental illness?

School curricula. To what extent and how are mental health issues part of teaching curricula? What do teachers need to adequately support young people who have a mental health problem? What kind of information is relevant to the needs and abilities of particular age groups?

Media images. What are the general themes in media reporting on mental illness? On which occasions is mental illness a newsworthy issue? How could the focus of media reporting be broadened to include positive aspects and evidence-based mental health information?

Targets. What should be achieved by an anti-stigma programme? Service users, families, mental health professionals, media representatives, health politicians and other groups will have different expectations regarding the outcome of anti-stigma efforts. As an input for programme planning, priorities of each group can be obtained.

Messages. What information is the programme to provide on mental health problems to fill the gap between a current lack of knowledge and a future desirable state of adequate mental health literacy? Which myths should be dispelled? How does the programme want to position the topic? Messages are the channels for bringing these points across.

Needs for support. What additional support is required for specific projects? This question arises at the outset of a programme and should be a regular element in monitoring the programme in action. People involved in projects should have a forum to regularly voice their experiences, concerns and needs for support.

CAPACITIES

Interests – Talents – Expertise. Among the stakeholder groups, who would be interested in contributing to anti-stigma activities? Do people have specific expertise (e.g. in fundraising, media relations, graphic design, research skills) that could be useful for the anti-stigma programme? What particular talents are there among service users (e.g. public speaking, professional skills, photography, art)?

Ideas – Concepts – Strategies. Which resources can be brought forward to achieve programme targets? Who can provide what type of useful expertise, contacts and previous experience with anti-stigma or health education efforts? Obtaining multiple perspectives enhances creativity.

Motivation - Commitment. Identifying those among the central stakeholders in the health professions, user and family organisations, politics, media, etc. who are motivated to become actively involved in anti-stigma efforts. Is stigma on the agenda of top-level management and/or decision-makers? Which factors produce motivation and what can be done to sustain commitment throughout an anti-stigma programme?

Fundraising. Gathering expertise and ideas on funding channels (e.g. inviting people with considerable experience with projects addressing mental health and other social issues, community leaders, representatives of government agencies, foundations and possible sponsors). Generating ideas for creative fundraising measures for specific projects.

Figure 6.2 Types of needs and capacities pertinent to anti-stigma programmes

Defining the specific groups a programme intends to work with is an obvious step in programme planning. Less obvious, but equally important to consider in defining a needs assessment strategy, is the fact that there are different levels of need, with different target groups associated with each [17]:

Level 1 (primary): Service recipients, i.e. those for whom a system or programme ultimately exists. Alternatively, 'primary-level needs' refers to the perspective of those who are to benefit from a new service or programme to be developed. Examples include clients, patients, students, information users and potential customers.

Level 2 (secondary): Service providers and policy makers, i.e. those who deliver services and thus affect the lives of service recipients, exerting a strong influence on level 1 needs. On the one hand, this implies a strong potential for these groups to be agents of change, on the other it may point to a need for changes in their knowledge, attitudes and behaviour. Target groups representing level 2 needs include health professionals, employers, administrators, policy makers and others.

Level 3 (tertiary): Resources and inputs into solutions. Examples of this level of need are buildings, facilities, supplies, equipment, skills, programme delivery systems, time allocations, legal regulations and budget requirements.

Ideally, a valid needs assessment is primarily directed at level 1. It seeks to determine the needs of the people for whom the organisation or programme exists. Primary-level target groups in anti-stigma programmes are people with mental illness and their families. Enquiring about their concrete experiences with stigmatising attitudes and discriminatory behaviour will provide valid information to identify the most important areas for intervention, and then define the relevant target groups at level 2 as well as level 3 resources to be deployed in alleviating stigma.

Whereas this sequence of determining needs may appear self-evident, research reveals that it is not: most needs assessments are actually conducted at levels 2 and 3 [18]. This may be a reflection of the fact that the majority of needs assessments are carried out under the auspices of an organisation and conducted by staff within it. Their attention is likely to be centred on obvious concerns in their daily practice, such as a lack of personnel or finance (level 3) or a need for training in a novel therapeutic intervention (level 2). Moving our perception beyond needs that strike us as relevant and urgent from a professional or organisational perspective, then, is the key to an effective needs assessment strategy. After all, we do not want to learn what we already know.

Steps in assessing needs and capacities – planning the process

Careful planning is required to conduct an effective needs assessment. The needs assessment process consists of three phases: (1) exploration and planning, (2) data gathering and (3) utilization [17].

1. Pre-assessment – exploration and planning

The starting phase serves to investigate what knowledge is already available on the needs of the target groups, to determine the focus and scope of the assessment and to gain commitment for all stages of the assessment [14].

From the start, a needs assessment should be a concerted effort with all relevant stakeholders involved. The first step therefore consists in setting up a needs assessment planning group and identifying a key person in charge of the process [32]. Due to the political in nature of needs assessments, it is recommended to select the needs assessment coordinator from outside the organisation or system where needs are to be identified. For example, facilitators could be found among social scientists at a university or college, with NGOs that may routinely scan for needs in their area of activity, or in the planning department of the local authority.

Next, it is important to ascertain what we already know about stigma, and its concrete impact in a particular local context. For example, one could draw on results of previous assessment or research, consult statistics on health care funding, or use available media databases to analyse mental health reporting in the press. Scanning for available information is important in order to avoid embarking on costly studies where relevant knowledge for planning an anti-stigma programme already exists.

Based on gaps identified concerning the information available, the purpose and scope of the needs assessment will be defined. Whose needs are to be better understood? What additional facts and opinions are needed to tailor effective anti-stigma activities? Which capacities are required for implementing a viable programme, and who could provide them? Following from these considerations, a specific set of questions should be developed that should be answered in the assessment.

Once the research question for the assessment is clear, the planning group will determine

1) what kind of data to gather

2) the sources from where to obtain the data

3) the methods best suited for data collection, and

4) how the data should be used.

It is important not to lose sight of the intended application of needs assessment data to make sure the right kind of data will be collected with the adequate amount of detail. Resources for an anti-stigma programme may be scarce and should thus be used wisely from the very start of the process.

2. Assessment – data gathering

The task of the assessment phase is to document the 'what is' status, compare it with the vision of 'what should be', and to determine the magnitude of the needs and their causes [14].

At the outset of data collection, it is important to define which level of need (levels 1, 2, and/or 3, see above) the assessment aims at. This step can serve to review the needs assessment strategy regarding whether it takes adequate account of the needs of people with mental illness and their families. For instance, a spectacular event such as a crime committed by a supposedly mentally ill perpetrator has produced a huge media interest, primarily the kind of coverage that reinforces negative stereotypes of mental illness (for examples, see [19]). The planning group may be incited to focus its assessment on the attitudes of journalists as changing their reporting may appear the most pressing issue in the current situation. However, there might be other aspects of stigma and discrimination that impact more strongly and directly on the daily lives of those with mental illness, such as an increasing exclusion from the labour market or the treatment of people with mental illness in medical emergency rooms. Needs assessors may lose sight of these other concerns in their planning in view of a dramatic event that seems to call for immediate action.

Once levels of assessment have been defined, desired measurable 'end states' must be determined for each level. For an anti-stigma programme, such goals include:

Level 1:

- Increase the proportion of people with mental illness working in regular jobs by 5%.

- Have user and family representatives on all mental health boards and service planning bodies.
- Eliminate legal discrimination (e.g., change health insurance policies excluding coverage for mental health problems).

Level 2:

- Reduce stress and burnout among mental health professionals to improve quality of care.
- Reduce inadequate use of language in media reports on mental health by 20%.
- Set up a 'hotline' for teachers who seek advice on mental health problems among their students.
- Enhance police officers' de-escalation skills in contact with people in acute psychotic states and reduce the rate of physical coercion by 20%.

Level 3:

- Increase the proportion of health care funds spent on mental health services by 3% in 2 years.
- Acquire a building to open an integration firm (e.g., a hotel, a graphic design office, a shop) to employ people with mental illness in regular jobs.
- Establish a crisis intervention service to prevent hospitalization in acute phases and reduce care-giver burden among the caring families.

Next, the appropriate methods for data collection will be selected. Many options are available for conducting the assessment (see next section). Data analysis focuses on identifying the most pressing problem areas, and on determining discrepancies between the current state and a vision for the future. At the end of the assessment phase, all data collected will be synthesized and results will be summarized in a set of needs statements in tentative order of priority.

3. Post-assessment – utilization

In phase 3, final priorities are established, solution strategies are selected, and an action plan is developed, implemented and evaluated. In order to utilize findings from needs assessments in planning interventions, it is necessary to define selection criteria, examine alternative solutions, and choose and implement the strategy that has the highest potential of resolving the need [14, 17]. Criteria for assigning priorities among needs include:

- The magnitude of discrepancies between current and target states.
- Causes and contributing factors to the needs.
- The degree of difficulty in addressing the needs.
- The effect on other parts of the system or other needs if a specified need is met or not met.

- The costs of implementing solutions.

- Political and other factors that might affect efforts to solve the need, including community values, local and national priorities, and public expectations.

It is important to involve all relevant stakeholders in this process and inform those consulted in the needs assessment on the progress in developing interventions, as well as to allow them the opportunity to offer suggestions and input.

Strategies for assessing need: approaches and methods

Overview of methods

This section gives an overview of needs assessment methods. Methods will be introduced for assessing particular dimensions of needs and capacities. This overview starts with presenting methods for enquiring the **perspective of target groups** for anti-stigma activities. Special emphasis will be placed on focus groups, a method particularly suited for exploring the needs of service users and family members that has widely been used in the context of the WPA Global Programme against Stigma. Second, the reader will be acquainted with assessment methods for understanding the **context of anti-stigma activities**, i.e. on analysing public attitudes, media reporting, and policies and legal regulations.

A detailed outline of how to plan and conduct data collection using the methods portrayed here is beyond the scope of this chapter. For a more thorough understanding and practical guidelines, literature for further reading is recommended for each of the proposed approaches. Advantages and disadvantages of the different needs assessment methods are summarized in Table 6.3.

Enquiring target groups' perspectives

1. Individual methods – the interview

Purposes of interviewing
In assessing programmatic needs for anti-stigma efforts, interviews are particularly useful for two different purposes. First of all, they allow obtaining **information from service users and families**. In health research, the use of interviews is recommended to gather first-hand information on the patients' perspective concerning their expectations or experiences with regard to interventions [21]. However, as assessment methods focusing on the individual are costly and time consuming, the interview approach is proposed for assessing first-level needs from the perspective of **experts** among the programme's intended beneficiaries. Key informants include representatives of user and family associations as well as service users and relatives represented on mental health boards (e.g., as ombudspeople). Through their political activity, they are likely to be aware of the kind of grievances articulated within both groups. In addition, user and family activists can supply information on barriers and factors that have contributed to stigma, or about previous programmes or solutions and the reasons for their success or failure. Consequently, such expert interviews can produce a list of areas that should be examined further through other techniques, e.g., in focus groups (see below).

The second purpose for using interviews in the planning phase of anti-stigma programmes is to investigate the perspectives of **key stakeholders** in fighting stigma. Stakeholders are individuals with a particular interest in the topic that often goes hand in hand with specialized knowledge about the issues or needs, either because of their position within an organisation or community or because of their expertise [14]. Such key informants include the headteacher of the local school, the police chief, health politicians, mental health experts, a lawyer specializing in anti-discrimination legislation, or important employers in the region. Interviews with these stakeholders can identify central concerns from the perspective of those in the position to actually affect change. They can also reveal additional useful information such as organisational or system factors to consider, or existing documents, previous needs assessments and evaluations you could examine. Moreover, interviews have been found to be especially well suited for obtaining information from busy people [15]. By discussing in depth the areas they know best, the participants may feel that they are using their time to best advantage.

Planning for the interview
Planning includes determining the purpose of the interview and the kinds of information wanted, deciding on the type of interview suitable for the planned enquiry, developing the interview protocol, and selecting and training the interviewers.

Step 1: Deciding on the type of interview
Interviews can be classified according to the level of structure they offer in terms of question wording and response formats. On one end of the continuum, there is the **fully structured interview**. It uses closed-ended items where both questions and response options are prescribed. This technique is predominantly used in face-to-face or telephone surveys with large samples, which are discussed later in this chapter.

Since the purpose of an assessment should inform the choice of the data collection method, this section on approaches for exploring first-level needs will focus on **open-ended interviewing approaches**. These aim at gathering qualitative data, i.e. statements and themes rather than numbers. Closed questions, on the other hand, are less suited as they may reflect needs assessors' assumptions rather than allowing respondents to express stigma experiences in their own words.

There are three basic approaches to collecting data through qualitative interviews. The *informal conversational interview* relies entirely on the spontaneous generation of questions in the natural flow of interaction. It offers maximum flexibility to pursue information in whatever direction appears to be appropriate, depending on what emerges from a particular setting or from talking with one or two individuals in that setting [22]. However, the interviewer will have an overall guiding focus in mind that will inform his or her interviewing. In the context of anti-stigma programme development, this technique may be useful to get a general idea of how an anti-stigma initiative will be received by mental health experts through informally eliciting their ideas at a psychiatry congress.

With the *general interview guide approach,* the interviewer follows a set of questions and suggested follow-up questions that serve as a basic checklist during the interview to make sure that all relevant topics are covered. Beyond that, interviewers are free to vary the wording of questions as well as the order in which they are asked. Additional follow-up questions are asked if the interviewer believes they would yield useful information [15]. This approach is most useful for interviews carried out to assess need in the context of anti-stigma programmes. It permits interviewees to openly express their views and gives them the chance to lead the interviewer to areas of stigma they find most pressing. At the same time, the set of issues outlined in the interview guide ensures that all topics of interest to the needs assessor are covered. The interview guide approach, however, leaves a large share of the responsibility for the quality of data collection with the interviewer. Giving interviewers more leeway on how to actually conduct the interview requires substantial skill on their part and/or extensive interviewer training. Simultaneously, the rich body of information produced by qualitative interviews requires more time, expertise and essentially money for data analyses.

A third opportunity is thus the *standardized open-ended interview*. Here, a set of questions is prepared that is carefully worded and arranged with the intention of taking each respondent through the same questions with essentially the same words [22]. This approach is particularly useful if you have little time, money and interviewing expertise at hand for your needs assessment. For example, the interview is highly focused so that interview time is used effectively. Using a more standardized interview format also allows you to collect needs assessment data more quickly by using a number of different interviewers simultaneously. Pre-defined questions and written interviewer instructions help to minimize variability in skill and interviewing style and thus ensure the validity of the information gathered. Finally, efficiency can be increased as data analysis is facilitated by making responses easy to find and compare.

In summary, there are two central criteria for making decisions on how extensively to structure the interviews for assessing need [15]:

1. The more you want to discover needs rather than test knowledge, the less you should structure the interviews.

2. The less time and money you have for your project, the more you should structure your interviews.

Step 2: Developing the interview protocol
The protocol includes the format and instructions for the interviewer as well as the way the answers will be recorded, either in writing or by recording. A tape recording gives a complete picture of the interview, which is important for some interviews. You should be aware, however, that taping the interview may inhibit free expression. More importantly, tape recordings require time and money to transcribe. Word-for-word transcriptions take from 2 to 6 hours for every hour of interview time [23]. Overall, needs assessments do not require the same precision in recording data as rigorous academic research. Summarizing the interview is a good alternative to transcription. This involves transcribing critical statements in their entirety, but condensing other statements. For most needs assessments, however, effective note-taking during the interview is sufficient.

Step 3: Select the sample of respondents
With open-ended interviews, remember that data analysis is a more extensive undertaking. The less structured your interviews are, they more you may want to interview specific people. Therefore consider purposefully selecting a smaller sample of key people, rather than drawing a representative sample of the given population. In **purposive sampling**, individuals are selected because they represent a range of diverse and important perspectives. It is recommended that you interview 'knowledgeable insiders' who have the best perspective on anti-stigma needs within a particular community or organisation. These people are selected because they can offer a broader picture, for instance, of community issues or societal trends than you would obtain from a random sample [15]. Rather than aim at a large representative sample, you purposefully select 10 to 15 individuals who can offer critical insights. Make sure you include more people in your sample than you need to interview. Some individuals will decline to participate while others will be difficult to contact.

Step 4: Select and train the interviewers

With open-ended interviews, the interviewer essentially represents the data collection tool. As we know from survey research or psychological tests, considerable effort goes into developing assessment instruments to ensure the reliability and validity of the information obtained. With qualitative enquiry, data quality fundamentally depends on the skills of the interviewers and the rapport they can develop with interviewees.

Skilful interviewers are especially capable in active and empathic listening and enjoy one-to-one, face-to-face situations. The more knowledge they have of the needs assessment project, the better. Knowledgeable interviewers have more credibility with interviewees and can take informed decisions about which follow-up questions to ask and which leads to follow [15]. It is also preferable that interviewers do not have a personal stake in the outcome of the needs assessment. In terms of rapport with the respondents, research has shown that the best results are obtained by interviewers with whom interviewees can identify, especially when language, ethnicity, cultural background, sex or age could make a difference in the responses.

It is essential to train interviewers. The best training contains a combination of teaching, practice and supervision. In particular, interviewers should get the chance to experience how different ways to phrase a question can affect the type of information obtained from the interviewee's responses. For example, dichotomous questions such as 'Do you feel socially excluded because of your mental illness?' or 'Do you prefer concealing your mental health problems in the workplace?' provide interviewees with a grammatical structure suggesting a 'yes' or 'no' answer. By contrast, open-ended interviewing strives to get the person interviewed to talk – to talk about experiences, feelings, opinions and knowledge [22]. An example of how question wording can affect the quality of responses is given in Table 6.1. In addition to practising interviewing skills, interviewers need to understand the purpose of the interviews, why they are important, and how the information will be used. They need

Table 6.1 Question wording and interview outcomes. Example adapted from Quinn Patton, [22]

Actual question asked		Genuinely open-ended alternatives with richer responses	
Question:	Have you ever felt stigmatised because of your mental illness?	Q:	What has changed since you developed your mental health problem?
Answer:	Yeah, many times.	A:	First, people around me were all insecure. They didn't know how to deal with my illness and then gradually stayed away. My psychiatrist told me that I can forget about finishing my studies. And when I go to see my GP now with a sore throat or anything, he keeps wondering whether I'm not making it all up.
Q:	Did you try to hide your mental illness from others to avoid stigmatising responses?	Q:	How did you react to people treating you differently?
A:	That was part of it.	A:	Well, at first I didn't want to see anyone. I was so ashamed, confused. Then I felt really let down and got angry with my so-called friends who weren't around when I needed them most. Eventually, I joined a self-help group, which gave me confidence and helped me to talk to people about my illness. I also made new friends there.

instructions on contacting participants, handling ambiguous responses, and recording data [15]. This background information about the project should be taught by someone on the needs assessment committee.

Step 5: Conducting the interview
Before setting out, the interviewer explains the purpose of the interview and how the results are going to be used, and assures the interviewee of confidentially. The actual interview generally begins with questions that are non-threatening and relatively easy to answer, thereby enabling the respondent to be at ease. Potentially threatening questions, e.g., about personal attitudes or own discriminating behaviours, should be asked near the middle of the interview, while demographic information should be obtained at the end [14, 15].

Probing techniques are an essential part of interviewing. Probes are used to gain greater detail, elaboration or clarification. Who, what, when, where or how questions can encourage respondents to provide more detailed information. Silence is also an effective elaboration probe. Skilful interviewing involves resisting the temptation to fill gaps in the conversation. Probing too soon can result in missing important information that the respondent may have otherwise volunteered. Sometimes, interviewees may offer unclear, contradictory or irrelevant answers. To clarify them, interviewers can ask neutral questions such as 'What do you mean?' or 'Why do you say that?', restate the original question, or summarize what has been said so far to encourage additional comments.

Step 6: Analysing interview data
To analyse interview data, read through your notes or a summary of the tape recording and look for pertinent themes. In this, you can use the questions asked during the interview to suggest categories for data analysis. Additional categories may emerge from the responses of the participants. Options for analysing qualitative needs assessment data will be discussed in more detail in the section on focus groups.

Recommendations for further reading
The reader has been familiarized with some central considerations in planning and conducting interviews. To obtain a more thorough understanding, the section on qualitative interviewing (pp. 339–427) in Michael Quinn Patton's excellent textbook on *Qualitative Research and Evaluation Methods* [22] gives a very instructive introduction. It provides a comprehensive overview of the issues at stake, including an outstanding discussion of question options, and presents many illustrative practice examples. Further helpful references on interviewing from a social science point of view include [24] and [25]. For those wanting to learn more about the use of qualitative interviews in the context of health care and health promotion, [15] and [26] provide useful sources of information.

2. Group methods – focus groups

Focus groups are group discussions involving 8–12 participants and are guided by a facilitator. Their purpose is to discuss a limited number of issues in order to identify a range of opinions and ideas. Originally, focus groups were used in market research to identify costumer preferences so that products could be matched to perceived wants and needs, and effective communication strategies developed.

Effective anti-stigma programmes have to be based on the needs of specific groups. Interventions must be appropriately tailored to these needs, and communicated in ways that the programmes' target groups will understand. Because focus groups start from the needs and experiences of those who experience stigma and discrimination, they help developers of anti-stigma programmes address important and concrete needs.

More specifically, they:

- Empower service users and family members by acknowledging their expert role and soliciting their assistance in defining effective interventions.

- Help identify and recruit interested and qualified individuals for programme task groups.

- Involve all members from relevant groups in programme development and so help sustain ongoing support throughout the programme.

- Help balance the interests of programme planners with the perceived needs of the intended beneficiaries of the programme.

Why focus groups to examine level 1 needs among service users and family members?
Focus groups produce a rich body of data expressed in participants' own words. They allow respondents to qualify their responses and explain their reasoning. In contrast with individual interviews, the facilitator addresses a number of issues (foci) for discussion and assures that the discussion remains on the subject of interest. Beyond that, interference with the discussion is kept to a minimum, which aims to create a communication situation which bears close resemblance to 'naturally occurring interaction' [27]. In fact, group participants often 'forget' the presence of the facilitator and begin discussing between themselves. In addition, a guided discussion among people who share a central part of their experiences (e.g., suffering from mental illness) encourages participants to articulate grievances and criticisms. Consequently, focus groups can help avoid social desirability bias which can limit the validity of results in face-to-face interview situations [21]. The group dynamics further stimulate thinking, provide a wider range of contributions, and yield information that may be missed or withheld in an individual interview or questionnaire. Therefore, in-depth information from focus groups is one important basis for targeting anti-stigma programming.

When to use focus groups?
Service users, families, mental health professionals, media representatives, health politicians and other groups all have different expectations regarding the outcome of anti-stigma efforts. The process of defining target groups and developing effective interventions require an in-depth understanding of these different perspectives. Focus groups can be used at different stages in programme development to:

- Understand how stigma and discrimination affect the lives of people with mental illness and their families, and what they feel needs to be done to reduce the burden of stigma in their daily lives. As participants share a similar living situation, focus groups provide a safe environment that facilitates expressions on difficult or hurtful subjects such as stigma. Discussions among like-minded individuals can also activate stigma-coping strategies and help create social network ties through which participants may support each other beyond the focus group session.

- Generate ideas and concepts to be used as input for programme planning. With their open atmosphere, focus groups are well suited to creating ideas. Based on these ideas, basic concepts for the anti-stigma programme can be developed.

- Create anti-stigma messages including what information the programme will provide on mental health problems, which myths should be dispelled, and how the programme will position the topic. Focus groups can be helpful in developing messages and testing them with different target groups.

- Monitor the programme. Focus groups can be particularly useful for understanding the needs of project teams. Possible needs arising in the course of the programme include a need for training, consultation, additional staff, special expertise and other resources.

Conducting focus groups

Successful focus group meetings require careful planning and preparation. You should consider the following steps.

Step 1: Define the problem and formulate the main question

It is important to be clear about the concepts or issues that you want to investigate. A good question to start an anti-stigma needs assessment is 'When and where do people with mental illness experience stigma that is a consequence of the illness?' Having a clear understanding of the underlying concepts such as stigma, discrimination, exclusion, disadvantage or anticipated stigmatisation is particularly important as you will use these terms to pose questions to focus groups' participants and to generate discussion.

Step 2: Identify eligible focus group participants

A thorough needs assessment will capture the views of different groups, such as service users, men or women with a mental illness, family members, health care professionals, clergy, journalists or film-makers. Plan separate sessions for each group. Participants who share similar key characteristics will more easily identify with each others' experiences. This will help participants feel more comfortable in the group and facilitate discussion. The goal is to create homogeneous groups of participants with respect to the key characteristics you have identified.

The number of focus groups required depends on your purpose. When exploring a broad and complex topic such as experiences with stigma, you may want to run several groups, continuing until you cease getting new information (termed 'saturation'). This usually occurs within 4–6 groups. When addressing a more specific question, such as how individuals cope with stigma, you may need fewer sessions until you reach the saturation point. For an even more specific and concrete purpose, such as testing audience reactions to a slogan or identifying needs for support in an action team, a single session with each target group may be all that is required.

Step 3: Developing discussion questions and probes

Identify the main issues to be discussed and formulate open-ended questions for each issue. Each open-ended question should have a series of sub-questions and probes to assist the facilitator in generating discussion and eliciting a broad range of responses. The main questions, sub-questions and probes form the discussion guide. This is an important tool for the facilitator to orient the group discussion and manage the time. An example of a discussion guide for enquiring subjective perspectives of stigma is given in Figure 6.3.

An in-depth exploration of a few concepts is preferable to brief exploration of a larger number of issues. Therefore, the number of issues to be addressed in a focus group should be limited to no more than three or four.

Questions do not need to be followed in strict sequence and probes should only be used if the group does not react to an issue or offers little information. Otherwise, the goal is to use the questions to initiate a natural and free-flowing conversation among the group members. It is important to be as non-directive as possible to encourage a broad range of contributions.

TOPIC 1: STIGMATISATION EXPERIENCES

Opening question:

What has changed for you after you first developed schizophrenia? Tell me concrete incidences and stories that you experienced! [if necessary, probe: work, family, friends, education, everyday life]

Further questions (alternative):

Were there situations in which you felt excluded or misunderstood? [if necessary, probe: when? where? can you describe other situations than you have already described?]

Did you tell other people that you had schizophrenia? [if necessary, probe: whom? when? why? why not?]

How did people around you react when they found out you had schizophrenia? [if necessary, probe: withdrawal, interest, gossip, support?]

TOPIC 2: SUGGESTIONS FOR ANTI-STIGMA INTERVENTIONS

Questions (alternative):

What should be done about negative stereotypes/discrimination because of schizophrenia?

How would you like people to react to the fact that you have schizophrenia?

How, do you think, could these situations (described earlier) be avoided/improved?

What kind of information would be important?

Who/which groups in particular should be addressed?

[probe for concrete ideas when suggestions are given (e.g. storyline of a film, contents of a newspaper article, strategies for political lobbying, etc.)]

Figure 6.3 Focus group guidelines for obtaining subjective perspectives of stigma experienced by people with schizophrenia

Step 4: Select and train a facilitator and co-facilitator

The facilitator is the main data collection tool. It is important to make a careful choice based on the purpose of the project, the characteristics of the focus group participants, and the type of facilitator that would best fit with the group to obtain useful data. A good focus group facilitator will create an open and tolerant atmosphere in which each participant feels free to offer opinions. They will have worked with groups in the past and have basic interviewing skills (attentiveness, preparation, ability with the skilful phrasing of questions, and genuine interest).

It is advisable to have a co-facilitator whose primary responsibilities are careful note-taking and helping the facilitator to generate discussion. Notes are the basis of the analysis so careful note-taking is crucial to the success of the focus group. It is best if all groups are managed by the same team of facilitators. This will improve comparability of results across groups. If time constraints require several focus groups to be carried on simultaneously, careful training of facilitators should aim for a relatively uniform moderating style.

Step 5: Establishing the groups

Send personal or written invitations at least two weeks in advance of your focus group session and confirm attendance. In your letter of invitation state the purpose of the group, the nature and the benefits of the participation, how the information will be used, and how individuals' privacy and confidentiality will be protected.

Different recruitment strategies may be necessary for different groups. People with serious mental illness and their relatives may be recruited though mental health programmes, advocacy organisations, or local mental health providers. Always invite more people than required to allow for drop-outs. Follow-up contact with participants, through either mail reminders or telephone calls, will help to reduce drop-outs. Providing support for transportation costs and parking may increase your turn-out. Also, depending on the local context, it may be appropriate to offer small financial incentives for participants. In this case, additional funds have to be allocated for this in the overall programme budget.

Time the groups carefully so that they do not compete with other important local events. Arrange the focus group sessions to take place in a comfortable and easily accessible environment. Create a relaxed atmosphere for the discussion through informal seating, and by providing beverages and light snacks. Whenever possible, hold groups with service users outside of the hospital or mental health programme.

Step 6: Running the focus group session(s)
Before participants arrive, set up and test any technical equipment that you plan to use, such as a tape recorder or video camera. Start the session with an introduction by the facilitator. Explain how members were selected, the purpose of the project, how the data will be handled, and how results will be used. Obtain informed consent to record the session.

Occasionally you will have more people in attendance than you anticipated. If you have too many people to run an effective group, split the group and have the co-facilitator lead the second group. If your attendance is low, you will have to reconsider your recruitment strategy. Too few group participants may render the data incomplete and incomparable with other groups.

Begin the discussion with a general question and ask all participants to respond. A question about some aspect of their experience will break the ice and create commonalities between group members. Then follow the discussion guideline you have prepared, using probes to generate more detail or to re-focus the discussion if it wanders off track. When the discussion is complete, thank the participants and solicit their advice on how you could improve future sessions.

Problems often arise in the course of moderating focus groups. Some of the most frequently experienced problems are as follows.

- The presence of a dominant group member. While they may provide a great deal of useful information, they may discourage other participants from entering the discussion, force agreement with their own views, or even attempt to take over the facilitator's role. If given too much room for expression, they are a major source of bias in focus group research. To defuse the situation, be appreciative of the dominant individual's knowledge, but explain that the opinions of others are equally important. You may need to tell them firmly, but politely, to wait their turn to speak. Establishing clear ground rules for communication at the outset may help to prevent this problem.

- Censoring and conformity are common processes in group interaction. In focus groups, participants may withhold comments through lack of trust, or tailor statements in accordance with their perceived expectations of the facilitator or other members of the group. At the outset, asking participants to describe concrete experiences, rather than having them provide opinions, can reduce this propensity.

- Focus group discussions may become heated as people begin to express different views. Two participants may begin to argue and exclude everyone else from the discussion. Working in smaller groups can overcome this problem. Assign the two people arguing to one group in order to encourage their cooperation. By making cooperation an explicit goal of the exercise, they will be faced with the possibility of group sanctions if they are unable to work together.

- Topics you wish to address may be too abstract for participants. This happens frequently when participants are asked to envision solutions. They may not see themselves in a position to implement change, or such solutions may be too far away from their every-day problems to be readily grasped. This situation may be alleviated by introducing games or stories. For example, you may ask the group to imagine that they are journal-ists commissioned to write an article on schizophrenia for a magazine, or consultants to a movie that features a character who has schizophrenia.

- Participants may feel embarrassed to share experiences. One option for overcoming this problem is to ask them to write down their views. A second option is to split the focus group into smaller subgroups, asking each to prepare a brief report. These strategies will assist participants in becoming clear about what they have to say and allow them to be selective in preparing and making their statements. An expansion of this method is to have people write experiences down anonymously on identical sheets of paper, put them in the middle of the table, shuffle them and let people draw statements to be read out. Unpleasant experiences are mentioned but without personal identifiers.

- With quieter participants, direct questions can be used to probe whether their silence means agreement, disagreement or unwillingness to respond, or whether the participant has nothing more to say.

Focus groups are intellectually and emotionally taxing for the facilitators. No more than three focus group sessions should be scheduled per week to allow facilitators sufficient time to debrief, review notes, identify themes to take up in the next sessions, look for improvements, and replenish energy levels.

Analysing focus group data

Material from focus groups can be used in a variety of ways. Hence there are different levels of analysis, ranging from providing an overview of a broad issue, to the detailed analysis of one particular aspect of experience. Ensure that the data analysis strategy answers the questions posed by your needs assessment project. A summary of focus group applications is provided in Table 6.2.

In-depth analysis   In-depth analyses are ideal where there are a small number of groups, the focus is relatively narrow, and the research question is specific. An example of a research question that is amenable to this analysis is: *How do families of people with schizophre-nia cope with the fact that friends and relatives abandon them after the illness begins?* A thorough analysis would use a full set of verbatim transcripts that have been prepared from tapes. The process is inductive. Categories are formed from themes that emerge when read-ing the text. Coding uses a cut and paste procedure. The coding system evolves throughout the course of analysis.

It is important to develop a coding guide that clearly defines the codes to be used and provides criteria for what kind of information is to be coded under which heading. To

Table 6.2 Summary of focus group applications

Purpose	In-depth analysis of a specific research question	Explorative, broader sampling population	Concrete purpose, e.g., developing messages, testing questionnaire items, identifying needs for support in project teams
Possible questions	How do university students with recent onset of schizophrenia cope with stigma?	How is stigma experienced from the subjective perspective of people with schizophrenia?	What are the training needs of people with schizophrenia in working with the media?
Number of focus groups	2–4	4–6	1–4
Data analysis	In-depth analysis: Use of a full set of transcripts Inductive coding: Generating categories (coping styles) from the respondents' own words	Exploratory analysis: Coding of a set of notes Search for patterns of experiences Use of transcripts possible for illustrative purposes	High-level analysis: Select relevant information from the notes or materials produced in the focus group (e.g., flipcharts, drawings, etc.)
Duration	6–10 months	4–6 months	1–3 months
Cost	high	medium	low

ensure that codes are reliably identified, coding should be done by two researchers working independently. Resulting codes are discussed and discrepancies identified and resolved. The final step is the interpretation of patterns in the material. For example, one may look for types of people reacting to stigmatisation in a particular manner, or develop a typology of coping styles that could serve as the basis for a stigma-coping training programme for family members. Analysis can be further facilitated by breaking it down according to 'sub-questions' to avoid including too many topics. Here, the text should be analysed for one aspect at a time. Also, several computer software packages for qualitative analysis are available and facilitate coding by allowing simultaneous access to the coding system and the coded text.

Exploratory analysis Exploratory analysis typically covers a broad range of issues derived from a larger number of groups. For example, one may be interested in identifying stigma experiences from service users, family members, and mental health professionals. Given such a broad research objective, verbatim transcripts are not required. An analysis of the notes taken by the co-facilitators during sessions is sufficient. Notes are scanned for general themes or categories of experience. The categories that are produced in this way can then be illustrated with quotes transcribed from the tapes.

High-level analysis A high level analysis may be conducted to generate ideas, or to develop or test questionnaire items or media materials. In such cases, transcription is rarely required. Instead, a more straightforward summary of the contents can be developed by selecting relevant information from the session notes. In addition, materials produced during the focus group session such as drawings, flipchart sheets summarizing the results of brainstorming sessions, or associative comments on a proposed slogan written down by each participant can be used. If the material provides information on a variety of topics, it is advisable to break down the analysis into manageable subsets. Topics relevant for analysis usually correspond with issues listed in the interview guide and the focus group objectives.

Problems in analysing focus group data
Focus group data are rich, complex, and the product of group dynamics. Therefore, focus groups do not lend themselves to understanding individual views or making comparisons between participants. While the group dynamics occurring in a guided, but relatively open, discussion are an important argument for the use of focus groups for specific purposes, they complicate an analysis of data at the level of the person. If the goal is to understand a problem at the individual level, then an interview, rather than a focus group, is the better approach.

One challenge in the in-depth analysis of focus group data is that several participants may speak at the same time, making it difficult to distinguish individual statements on the tape or identify individual perspectives. A skilled facilitator may prevent this by asking people to repeat themselves or by stopping the discussion when participants speak simultaneously.

Recommendations for further reading
A very practical summary on focus groups is given in [28]. This handy paperback gives an overview of the uses of focus groups, research designs, conducting focus groups and analysing focus group data. It also compares focus groups with other methods such as interviews or participant observation. For a comprehensive insight, the *Focus Group Kit* [29] provides you with plenty of resources and practical examples on how to run successful focus groups, from the initial planning stages to asking questions, to facilitating, to the final analysis and reporting of your project. [30] represents another useful handbook you may wish to consult.

Evaluating the context for designing and implementing effective anti-stigma interventions

No matter how specific or small-scale the programme you have in mind may be, all your activities against stigma are always embedded in a wider social, cultural and political context. It is therefore necessary to understand the environment in which anti-stigma activities take place. Knowledge of the wider environment is important for two reasons. First, it provides potential **resources** for anti-stigma action, such as a particular journalist who stands out in the overall negative reporting on the mental health issues and hence could become an important ally in sensitizing media representatives to the importance of responsible reporting. Likewise, a local health politician who successfully fought for the establishment of a housing project for people with chronic mental illness against strong resistance in the neighbourhood may be interested in counteracting discrimination on a wider scale.

Second, however, the wider context of anti-stigma activities also presents **obstacles and constraints** for successful action. For example, it is likely to be difficult to obtain funding for an issue that might not be at the top of local politicians' or potential sponsors' agendas. Also, stereotypical attitudes among the general public or key opinion leaders may mask their view for there actually being stigma in place, as discriminatory action may be seen as a 'normal' reaction to deviant, incomprehensible behaviour or to a perceived danger represented by people with mental illness. Yet, in the context of anti-stigma programmes, these obstacles may lead the way to defining targets for anti-stigma action. As discussed earlier, these may indicate a need, i.e. the necessity to fill the gap between the current situation and a future

Table 6.3 Overview of needs assessment methods

Assessment method	Advantages	Disadvantages	Tips	Possible use in the context of anti-stigma programmes
Interviews	– Record multiple perspectives – Minimal cost – Allows for clarification	– Requires much time – Difficult to quantify	– Identify groups to interview – Use active listening – Prepare specific questions and focus points	– Interview key people in the community (e.g., school headmaster, head of the police, health politicians) – Obtain expert perspective on mental health literacy
Focus groups	– Allows brainstorming – Discussion among participants – minimal interference from the researcher – Allow participants to qualify their responses – Synergetic effect of the group setting – Encourage the articulation of grievances by reducing social desirability	– Dominant personalities – Time constraints – Difficult to analyse – Difficult to capture various viewpoints	– Conduct groups with all relevant stakeholders – Make field notes and tape the session – Ask participants to think about key issues beforehand – Set up ground rules	– Exploring stigma experiences of people with mental illness and their families – Generating ideas for anti-stigma strategies – Developing anti-stigma messages – Gathering expertise on funding channels
Surveys	– Allow to gather representative data – Allow participants time to think – Easiest to analyse/quantify – Little time required to administer – Anonymity	– Development time – High cost – Low returns – Data gathering through the lens of the researcher – Low return rate	– Keep questions basic and clear – If possible, use uniform response format – Pilot questionnaire first – Maximize return: follow-up calls – Assure participants' confidentiality	– Studying public opinion on mental illness – Ascertaining views of target groups (e.g., teachers) about specific issues (e.g., mental health promotion at school)
Analysis of existing data	– Easy to analyse/quantify – Minimal cost – Provides evidence of ongoing trends and problems	– May be outdated or incomplete – Data could have been selectively edited – May not be helpful in identifying cause of problem	– Determine ethical and legal constraints of data use – Formulate questions to be answered by reviewing documents – Consider search time vs. survey time – Check validity: interview authors	– Policy analysis (health and social policy, insurance practices) to identify discrimination against people with mental illness – Review human rights legislation to see whether it applies to people with mental illness

Adapted from NOAA Coastal Services Center – www.csc.noaa.gov/cms/cls/needs_assessment.html

desirable state. Analysing the environment in which anti-stigma activities take place is thus a central aspect of successful needs and capacity assessment strategy.

As may be evident from examples for resources and obstacles for action against stigma given above, there are three main avenues to pursue in obtaining context information for developing effective anti-stigma interventions:

1) understanding attitudes of the general public and important stakeholders;

2) analysing media images of mental illness;

3) studying policies and legal regulations to detect where structural discrimination against people with mental illness is in place.

For each of these three strategies, planners will be acquainted with some central steps and tasks to provide a basic understanding of the issues involved.

1. Assessing population and stakeholder attitudes: surveys

Definition and purpose

A survey is defined as

> a structured process for collecting primarily quantitative data directly from individuals by asking questions. It can show the distribution of certain characteristics within a population, usually by surveying only a small proportion of that population. [31]

Surveys are used when needs assessors require generalizable information about particular topics. This means they aim to make inferences about an entire population (e.g., all mental health professionals, the general public in a country, all journalists) on the basis of their data. This requires adopting an appropriate sampling strategy, i.e. a procedure to select a group of people for the survey that adequately represents the population one intends to study. Further, it is important that the topics addressed assume approximately the same meaning for everybody questioned, and that questions can be understood identically by persons coming from different contexts or social groups [21].

Not only do surveys (1) provide context information for programme activities, they are also used to (2) broaden planners' understanding of first-level needs by quantifying their scope. Once the nature of problems as well as priorities for action have been understood through qualitative inquiry, knowing its frequency and distribution in potential target groups is essential to effectively focus an anti-stigma programme [32]. Finally, needs assessment surveys can (3) provide baseline information against which the success of programme activities can be judged. Next, the steps and tasks in conducting a survey will be outlined.

Step 1: Deciding on survey objectives

Starting out with a survey, you first need to decide on the objectives of the survey. This implies determining exactly what you want to learn from the individuals you plan to survey. Having a clear idea before you begin will guide you through the whole survey process and can save valuable time for both you and your participants [15].

Ideally, this is done by formulating a research question, i.e. phrasing the topic of interest in one concrete question. For anti-stigma programmes, this question may read as follows:

1) What do people know about mental health problems? and/or

2) Which treatment methods do they perceive as helpful? and/or

3) What are the common stereotypes held about people with mental illness? and/or

4) How would people react towards someone with mental illness in important social situations?

These questions target different levels of public or target group opinion. Questions 1 and 2 would guide the design of a survey aimed at testing *knowledge* about mental health problems and available help-seeking options, which is also described as *mental health literacy* [33]. Identifying gaps in mental health literacy is particularly important in assessing needs for programmes aiming at improving prevention and fostering adequate help-seeking. Question 3 taps public *attitudes* about people with mental illness, and question 4 gauges hypothetical *behaviour* towards them. Among these levels, data on the scope, nature and distribution of stigmatizing behaviours should be the main aim of the survey as the latter most strongly affect the concrete burden of stigma in service users' and families' lives [32].

Not only does the survey objective determine what kind of information the assessment will provide, but it also needs to guide the whole process of survey development, implementation and analysis. For example, a survey aiming at measuring mental health literacy of the *general public* will have to formulate questions in such a way that they are relevant and understandable for *lay persons* rather than testing specialist medical knowledge. When attitudes of mental health professionals are being surveyed, on the other hand, questions used in attitude surveys among the general public may be useful to make comparisons. However, professionals' contact with people who have a mental illness mainly takes place in the context of therapeutic relationships, when those suffering from mental illness are their patients or clients. Therefore, attitude questions should specifically refer to providing care for mental illness, e.g., by asking about treatment philosophies.

Step 2: Developing a budget
Before beginning to develop a survey, planners need to be aware of how much money they can spend. Developing a budget is the second step in conducting an assessment. Together with the survey objective, the budget will guide the selection of survey methods and will facilitate decision-making on central planning questions such as deciding whom to hire to assist with the survey, how many people to include in the study, and what kind of and how much data analysis to do.

Step 3: Questionnaire design
Next, the survey objectives have to be operationalized, i.e. needs assessors must **develop questions** that adequately measure the context variables they decided to survey.

When it comes to assessing programmatic needs for anti-stigma activities, there is plenty of experience with surveys from the World Psychiatric Association's Global Programme to Fight Stigma and Discrimination because of Schizophrenia. Several assessment tools have been developed in the context of the programme, for example social distance questions to measure the general public's behavioural intentions towards people with schizophrenia or surveys to study the attitudes of journalists. Many useful programme materials are available on the programme's website at www.openthedoors.com. On the site, you can also find contact details of colleagues in different countries who will be happy to share their expertise and experiences. So before you set out to develop your own survey questions, it is always a good idea to see what assessment tools are already available. Apart from saving valuable time and resources, drawing on existing materials also offers the advantage that these tools have already been used in the field and may have been tested for their reliability and validity. So using them will also increase the quality of the data you obtain from your assessments.

In case you have specific assessment objectives that have not been studied elsewhere, the following aspects have to be borne in mind in developing questions:

- the kind of survey you are planning (e.g., mail survey, telephone survey, Internet survey, face-to-face survey);

- the population you intend to survey (e.g., the general public, journalists, mental health professionals);

- the kind of data analysis you plan to carry out.

For example, a mail survey should include primarily 'closed' questions, which give the respondent a choice of answers to select. Examples include responding yes or no, indicating how frequently a certain situation applies, or rank-ordering several options [15]. Through this, respondents are required to express their opinion through a scale point and thus produce quantitative information. Quantitative scales available to record responses include the five-step Likert scale (e.g., ranging from 'strongly agree' to 'strongly disagree') or scales using semantic differentials (e.g., between 'hurts' and 'doesn't hurt'), usually giving seven intervals allowing respondents to quantify their position between the extreme poles [21]. A good summary of different scales is provided in [34].

'Open-ended' questions allow participants to generate answers themselves. In surveys, these should be used as little as possible, as they (1) do not provide quantifiable information and thus (2) require considerable effort in data analysis (developing a coding scheme, etc.). In mail surveys especially, the number of open-ended questions should be limited since here respondents' motivation will be lower than in a face-to-face or telephone interview situation. Hence a mailed survey should be as simple and convenient as possible. This means that questions and response options must be clear and short, and the questionnaire should have an attractive layout which guides respondents through the questions in a 'look-and-feel' fashion.

Put yourself in your respondents' shoes also in deciding on the **order of questions**. To keep them from fatigue and frustration in filling in the questionnaire, start with questions that build interest in your survey and are relatively easy to answer. The following questions should be ordered in a manner that will seem logical to respondents [35]. Place difficult or potentially threatening questions in the middle of the questionnaire, as you want respondents to answer these questions after they have warmed up, but before they get tired [15]. Finally, place demographic questions (e.g., about respondents' age, income and family status) at the end, as these may lead some respondents to interrupt answering the survey. Also, demographic questions are answered quickly which makes them convenient at the end when respondents may already be tired.

Once an initial set of questions has been developed, they must be **tested and revised.** The following steps are recommended for testing questions:

- Seek to establish content validity by sharing them with colleagues who have experience with or expertise in the subject of the survey.

- Solicit the opinions of people who will analyse the data.

- Ask them to critique the questions and suggest ways to improve the wording.

- Ask them to tell you what they think the questions mean.

These people should be informed about the scope and purpose of your assessment and be asked to use a consistent format in providing written feedback. Taking time to revise your questions is the best way to diminish measurement error in responses, thereby increasing reliability and validity of your survey [15].

Step 4: Piloting the questionnaire
Before entering the field with your survey, you should allow time to **conduct a pilot test**. This investment should result in an effective format and response rate. For larger research projects, several steps are suggested for pilot testing, including peer critique of a draft questionnaire, revision and testing with friends and colleagues, pilot testing with a small sample of respondents, written comments from interviewers and respondents, and pilot testing again [15]. However, extensive pilot testing like this is likely to exceed the resources of many anti-stigma programmes. After all, the assessment of programmatic needs is only the first (though crucial) step of putting activities into place – so it must not absorb the lion's share of project funds. Piloting a survey should nevertheless not be bypassed. An economical way to carry out a pilot test is to find a group of people to practise filling in the questionnaire. For this, select a small sample of people ($n \leq 20$) who are similar to those who will participate in the survey, and then administer the questionnaire to them under 'real-life conditions'. Ask them to identify confusing questions, state the reasoning they used to answer the questionnaire and to suggest improvements for question wording and response options on an extra page at the end of the questionnaire.

Step 5: Conducting the assessment
Administering a survey requires considerable expertise and resources, for example access to address databases of the target groups to be questioned, computer algorithms for selecting a sample, specially trained staff to conduct the interviews, telecommunication facilities for telephone or Internet surveys, and administrative support in coordinating the fieldwork. Therefore, it may be worth considering contracting **an external survey firm** to conduct the survey for you. These have trained interview crews and survey staff, plenty of experience with fieldwork, and have the relevant networks and resources to organise a smooth and professional survey. Within the WPA Global Programme to Fight Stigma and Discrimination because of Schizophrenia, needs assessment surveys in many countries have been conducted in cooperation with reputable research firms. Experiences and lessons learnt are summarised in the programme's training manual [32].

Step 6: Analysing survey data
Once you have gathered your data, they will have to be summarized in a suitable way to render them useful for the programme planners. Data analysis may be one of the last steps in your survey, but it is advisable to plan for it from the very beginning. In this way, you can ensure that the right data are collected and that you will have them available in the form that is required for the analysis [32]. Depending on the purpose of a survey, varying degrees of complexity are possible in analysing the data. In the context of a needs assessment, sophisticated statistical tests are typically not necessary. Rather, simple descriptive statistics such as frequency distributions, the range of responses and the most appropriate measure of central tendency (mean, median or mode) are usually sufficient for analysing programmatic needs [15]. For determining the direction of anti-stigma activities, your results should show levels of stigmatising behaviours and practices in the sample as a whole and in sub-groups defined on the basis of relevant social and demographic indicators [32].

Recommendations for further reading

There is ample literature on the design and implementation of surveys. Detailed background information on planning considerations as well as useful knowledge on how to put a survey into practice are provided in [31, 35–37]. [15] and [32] give excellent overviews of the concrete steps in conducting a survey in the context of a local needs assessment.

2. Assessing public images of mental illness – media analyses

The media play a decisive role in disseminating public images of mental illness. Only a minority of people have direct access to first-hand information on mental illness. Public perceptions about mental health issues are therefore largely informed by images and information circulated by the mass media.

Media representations of mental illness have been shown to reflect common stereotypes present in public opinion: reporting focuses on severe mental disorders, most media images emphasize bizarre behaviour and create the impression that there is a strong association between mental illness and violence [19, 38, 39]. This stereotype of unpredictability and violence has been found to be most strongly associated with people rejecting social relationships with people with mental illness and engaging in discriminatory behaviours [40]. Accordingly, there is good reason to include an analysis of media representations of mental illness in the needs assessment for effective anti-stigma strategies.

Here, it is of particular importance to consider how the media in your local context deal with news and stories about mental health and illness. For, at the local scale, you stand the best chance to actually affect media reporting. When analysing the content of your local newspaper, for instance, you can identify which journalists specialize on topics related to mental health and try to involve them with your local action group. You can further obtain an insight into what makes mental illness a 'newsworthy event' and tailor you public relations strategy accordingly. Also, focussing your project on a limited number of media products will allow you to define clear, measurable goals for your programme. For example, you may seek to increase the proportion of positive reports on mental health issues in the local newspaper by 5%.

The first step in analysing media images is to decide on the **type of media** (newspapers, magazines, radio broadcasts, television programmes) you are going to study. Criteria on which you can base your decision include circulation data (i.e. how many people a particular medium reaches), accessibility of information, and the effort required to analyse media content. Several methods are available for media analysis.

Content analysis is the technique most commonly used in analysing media reporting. It is a systematic method used to turn items (mainly texts) into content categories. It starts with developing explicit rules of coding and enables large quantities of data to be categorized with relative ease. It focuses on quantitative techniques such as frequency counts, concordances and collocation measurements and a number of clustering techniques for codes derived from textual, audio or visual data, sometimes also referred to as 'text mining' or 'data mining'. In addition, content can be analysed in an interpretive fashion, e.g., by describing common themes in the reporting about mental health issues. This is referred to as 'qualitative content analysis'.

Frame analysis looks for key themes within a text and shows how cultural themes shape our understanding of events. For example, you could develop a list of common stereotypes of mental illness such as dangerousness, unpredictability, incompetence or untreatability, and analyse in which ways these are reinforced in news items, TV programmes or feature films. Frame analysis of media content can also show how aspects of the language and structure of news items emphasize certain aspects and omit others, and thus contribute to our understanding of processes of stereotyping.

Discourse analysis examines how the social world is constituted through discourse between social actors. Used in the context of media analysis on mental illness, it can identify

1) the perspectives of actors present in the media, such as health professionals, politicians, user and family organizations, or the police;

2) the views on mental health and illness they are promoting;

3) to what extent their perspective is portrayed in the media; and

4) to what extent these views contribute to stigma or to fighting it.

Assume that your analysis of first-level needs, i.e. service user and family views, has revealed that people with mental illness face disadvantages due to a lack of adequate information on mental illness among the public. In this case, your needs analysis could use this method and focus on the extent to which and the contexts in which mental health professionals provide information that dispels myths and stereotypes, and to which service users and family members are represented in the media.

In practical terms, conducting a professional media analysis can be very time-consuming and costly. There are different options which can make media analysis feasible as a needs assessment strategy, even though you may be on a tight budget:

1. *Subscribe to a media service for a certain period.* These services have access to electronic databases on all media content and can carry out structured searches for you. You have to provide them with a list of keywords, and they select the relevant media items and send results to you in the shape of a newsletter.

2. *Use electronic databases or archives of media content.* These are commonly available online on the newspapers' or TV programmes' websites and can be searched for a small fee. Some daily papers produce content archives on CD-ROMs which can be accessed at public or university libraries.

3. *Co-operate with the Department of Media Science and Communication at a local university or college.* They often routinely carry out media analyses and may have both relevant databases and specific software that searches, organises and annotates textual or multimedia data available, and may allow you to use it. Another option is locating media science students who may be interested to do a thesis project on mental health reporting and could conduct the assessment for you within the framework of their research.

4. *Find regular readers of particular papers or magazines among your local action committee.* Ask them to identify relevant articles over a period of one month and collect them in a media folder. You could use a committee meeting to go through these materials and locate (1) general themes and (2) occasions on which mental health becomes relevant as a news item. Decide on the necessary steps to change reporting patterns based on this information.

Recommendations for further reading

If you would like to learn more about media analysis, Klaus Krippendorff's classic textbook on content analysis gives a comprehensive overview and describes different strategies of analysis [41]. A concise introduction into the concept of content analysis and its uses is provided in [42]. Both [43] and [44] provide readers with a clearly written, user-friendly, hands-on guide to media research techniques.

3. Analysing documents and existing information: health-related data, policies and legal regulations

Beyond doubt, needs assessments require the collection of original data. However, it would be a serious oversight if existing sources of data were not considered. They, too, can produce valuable facts and figures about need. For instance, other researchers may have already collected data on particular areas of need. Examples of useful secondary information include national survey data on public images of mental illness or research reports on media content.

Additional background and supplementary information can also be obtained from analysing raw data and published data summaries on **health and social indicators** relevant to understanding the effects of stigma on a structural level. Here, statistics on health care funding in the different medical specialties, employment rates of people with mental illness, physical health problems experienced by mentally ill people as well as epidemiological data on the prevalence of untreated mental illness among the population can supply important information in deciding on the priorities of anti-stigma action. Sources of these data include libraries, reports of experts and authorities, and census data as well as agency and organisational reports.

Existing information can be obtained from local, national and international sources. Examples of data sources at the local level include those maintained by the statistics section of a local health department, economic and human resources information available from a human services office, and regional data collected by a health planning agency. Highly regarded international sources include those provided by the World Health Organization, such as *World Health Statistics, Weekly Epidemiological Record* [15] and the *World Mental Health Survey* (www.hcp.med.harvard.edu/wmh/index.php). These sources provide health-related statistical data.

Additionally, planners of anti-stigma programmes may be interested in understanding where **policies or legal regulations** discriminate against people with mental illness. Structural discrimination chiefly comes into being through decision-making routines that may not necessarily explicitly refer to people with mental illness, but put them at a disadvantage. For example, the National Monitoring Body for the Insurance Trade in Germany confirmed that it is common practice for insurance companies to classify people with mental illness as chronically ill, and thus as a high-risk group. As a consequence, treatment for mental illness is generally excluded in travel health insurance packages. If one considers the economic situation of people with mental illness, however, it is likely that the majority of them are not actually in a position to afford holidays abroad. Thus considering people with mental illness as a high-risk group does not have a rational basis when it comes to travel insurance [45]. Similarly, legal discrimination was detected in Austrian law. For example, legal texts still use outdated, discriminating terminology such as 'mentally abnormal'. In addition, the social and health insurance systems are described as drawing on a clear dichotomy between health and illness, which does not adequately reflect the nature of mental health problems. Consequently, rehabilitation measures and complementary services for people suffering from mental illness are frequently not offered or financed by public insurance. Further, Austrian civil and canon law contains rules that allow declaring a marriage invalid if one of the partners develops a mental illness [46].

Analysing laws and policies first of all requires identifying the kinds of legal provisions that may discriminate against people with mental illness, thereby limiting the scope of your analysis to the relevant documents. This information can be obtained from the analysis of first-level needs, i.e. the areas in which people with mental illness and their families experience discrimination in their daily lives. Furthermore, needs assessors may wish to consult with legal experts in identifying the pertinent laws to examine. The Austrian study, for example, combined these two strategies and decided to investigate the following laws as potentially discriminating: the social security system, civil commitment, legal rules related to obtaining a driving licence, family and canon law, and inheritance regulations [46].

It may also be worthwhile for needs assessment groups to consider cooperating with national or regional anti-discrimination bodies. These often employ legal experts who know what type of laws and policies to scrutinize for discriminatory practices. Moreover, they may be interested in conducting an enquiry into the legal situation of people with mental illness and could thus be a competent partner in assessing anti-stigma needs.

Scanning the health statistics, legal regulations and policy documents for relevant existing data pointing to mental-health-related stigma, then, helps to avoid investing resources in an assessment that does not actually produce novel insights. Conducting a survey, especially, requires a considerable budget. If one based decisions about programmatic needs regarding attitude change among the public on available survey data, these funds could be transferred to data collection on other areas of need on which no relevant data exist to date.

While drawing on existing data can save valuable time and resources in assessing need, there is a note of caution: sources providing such information should only be used after carefully analysing their quality. Questions needs assessors should raise include how the data have been obtained, when they have been collected and whether the information is in-depth. When consulting health and social indicators, they can only interpret the data appropriately if they understand what has been included or excluded from records, why such decisions were made, and how variables have been defined [17].

In summary, in taking decisions about need on the basis of existing data, make sure that the data were obtained recently, addressed the same survey population, and provide information in a format that is conducive to taking decisions about needs. Further, bear in mind that data from documents and records represent the current status of a situation. In order to make inferences about needs and capacities, discrepancies have to be determined in comparison with standards [17]. Where standards do not exist, the current status must be related to a desirable future state that can be expressed as the target your anti-stigma programme seeks to achieve. One such goal could be the inclusion of the mentally ill in national anti-discrimination legislation when needs analysis has identified that these laws currently do not take account of discrimination on the grounds of a person's mental health [47].

Recommendations for further reading
[47] presents a detailed study of social attitudes and responses to people with mental illness in the USA and the UK, contrasting anti-discrimination legislation in the two countries. For those with an interest in the theoretical background and methodology of policy analysis, [48] will make for an interesting read. From the perspective of political science, this book provides practical advice about how to actually conduct policy analysis and demonstrates

the use of advanced analytic techniques. The use of existing data as a source of information about needs is described in [15] and [17].

Translating needs assessment results into practice

Setting priorities on needs

At first glance, it appears obvious that all needs assessment activities should be geared towards defining priorities for action. However, many needs assessments do not actually include such a step – they stop at data analysis: [18] analysed 125 needs assessments reported after 1981 and found that *fewer than half* gave attention to priorities for action. To counteract this apparent blind spot, the following section focuses specially on priority setting approaches.

Simple approaches

Where the situation concerning needs is not complex, simple decision-making procedures can be used to set priorities. These include paired comparisons, rank ordering and zero-sum games [17]. Here, criteria for decision-making are not spelt out in any detail. In addition, these techniques are easy to use and understand, and allow programme developers to complete decision-making in rapid order. In the context of anti-stigma programmes, they can be useful in smaller-scale projects with a local or regional focus that largely rely on their own funds or voluntary work. This being said, these locally based projects are often particularly effective in improving the lives of people with mental illness. They can focus their activities on concrete problems in the local context, may be less removed from the programme's target groups than larger-scale projects through community ties, and frequently organise a continuous flow of activities, thus enhancing their impact and fostering programme sustainability. The success of programmes against stigma, then, does not only depend on their scale and the funds they have available, but just as crucially on the commitment, creativity and social networks of programme activists. Therefore simple priority setting is a feasible strategy for many anti-stigma programmes.

Multi-criteria approaches

Anti-stigma efforts aiming to affect change on a national or even international scale, however, often depend on external support and require a large commitment of resources. Here, priorities may need to be defended to external constituencies such as political bodies or sponsors. With such a scenario, a multi-criteria approach to priority-setting will be a good option.

Here, two basic dimensions are considered in judging needs: **importance** and **feasibility** [49]. A set of criteria is defined on each of these dimensions. Important criteria include the number of individuals affected, the contribution to organisational goals, the need for immediate action, and the magnitude of discrepancy between a need and the desired status for an area of concern. Availability of resources, the expected efficacy on an intervention, and commitment to change on the part of relevant stakeholders are examples for feasibility criteria [17]. Needs are judged against these defined criteria, and then criteria scores are combined to a total priority score.

Advantages of this approach include that well-thought-out criteria are explicit and can be weighted and that the technique allows taking account of interaction among criteria. Decisions on priorities can thus be made in a transparent and accountable fashion.

Disaggregated prioritization

This approach places criteria in a rank order. Next, a need candidate is screened through each criterion, starting with the highest-ranked one first. This process is particularly useful when programme developers have to deal with a complex set of needs and have drawn up a set of multiple criteria on which to base their decision-making. Ordered criteria, used one at a time, allow keeping the focus of prioritizing on a single criterion, which may facilitate insights that may have otherwise been clouded in the complexity of needs assessment findings. Ranking is a useful strategy whenever it is desirable to simplify the prioritizing process. This may be the case when multiple needs compete for limited resources or when developers of anti-stigma programmes are under time pressure, for example leading up to a deadline for a funding application.

Risk assessment

Another way to view needs-based priorities is in terms of the risks associated with not attending to or resolving a need. This method should be contemplated in situations in which not meeting a need has a major impact. In fact, the cost of choosing to address one need at the expense of another may outstrip the benefit incurred by your entire programme directed at that need.

Consider the following situation. After local government has decided to curb health care funds, the health board decides to outsource its housing projects for people with severe mental illness to a private company from the beginning of the following year. The company will continue to run them, but will increase the monthly fees charged to residents. You know from your needs assessment that their average income is barely enough to get by, and only a small share of residents can count on financial help from family members. At the same time, you identified a need to improve the mental health literacy among the general population as a large share of mental health problems remains untreated. Because of its scope, the latter problem may be high on your agenda. The first need, however, may, at worst, lead dozens of mentally ill people into homelessness, with serious consequences for their health and life. Further, the risk will increase with the passage of time (greater time risk). An urgent response is called for. Deciding not to act on it may also question the credibility of your public awareness campaign. You may be challenged for encouraging people to seek treatment for mental health problems, while the health system fails to sufficiently provide for those treated for severe psychiatric illnesses. Consequently, support and buy-in for your programme may drop (internal moral risk). Some level of risk assessment should therefore be carried out in deciding on priorities for anti-stigma interventions. A detailed discussion of different types of risks and ways to measure them is provided by [17].

Selecting solution strategies and developing an action plan

Priorities for action do not yet make an effective anti-stigma programme. Before being able to embark on concrete projects, developers of programmes against stigma need to identify appropriate solution strategies to resolve high-priority needs.

Reviewing the relevant literature to identify potential solution strategies and possible exemplary sites can be a good starting point. Without doubt, the literature and the Web will offer plenty of project descriptions which may be pertinent to addressing the problems you identified. However, try to limit your search to interventions that have been evaluated and where there is evidence with respect to their effectiveness. This simultaneously introduces a quality criterion and reduces the amount of information you obtain to manageable dimensions.

Locating experts and asking for their input regarding ways to resolve problems is another worthwhile strategy in developing solutions. Not only can they share their experience with anti-stigma activities, but they can also point you to fruitful avenues to explore in existing sources. Cooperation with experts also facilitates benchmarking with other similar groups and organisations that have handled anti-stigma needs. Contacting colleagues working to fight stigma in your country or region, you may be able to arrange site visits where you can observe their projects in action and discuss the pros and cons of solution strategies with their protagonists.

An action plan for your programme determines the best solution strategies for the central areas of needs and outlines how to translate them into concrete interventions. Develop an overall action plan for coordinating your project and specific action plans for each activity you decided to embark on. Your plan should specify who is in charge of each project, the staff required to put it into practice, and communication pathways with project recipients. It should contain clear descriptions of each measure, outline a project schedule, and allocate a budget. Whatever project you plan, make sure to obtain the support and commitment of the leadership of your organisation. This is important to ensure that the programme is present on the organisation's agenda, to secure the necessary funds, and to foster project sustainability [32]. To be effective in the long run, anti-stigma programmes should eventually become integrated into organisational routines and practices. It has been shown to be worthwhile to plan for programme continuity from the outset. The German school project 'Crazy? So what!', for example, liaised closely with educational policy from the early stages of the planning process. For instance, their intervention drew on policies suggesting that schools should play a more important role in developing students' social competencies by including a preventive component aiming to strengthen young people's coping capacities. After successful pilot interventions at Leipzig schools [50], the national NGO Aktion Mensch decided to provide funding to train 20 regional project teams across Germany with the aim of installing the project as a regular feature of secondary education (www.verrueckt-na-und.de/html/english.html).

From needs to action – examples from the WPA Global Programme against Stigma

So far, this chapter has introduced methods to assess programmatic needs and to translate needs into programme priorities. Using examples from four countries participating in the World Psychiatric Association's Global Programme against Stigma, this section will illustrate how this process may look in practice.

Canada

The Canadian province of Alberta was the pilot site for WPA's anti-stigma efforts. The pilot programme sought to test different avenues of anti-stigma action in order to gather as much experiential data as possible for future participants. Therefore they addressed a large collection of target groups, one of them being health care professionals. As part of their needs assessment, they conducted a survey among people with schizophrenia about their experiences with treatment in emergency situations. At the same time, hospitals were asked to complete a questionnaire regarding their provisions for psychiatric emergencies at their emergency rooms (ER). Surveys were designed to elicit information on matters highly relevant to the treatment of people with schizophrenia, including privacy, security (for patients and staff), policies on patient rights and the use of restraints, staff training in mental health and crisis management, waiting times and patient and family satisfaction with services (Thompson *et al.* in [51] pp. 229–233). Results revealed deficits at some hospitals, such as limited availability of staff with special qualifications regarding the handling of mental health emergencies, a lack of routine procedures to inform patients with schizophrenia and their families of their rights, insufficient training of emergency staff in managing mental health crises, the absence of client satisfaction data, and some degree of neglect and marginalization of ER psychiatry on the part of 'mainstream' psychiatry and mental health and the ER departments.

In discussing needs assessment results, programme planners paid attention to the specific situation in the hospitals surveyed. In the priority-setting process, however, the group found that the most important issue is whether or not psychiatric patients in emergency departments are treated appropriately. As a result, their programme focussed on developing and adopting acceptable standards and practices by each hospital with an ER. To this end, the group submitted the results of their research and the following five recommendations to hospital directors and emergency room directors:

- That the examination and interview process and space are adequate for safety, security and privacy of patients and staff.

- That there are enough interview rooms available to ensure privacy during interviews in most situations.

- That these interviews are located near or with easy access to hospital security personnel.

- That security staff are available in a timely, as needed, basis.

- That a policy is in place for governing the use of restraints.

The local action group discussed the findings with the individuals in charge and then followed up on the progress of these recommendations. In addition, discussions were held with the Canadian Council on Health Services Accreditation and Regional Health Authorities. By focusing on this specific point of encounter and stigmatising experiences, the Canadian group was able to effect one of the greatest changes achieved by the programme: the adoption of these recommendations as part of the national hospital accreditation process [51].

Germany

The German anti-stigma centre in Leipzig has long-standing expertise in surveying public attitudes towards the mentally ill. Results consistently revealed a predominantly negative picture. It was therefore the initial assumption of the local action team that improving public attitudes should be the primary goal of their programme. A public awareness campaign seemed to be the way ahead. To obtain the views of the intended beneficiaries of the programme, they conducted focus groups with people suffering from schizophrenia, their family members and mental health professionals. Needs assessment results showed that, from their point of view, stigma went beyond social rejection. Besides disadvantages experienced in the context of interpersonal interaction, focus groups revealed three additional dimensions of stigma: public images of mental illness, limited access to social roles and structural discrimination [52]. These findings led programme developers to expand their spectrum of interventions. In order to have sufficient resources available to address all these problems, they abandoned the idea of a public relations campaign in favour of setting up the association 'Irrsinnig Menschlich e.V.' which focuses on public relations in the field of mental health and psychiatry. The association was to develop several strands of action, on a smaller scale but on a continuous basis:

- *To improve public attitudes*, a school project was initiated, aiming to counteract stereo-types about mental illness before they arise or become reinforced.

- *More accurate media representations* were to be accomplished by supporting journal-ists in their research on mental health issues and simultaneously training people with mental illness as well as mental health professionals to work with the media.

- A third line of action aims *to tackle structural discrimination*. In 2003, Irrsinnig Menschlich e.V. created the 'Courage Award' for politicians committed to equal rights for people with mental illness, which invites proposals from all over Germany and has been receiving considerable media attention and support from prominent public figures.

The Leipzig project provides an example of how priority-setting does not necessarily require to address one need at the expense of another. Rather, a time schedule was developed to implement projects tackling the crucial needs in a gradual fashion. This took place within the framework of the association which ensured a continuous presence of anti-stigma messages in the public discourse.

Morocco

As in other developing countries, needs assessment in Morocco has indicated significant involvement of the family in the lives of patients. Not least, this is due to a lack of mental health services in the country: only 300 psychiatrists cater for a population of 30 million. Interviews with people treated for schizophrenia at outpatient clinics at the two psychiatric hospitals in Casablanca revealed that the majority had lost their jobs and friends, and that 95% of patients lived with their families throughout the duration of the illness, on average more than 10 years. Many relatives faced significant stigma themselves, in particular from neighbours in their communities. As a result, they tried to conceal the fact that their family member had a mental illness and to protect them by not letting them leave the community or hold a job [51].

Based on these results, Moroccan programme developers reasoned that information alone would not be sufficient to fight the stigma associated with schizophrenia. Instead, their first interventions targeted patients with schizophrenia and their families. Weekly meetings were organized with patients in inpatient settings at hospitals to explore the topic of stigma and how to best fight it. The groups explored coping strategies for both patients and families. Experiences from these groups resulted in a second wave of needs assessment. Focus groups were conducted to examine first-hand experiences of stigma and its effects on prognosis of the illness, revealing three dimensions of stigma [53]:

- *The image of the illness itself.* For example, 'aggressiveness' and 'dangerousness' were characteristics often associated with schizophrenia.

- *The stigma of interpersonal interactions.* This included the 'social isolation' reported by those living with schizophrenia and their families.

- *Structural discrimination.* Here, people with schizophrenia reported the lack of rehabilitation services as being the most serious structural disadvantage they face. Family members expressed a particular concern about the quality of available care.

Programme developers concluded from these data that they must first educate individuals with schizophrenia and family members about the illness, about available treatment options and about ways to improve the quality of life of those living with schizophrenia. The Moroccan programme also works in close cooperation with two family associations specially focused on schizophrenia. These groups sponsor seminars on the stigma of schizophrenia for their members [51].

Given the strained situation of mental health care in the country, the programme additionally engaged in lobbying the Moroccan Parliament concerning the availability of medications, the rights of the mentally ill, and their treatment by police and officials in the penal system. Also, they specifically targeted the medical profession, whose members were found to hold strongly stigmatising views. Interventions included an article in a journal for general practitioners and hosting an on-line forum discussion on the stigma of mental illness at the website of the *Maghrebian Journal of Psychiatry* [51].

As we have seen, the Moroccan programme planners started their assessment by exploring first-level needs. To substantiate these findings, they consulted existing data sources on the levels of mental health service provision and surveyed general practitioners regarding their knowledge of schizophrenia. As part of their priority-setting, they explicitly consulted feasibility criteria. This becomes particularly crucial when programmes are confronted with a scarcity of resources, both for their anti-stigma activities and for mental health services in general. Consequently, the two major avenues of fighting stigma in Morocco were (1) strengthening support networks for the family members who currently provide the bulk of care of people with schizophrenia and (2) preparing the ground for better access to adequate treatment for mental health problems by educating the medical community.

Switzerland

In Switzerland, a survey on public attitudes has shown that a large share of the population is little informed about mental health problems and would prefer to avoid social contact with someone suffering from mental illness [54]. This motivated leading mental health professionals to initiate activities to tackle stigma and discrimination. Focus groups with patients and family members were conducted in Geneva and Zurich to assess programmatic needs. Contrary to what programme planners would have expected from their survey findings, results revealed that service users experience a large share of stigma as part of their psychiatric treatment. Stigmatising aspects of their relationship with mental health providers included a lack of interest in their person and the history of their mental health problem, the fact that a psychiatric diagnosis is often given with a negative prognosis and impersonal treatment during inpatient care.

Following up on these findings, a survey was conducted on mental health professionals' attitudes towards people with mental illness. Confirming the results of the focus groups, mental health professionals were found to hold equally stigmatising views as does the general public. Regarding some aspects, such as the assumption that people with mental illness are dangerous or unreliable, psychiatrists' attitudes were even more negative than those of the general population [55].

A review of the literature on factors contributing to stigma suggested that, in actual fact, regular personal contact with someone suffering from mental illness was found to be the most effective way to reduce stigma or to prevent it from occurring in the first place. According to these findings, then, mental health professionals should hold few stereotyping views about their patients. This contradictory evidence raised questions about the type of contact mental health providers entertain with people with mental illness.

Here it becomes evident that, while work in psychiatry can be highly rewarding, interesting and challenging in a positive sense, mental health professionals are confronted with an array of psychosocial stressors. In fact, the very nature of health service work is such that it promotes and maintains a negative perception of clients: professionals' contact with patients is usually limited to times of acute crisis and focused on improving symptoms and illness-related deficits. At the same time, patients may not always follow professionals' advice, thus negatively affecting their sense of achievement. These pressures may lead to an emotional withdrawal from client contact and foster therapeutic pessimism – exactly those aspects of mental health professionals' behaviour that service users and family members experienced to be stigmatising.

However, mental health professionals are guided by their desire to provide effective treatment and care. Hence it is likely that most stigma in the context of treatment relationships occurs unintentionally. Rather, it may be a response to increasing pressures on mental health services, coupled with little individual control and a lack of recognition of one's own commitment by colleagues or superiors, or indeed by patients. This situation has been found to bear the risk of burnout: feelings of emotional exhaustion, increasing distancing from one's patients in an attempt to cope with excessive demands, and finally a negative perception of one's work performance [56].

Swiss programme planners therefore decided to focus their anti-stigma efforts on mental health professionals, following two aims:

1. supporting mental health professionals in managing work-related stressors and preventing job burnout;

2. developing resources to foster cooperative treatment relationships and thus reduce both the risk of burnout and ensuing negative behaviours towards clients.

Interventions include training modules on stress management and empowerment competencies such as shared clinical decision-making, as well as a nationwide staff survey on work-related stress and resources. Mental health services taking part in the survey are given feedback on their results and receive recommendations concerning organisational measures to reduce the risk of burnout and enhance a positive work climate. Further, contact with service users in competent roles will be a central element of the training programme to counteract the negative perspective inherent in the helping relationship [57].

Final considerations on assessing programmatic needs

The practical examples outlined above emphasize that programmatic needs on the stigma of mental illness can vary significantly, depending on local context variables. These experiences further illustrate that, frequently, programme developers' initial assumptions on the most crucial problems to be tackled have been supplemented, if not contradicted, through collecting needs assessment data. This highlights the importance of assessing need in targeting effective anti-stigma interventions.

Examples also highlight that exploring anti-stigma needs must not stop at collecting and analysing data. Failing to use data to make programme choices and set priorities has been noted as one of the most common mistakes in conducting a needs assessment [14]. This does not necessarily imply that needs analysis is not followed by action to resolve the problems identified. Rather, planning for programme activities may not take sufficient account of needs assessment findings and go ahead according to the best of programme planners' knowledge.

This is likely to jeopardize the success of their programme. For one, the most important problems may remain unattended, with serious consequences for people's lives and the provision of adequate psychiatric care. Indeed, failing to act on needs assessment findings may be particularly counterproductive in the context of anti-stigma activities. Research on programme effectiveness has found that raising awareness of stigmatising views by administering an opinion survey may actually emphasize negative attitudes if the assessment is not followed by an intervention. This was assumed to be due to the potential of negative statements in the attitude questionnaire to activate participants' prejudicial cultural beliefs regarding mental illness [58].

A further risk of falling short of translating needs assessment results into action may be less apparent, but equally important: assessing programmatic needs is a political process. In actual fact, conducting a needs assessment already constitutes an intervention. When decision-makers commence to initiate an evaluation of needs and problems, awareness is raised among members of the organisation and the public. Attention to a problem, then, creates the expectation that something will be done about the issues identified. Failing to do so may lead collaborators, partner organisations and sponsors to have second thoughts about supporting the programme or to lose trust in the project leadership.

Beyond acting upon their needs, those with a mental illness and their relatives should be an integral part of anti-stigma programme activities. For research on public attitudes agrees that positive personal contact with people to whom common stereotypes are applied is the single most effective predictor to alter negative conceptions as well as discriminatory practices [59–61]. Their active involvement further enhances social integration and self-esteem, thus contributing to user empowerment for an active participation in society, as well as positively affecting both their well-being and their symptomatology [62–64].

As R., a young man who has had schizophrenia and participated in the project team of the German school project 'Crazy? So what!', confirms:

Eight years ago I became ill: I developed schizophrenia, triggered by taking drugs. I've been feeling better now for two years. But I do have to take good care of myself. But hiding because of that? These times are over. I finally want to live now! Talking to the students is exhausting, but also really great. I like being among people. The kids are very open-minded, have hardly any reservations. And what's the best for me: they discover that there are a lot more commonalities than differences between us, that their images of 'the crazy ones' are not true. It feels really good to contribute to achieving that we finally can talk openly about mental illness, and that nobody has to hide because of a mental health problem. [65]

This insight has guided the approach of the World Psychiatric Association's global programme 'Open the Doors' against stigma and discrimination because of schizophrenia [20, 51]. It builds on cooperation between mental health experts and those experts who know what stigma and discrimination entail from their everyday experience: people with mental illness and their families. The success of programme activities in 20 countries confirms that these groups must be important partners in programmes to reduce stigma and discrimination from the outset. And effective anti-stigma activities start with assessing programmatic needs.

References

1. Link, B. (1982) Mental patient status, work, and income: an examination of the effects of a psychiatric label. *American Sociological Review* **47**, 202–215.
2. Link, B.G., Cullen, F.T., Frank, J. and Wozniak, J.F. (1987) The social rejection of former mental patients: understanding why labels matter. *American Journal of Sociology* **92**, 1461–1500.
3. Fink, P.J. and Tasman, A. (1992) *Stigma and Mental Illness* (1st edn). Washington DC: American Psychiatric Press.
4. Rosenfield, S. (1997) Labelling mental illness: the effects of received services and perceived stigma on life satisfaction. *American Sociological Review* **62**, 660–672.
5. Sirey, J.A., Bruce, M.L., Alexopoulos, G.S., Friedman, M.S., Perlick, D.A. and Meyers, B.S. (2002) Perceived stigma and patient-related severity of illness as predictors of antidepressant drug adherence. *Psychiatric Services* **52**, 1615–1620.
6. Sartorius, N. (2002) Iatrogenic stigma of mental illness. *British Medical Journal* **324**, 1470–1471.
7. World Psychiatric Association (1998) *Open the Doors. WPA Global Programme to Reduce Stigma and Discrimination because of Schizophrenia. Volume1: Guidelines for Programme Implementation*. Geneva: World Psychiatric Association.
8. Angermeyer, M.C. and Matschinger, H. (1995) *Auswirkungen der Reform der psychiatrischen Versorgung in den neuen Ländern der Bundesrepublik Deutschland auf die Einstellung der Bevölkerung zur Psychiatrie und zu psychisch Kranken*. Baden-Baden: Nomos Verlagsgesellschaft. Schriftenreihe des Bundesministeriums für Gesundheit, Vol. 59.
9. Thompson, A.H., Stuart, H., Bland, R.C., Arboleda-Flórez, J., Warner, R. and Dickson, R.A. (2002) Attitudes about schizophrenia from the pilot site of the WPA worldwide campaign against the stigma of schizophrenia. *Social Psychiatry and Psychiatric Epidemiology* **37**, 475–482.
10. Angermeyer, M.C. and Matschinger, H. (2003) The stigma of mental illness: effects of labelling on public attitudes towards people with mental disorder. *Acta Psychiatrica Scandinavica* **108**, 304–309.
11. Farina, A. and Felner, R.D. (1973) Employment interviewer reactions to former mental patients. *Journal of Abnormal Psychology* **82**, 268–272.
12. Farina, A., Thaw, J. and Lovern, J.D. (1974) People's reactions to former mental patients moving to their neighbourhood. *Journal of Community Psychology* **2**, 108–112.
13. Page, S. (1977) Effects of the mental illness label in attempts to obtain accommodation. *Canadian Journal of Behavioural Science* **9**, 193–199.
14. Witkin, B.R. and Altschuld, J.W. (1995) *Planning and Conducting Needs Assessments a Practical Guide* (1st edn). Thousand Oaks, CA, London, New Delhi: Sage.
15. Gilmore, G.D. and Campbell, M.D. (1996) *Needs and Capacity Assessment Strategies for Health Education and Health Promotion* (3rd edn). Boston, Toronto, London, Singapore: Jones and Bartlett.
16. Reviere, R., Berkowitz, S., Carter, C.C. and Gergusan, C.G. (1996) *Needs Assessment: a Creative and Practical Guide for Social Scientists*. Washington, DC: Taylor and Francis.
17. Altschuld, J.W. and Witkin, B.R. *From Needs Assessment to Action. Transforming Needs into Solution Strategies*. Thousand Oaks, CA, London, New Delhi: Sage.
18. Witkin, B.R. (1994) Needs assessment since 1981: the state of practice. *Evaluation Practice* **15**, 17–27.
19. Angermeyer, M.C. and Schulze, B. (2001) Reinforcing stereotypes: how the focus on forensic cases in news reporting may influence on public attitudes towards the mentally ill. *International Journal of Law and Psychiatry* **24**, 1–19.
20. Sartorius, N. (1998) Stigma: what can psychiatrists do about it? *The Lancet* **352**, 1058–1059.

21. Øvretveit, J. (2002) *Action Evaluation of Health Programmes and Changes. A Handbook for a User-Focused Approach*. Abingdon: Radcliffe Medical Press.
22. Quinn Patton, M. (2002) *Qualitative Research and Evaluation Methods* (3rd edn). Thousand Oaks, CA, London, New Delhi: Sage.
23. Gordon, R.L. (1998) *Basic Interviewing Skills Prospect*. Heights, IL: Waveland Press.
24. Kvale, S. (1999) *InterViews. An Introduction to Qualitative Interviewing*. Thousand Oaks, CA, London, New Delhi: Sage.
25. Rubin, H.J. and Rubin, I.S. (1995) *Qualitative Interviewing. The Art of Hearing Data*. Thousand Oaks, CA, London, New Delhi: Sage.
26. Britten, N. (1995) Qualitative interviews in medical research. *British Medical Journal*, **311**, 251–253.
27. Morgan, D. (1993) *Successful Focus Groups London*, Newbury Park, CA: Sage.
28. Morgan, D. (1997) *Focus Groups as Qualitative Research*. Newbury Park, CA: Sage.
29. Morgan, D. and Krueger, R. (1997) *The Focus Group Kit. Volumes 1–6*. London, Newbury Park, CA: Sage.
30. Krueger, R. (2000) *Focus Groups: a Practical Guide for Applied Research* (2nd edn). Thousand Oaks, CA: Sage.
31. Fowler, F.J. (2002) *Survey Research Methods*. Thousand Oaks, CA: Sage.
32. Stuart H. (ed.) (2005) *The WPA Global Programme to Reduce Stigma and Discrimination because of Schizophrenia. Schizophrenia – Open the Doors. Training Manual*. Geneva: World Psychiatric Association.
33. Jorm, A.F. (2000) Mental health literacy: Public knowledge and beliefs about mental disorders. *British Journal of Psychiatry*, **177**, 396–401.
34. Breakwell, G. and Millward, L. (1995) *Basic Evaluation Methods*. Leicester: British Psychological Society Books.
35. Dillman, D.A. (2000) *Mail and Internet Surveys: the Tailored Design Method* (2nd edn). New York: John Wiley & Sons.
36. Salant, P. and Dillman, D.A. (1994) *How to Conduct Your Own Survey*. New York: John Wiley & Sons.
37. Sudman, S. and Bradburn, N.M. (1983) *Asking Questions: a Practical Guide to Questionnaire Design*. San Francisco: Jossey-Bass Publishers.
38. Wahl, O.F. (1992) Mass media images of mental illness: a review of the literature. *Journal of Community Psychology* **20**, 343–352.
39. Philo, G. (1996) *Media and Mental Distress*. Harlow: Addison Wesley Longmann.
40. Angermeyer, M.C. and Matschinger, H. The stereotype of schizophrenia and its impact on the discrimination of people with schizophrenia: results from a representative survey in Germany. *Schizophrenia Bulletin* **30**, 1049–1061.
41. Krippendorff, K. (2004) *Content Analysis: an Introduction to its Methodology*. Thousand Oaks, CA: Sage.
42. Roberts, C.W. (2001) Content analysis. In N.J. Smelser and P.B. Balthes (eds). *International Encyclopedia of the Social and Behavioural Sciences* (pp. 2697–2702), Amsterdam: Elsevier.
43. Berger, A.A. (2004) *Media Analysis Techniques* (3rd edn). Thousand Oaks, CA: Sage.
44. Altheide, D.L. (1996) *Qualitative Media Analysis*. Thousand Oaks, CA: Sage.
45. Schulze, B. (2004) Stigmatisierungserfahrungen von Betroffenen und Angehörigen – Ergebnisse von Fokusgruppeninterviews (Stigmatisation experiences of service users and families: results of focus group interviews). In W. Gaebel, W. Rossler and H.-J. Möller (eds). *Stigma – Diskriminierung – Bewältigung. Der Umgang mit sozialer Ausgrenzung psychisch Kranker* (Stigma – Discrimination – Coping. Responding to the Social Exclusion of the Mentally Ill) (pp. 122–144). Stuttgart: Kohlhammer.
46. Gutiérrez-Lobos, K. (2002) Rechtliche Benachteiligung psychisch Kranker in Österreich (Legal discrimination of people with mental illness in Austria). *Neuropsychiatrie* **16**, 22–28.
47. Sayce, L. (2000) *From Psychiatric Patient to Citizen: Overcoming Discrimination and Social Exclusion*. Basingstoke: Macmillan.
48. Weimer, D.L. and Vining, A.R. (2005) *Policy Analysis: Concepts and Practice* (4th edn). Upper Saddle River, NJ: Prentice Hall.
49. Needs assessment in adult education. Edmonton, Alberta, Canada: Workshop sponsored by Faculty of Extension, University of Alberta, 1995.

50. Schulze, B., Richter-Werling, M., Matschinger, H. and Angermeyer, M.C. (2003) Crazy? So what! Effects of a school project on students' attitudes towards people with schizophrenia. *Acta Psychiatrica Scandinavica* **107**, 142–150.
51. Sartorius, N. and Schulze, H. (2005) *Reducing the Stigma of Mental Illness. A Report from a Global Programme of the World Psychiatric Association.* Cambridge: Cambridge University Press.
52. Schulze, B. and Angermeyer, M.C. (2003) Subjective experiences of stigma. A focus group study of schizophrenic patients, their relatives and mental health professionals. *Social Science and Medicine* **56**, 299–312.
53. Kadri, N., Manoudi, F., Berrada, S. and Moussaoui, D. (2004) Stigma impact on Moroccan families of patients with schizophrenia. *Canadian Journal of Psychiatry* **49**, 625–629.
54. Lauber, C., Nordt, C., Falcato, L. and Rossler, W. (2004) Factors influencing social distance toward people with mental illness. *Community Mental Health Journal* **40**, 265–274.
55. Nordt, C., Rossler, W. and Lauber C. (2006) Attitudes of mental health professionals towards people with schizophrenia and major depression. *Schizophrenia Bulletin* **32**, 709–714.
56. Maslach, C., Schaufeli, W.B. and Leiter, M.P. (2001) Job burnout. *Annual Review of Psychology* **52**, 397–422.
57. Schulze, B. and Rossler, W. (2005) New perspectives on reducing stigma: fighting burnout to enhance provider attitudes of recovery. *European Psychiatry* **20**, 222.
58. Ng, P. and Chan, K.F. (2000) Sex differences in opinion towards mental illness of secondary school students in Hong Kong. *International Journal of Social Psychiatry* **46**, 79–89.
59. Pettigrew, T.F. (1998) Intergroup contact theory. *Annual Review of Psychology* **49**, 65–85.
60. Penn, D.L. and Couture, S. (2003) Interpersonal contact and the stigma of mental illness: a review of the literature. *Journal of Mental Health* **12**, 291–305.
61. Corrigan, P.W., River, L.P., Lundin, R.K., Penn, D.L., Uphoff-Wasowski, K., Campion J *et al.* (2001) Three strategies for changing attributions about severe mental illness. *Schizophrenia Bulletin* **27**, 187–195.
62. Lehman, A.F. (1983) The well-being of chronic mental patients. *Archives of General Psychiatry* **40**, 369–373.
63. Breier, A., Schreiber, J.L., Dyer, J. and Pickar, D. (1991) National Institute of Mental Health longitudinal study of chronic schizophrenia. Prognosis and predictors of outcome. *Archives of General Psychiatry* **48**, 239–246.
64. Brekke, J.S., Levin, S., Wolkon, G.H., Sobel, E. and Slade, E. (1993) Psychosocial functioning and subjective experience in schizophrenia. *Schizophrenia Bulletin* **19**, 599–608.
65. Irrsinnig Menschlich e.V. (2002) 'Stark, wenn sich einer traut über seelische Probleme zu reden!' Verrückt? Na und! Das Schulprojekt von Irrsinnig Menschlich e.V.; Informationsbroschüre. ('Cool when someone dares to speak about mental health problems!' Crazy? So what! The School Project of the Association 'Irrsinnig Menschlich e.V.; Information Brochure.) Leipzig: Irrsinnig Menschlich e.V.

7 Using the Internet for fighting the stigma of schizophrenia

Hugh Schulze

President, c/Change inc., Chicago, USA

Introduction

In 1996, the World Psychiatric Association launched its global programme to fight stigma and discrimination because of schizophrenia. Just one year before, new Internet browsers and other innovations opened up unprecedented access to the World Wide Web. Over the next 10 years as the global programme to fight stigma expanded into two countries, Internet usage and international online communication grew exponentially.

The website of the global anti-stigma programme, www.openthedoors.com, was created to disseminate information about schizophrenia as well as the stigma and discrimination associated with it. To this day, those living with schizophrenia and their families and friends access the site daily – as do academicians, students and professionals from a wide range of disciplines. This chapter describes lessons learned from the eight years since the launch of www.openthedoors.com.

Internet growth and implications for mental health education

According to Nielsen/NetRatings and IDC estimates, in the decade between 1995 and 2005 global usage of the Internet rose from 16 million (or roughly 0.4% of the world's population) to nearly 972 million (or 15.2% of the population). In just five years, from 2000 to 2005, Internet usage on the continent of Africa rose 428.7% to 23,867,500. Usage in Asia is more than ten times as great, with an estimate of 327,066,713 for September 2005.

An 'Internet gap' has clearly existed between developed and developing countries. The World Summit on the Information Society, sponsored by the United Nations and the International Trade Union (www.itu.int), reported that 3% of those in Africa use the Internet, compared to 50% for G8 countries.

While the rates of increase vary from country to country, the rapid growth in use of the Internet continues globally. Search engines, such as Google and Yahoo, are making more and more information accessible in more and more languages.

At first glance, regarding issues of mental health, this increase in information may appear like a positive development. But are more questions – and concerns – raised as more information is made available? Does an increase in information lead to a reduction in stigma? Reports from the 20 countries participating in the WPA Global Programme to

Understanding the Stigma of Mental Illness: Theory and Interventions   Edited by Julio Arboleda-Flórez and Norman Sartorius
© 2008 John Wiley & Sons, Ltd

Fight the Stigma and Discrimination because of Schizophrenia have shown that increased knowledge does not necessarily lead to improved attitudes [1].

A search of Internet sites reveals that far more consumer and family groups are dealing with the question of stigma and discrimination because of schizophrenia than websites for academicians or health care professionals. While there is anecdotal evidence that online chat rooms and forums are providing online communities for consumers and family members to share information [2], little information is currently available on actual changes in attitudes based upon web-based interventions [3].

The WPA programme

Given the speed with which the Internet has developed as a communication medium, a few historical references may provide some perspective:

- The first version of the Netscape web browser was introduced in the second half of 1994.

- Microsoft's Internet Explorer was not released until August of the following year.

- Just one month earlier in 1995, Amazon.com first began selling books online.

When the World Psychiatric Association, under then-president Professor Norman Sartorius, launched the Global Programme to Fight the Stigma and Discrimination because of Schizophrenia in 1996, standard mail, telephone and fax were the primary channels of communication used by the forty psychiatrists and mental health professionals involved. The Internet was still being watched a bit warily. At that time, more than half of Internet users were in the United States and many wondered if this might be a passing Yankee fad.

By 1998, a significant shift was already under way. The use of e-mail had become the primary communication tool among programme participants. In September of that year, the Steering Committee of the programme agreed to establish a website to disseminate information being developed by the global experts. By 2005, at the World Congress of Psychiatry in Cairo, Egypt, more than 20 countries were participating in the global anti-stigma effort and the website had been translated from English into Arabic, German, Italian, Japanese, Portuguese and Spanish – more languages than for the websites of the World Health Organization or the United Nations.

Both the design and content of the website have been updated over time. However, the four main navigational portals or 'doors' have remained the same. These include an overview of the global programme, its mission and its members, an area for mental health professionals, an area for family members, friends and those living with schizophrenia, and finally an area for personal stories.

Opening doors

Enlisting the services of a marketing communications company, the programme's Steering Committee developed a name and logo that could be used to identify the efforts of the programme. 'Open the Doors' was selected for several reasons:

1. It quickly communicated one of the main goals of the programme: to assist in the reintegration of those living with schizophrenia back into society;

2. The three-word slogan, opening with an action verb, was a call to action;

3. Accompanied by the logo graphic of an opening door, it was easily translatable and understandable. The logo was subsequently translated into nine languages, including Arabic, Greek, Japanese and Portugese.

The brevity of this title (as opposed to its longer official title, World Psychiatric Association Global Programme to Fight the Stigma and Discrimination because of Schizophrenia, which confounded even a workable acronym) also made it applicable for use as an easy-to-remember URL address: www.openthedoors.com.

The domain '.com' was chosen over '.edu', given that such a domain denotes an affiliation with a specific academic institution. Similarly, while the World Psychiatric Association itself uses '.org' as a domain (www.wpanet.org), the .com registration has been the most common top-level domain for websites since the 1990s'. The top-level domain '.net' was originally intended to identify Internet service providers.

The group conducted a review of other websites dealing with stigma. Virtually all of the relatively few were (and still are) affiliated with consumer and family advocacy groups, such as www.nami.org of the National Alliance for the Mentally Ill in the United States and www.sane.org of the Schizophrenia Australia Foundation. These in turn focus on mental illnesses in general, unlike the WPA anti-stigma website which focuses solely on schizophrenia and its related stigma.

Box 7.1: Message boards and threaded discussions

The National Alliance for the Mentally Ill (www.nami.org) and other support organizations have discussion areas for those living with mental illness and their family members and friends. Visitors to the NAMI website are required to provide information on themselves such as an e-mail address and a password. The visitor is then given access to discussion areas on 'schizophrenia', 'major depression', 'anxiety', 'OCD' (obsessive-compulsive disorder) and 'Other Mental Disorders'. This last category includes eating disorders and PTSD (post-traumatic stress disorder).

In 2000, the Open the Doors programme created a message board whereby programme participants could share best practices or pose questions to other local action groups participating in the global effort. To ensure the information was kept to only those individuals involved in an intervention through the WPA anti-stigma effort, this discussion area was password-protected. All heads of sites were given the password.

After initial postings by members in the first few months, participation dropped off precipitously. Participants defaulted to using e-mail for regular questions or insights about the anti-stigma efforts. In 2002, this discussion board was discontinued.

Compared to other online discussion boards by support groups, this effort lacked:

- A large enough universe of active participants for involvement and responses to new postings;

- A time-critical need for information.

One recommendation for any future effort would be to allow access and postings from others involved in mental health education or anti-stigma programmes.

Developing Web content

The informational content to be presented on the WPA anti-stigma website was gathered into four navigational portals or 'doors':

1. *Global Programme.* This area is devoted to information on the global programme itself, including:

    a. Information on the five committees of the programme – the Steering, Awareness, Reintegration, Stigma and Review Committees.

    b. Downloadable materials, including reports, bibliographies and programme logos in different languages;

    c. Contact information for local action groups in each of the participating countries.

2. *Professionals.* The content of these pages is taken from Volume II of the programme materials which was assembled by 40 global mental health experts. Categories in this area include:

    a. Aetiology of schizophrenia

    b. Treatment information

    c. Links for professionals

3. *Family members and friends.* The content of these pages was taken from an educational handbook developed for the families and includes information on:

    a. Causes of schizophrenia

    b. Myths and stereotypes

    c. Reintegration.

4. *For personal stories.* This area was set aside to allow consumers and family members to post stories of the stigma they experienced, as well as practical steps to address that stigma.

Since 1998, the first area, with information on the *Global Programme*, has been updated on a regular basis. Much of the Professional and Consumer sections have remained the same. A few additional stories have been added to the last section. As of 2005, those stories include first-person accounts from Canada, India, Germany, the United Kingdom and the United States – all sites of the Global Programme.

Perhaps the most significant change has occurred at the 'Homepage' interface, where additional languages have been added as content has been translated. Each has been translated to varying degrees from the initial English content. The choice of what section(s) to translate was made by each local action group after an assessment of communication needs and the target audiences of their efforts.

The Arabic, Greek and Portuguese versions have both the 'Professionals' and 'Families and friends' sections fully translated. The Arabic and Greek versions also have amended introductions under the Global Programme section.

For the Italian translation, only the section for 'Professionals' has been translated. The German local action groups, on the other hand, have only translated the 'Families and friends' portion.

The local action group in Spain maintains a separate informational website, which is linked through the Open the Doors portal. Similarly, the Japanese local action group, while using a similar, linked architecture has content maintained in Japan.

The combination of languages can also help in directing search engines to the site. Cecilia Villares, director of the local action group in São Paulo, Brazil, observes that for Portuguese users: 'When someone types in esquizofrenia' (schizophrenia) in the Google search engine, the website does not appear in the first page. However, when you add *doença* (illness), *doença mental* (mental illness), *transtorno mental* (mental disorder), *estigma* (stigma), *discriminação* (discrimination), *sintomas* (symptoms), *tratamento* (treatment) – the openthedoors.com link has been among the first 10 or 15 sites listed.' Professor Villares reports having been contacted through the website by Portuguese and Brazilians living in other countries.

Website usage

Statistical data for website usage can sometimes be misleading. While 'hits' to a website are often reported, a 'hit' is reporting retrieval of data. A single page with two or three graphics would include those graphics as separate 'hits'. Simply arriving at a website is no indication that it was the destination intended. For example, as the box below reports, some web users who found openthedoors.com came to the website by searching for the rock group 'The Doors'.

Box 7.2: Searching for stigma

When developing webpages, programmers often insert software code, referred to as metatags, or keywords, in the page's HTML code. These metatags are like Exit signs on the information superhighway, directing search engines to relevant content in your site. For the month of October 2005, the top keyword used in search engines which brought visitors to www.openthedoors.com was 'schizofrenia'. A little more than a quarter of all keyword enquiries bringing traffic to the site (27.4%) of 1070 visitors typed 'schizofrenia' into the search engine. Other search engine enquiries included:

what causes schizophrenia – 3.2%

síntomas de la esquizofrenia – 3%

schizophrenia – 2.8%

One hundred and five visitors in October 2005 came to the website looking for information on the rock group 'The Doors'. This was followed closely by 'hereditariedade' (101 visitors).

At present, programs called 'spiders' and 'crawlers' are used by search engines to also check for content embedded in downloadable files on websites. These files might be in .pdf format, for example. Thus by posting articles or additional information in downloadable .pdf files, websites are able to achieve higher 'hit rates' and greater relevancy ratings to supplement efficiency with well-chosen metatags.

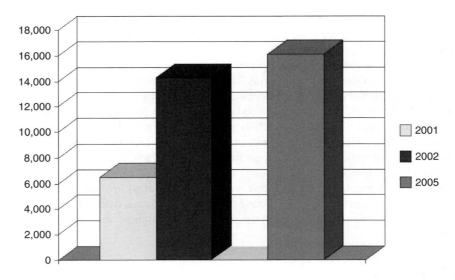

Figure 7.1   Visitors per month

A far more useful statistic is 'visitor' which identifies individuals who visited a site more than once and can be further refined as those who spent three minutes or more at the site. Simple statistical records from most Internet providers can also indicate the number of pages viewed, so that content developers are able to track what areas are most frequently visited.

As Figure 7.1 shows, in 2001, the average number of people spending three or more minutes at the site was 6500 per month. Of those, 112 visited more than 10 times. The average length of those visits was 9 minutes and 18 seconds.

Traffic to the website in 2002 peaked in October at 14,261 for the month. This spike in activity may have been due to interest following the WPA World Congress that was held in Yokohama in August. Several psychiatrists involved with the programme presented results on stigma interventions in Austria, Canada, Germany, Greece, Italy, Japan, Spain and the United States.

In 2005, the average number of visitors per month was 16,140 – roughly two and a half times the number of visitors four years earlier.

Statistical reports from 2003 to 2005 indicate that traffic from .com and .net domains (largely English-speaking users) accounted for roughly 46% of the traffic. (Another 20% were unidentifiable.) However, the leading country domain suffix, which resulted in 16,363 returning visitors, was .it (for Italy). This high percentage of Italian visitors to the site was confirmed by reviewing Page View statistics, which rank the relative traffic for individual pages of the site. Italian pages of the website ranked higher than all other languages save English – and were higher than many of the pages in English.

Visitors from different countries included (ranked in descending order):

Italy (.it) – 16,363

Brazil (.br) – 9139

Saudi Arabia (.sa) – 5653

Japan (.jp) – 5031

Germany (.de) – 2851

Greece (.gr) – 2478

Mexico (.mx) – 2231

Educational sites (.edu) – 2081

Again, these were individuals who visited for more than three minutes. These numbers are also lower than the actual total, given that some visitors from these countries might be included in the 60,501 visitors who were identified with the .com domain suffix.

Dr Chiara Buizza reports that the local action group in Italy has promoted the global website as an information resource. This has increased traffic in that country. She also cites a growing interest in stigma and stigma-related issues by the general public as one of the reasons the website is so frequently referenced.

Overall, one important corollary appears to be that where a local action group has been established by the WPA global programme, website traffic for that country and language increases as well. Each of the countries listed above has a local action group in place, save for Saudi Arabia and Mexico. The usage for these two countries, however, is undoubtedly a reflection of the translations available in Arabic and Spanish.

Statistical reports of website activity indicate people from well over 100 countries have visited the site. More specifically, the local action groups in the twenty countries involved report that the website has also directed many people to their own anti-stigma initiatives. This includes those living with schizophrenia and family members in need of further information, journalists seeking more information, mental health professionals seeking more information on the anti-stigma programme, and volunteers interested in supporting their efforts. In addition, the website has helped several local action groups to link up their efforts with other mental health and consumer organizations in their own country.

Mental health professionals who have learned of the programme and website have also contacted the WPA about starting a programme in their country. Several of those initiatives are in the planning stages as of this writing.

Website enquiries

E-mail enquiries also provide an insight into the use of the website by visitors. On average, messages from visitors are received every three to four days and fall into roughly four categories:

- Family members or friends asking for more specific information on symptoms. Many of these relate concerns or frustrations they may be encountering with a person close to them.

- Academicians and students, most often at university level, seeking more information, such as bibliographies for further study on schizophrenia or stigma.

- Individuals or groups may request to have links to their website placed on the openthe-doors.com website or offer to place links on their website.

- Anti-psychiatry activists also write to contradict information presented on the site or offer alternative therapeutic strategies such as mega-vitamins.

Responses are usually sent to the first three groups. For family members and friends, no information or online diagnosis is given but rather, based upon the specific enquiry, suggestions are made for speaking to a medical professional or local support group in that country.

Conclusions and recommendations

The website, www.openthedoors.com, has served four purposes for the WPA Global Programme to Fight the Stigma and Discrimination because of Schizophrenia:

1. It has provided a central informational resource on the programme internationally, including presentation of materials such as the programme bibliography, programme guidelines in Volume I and compendium of the latest information on schizophrenia and stigma, contained in Volume II.

2. It has provided information on the groups and activities in the twenty countries involved in the global effort.

3. It has served as an informational resource for the local action groups working in those countries, providing follow-up information after presentations or discussions.

4. More broadly, it has served as an informational resource – in eight languages – for those who are unaware of the programme itself but interested in topics such as schizophrenia and the stigma associated with it.

Moving forward, other website details being considered are: an online questionnaire and tool to assess knowledge of and attitudes about schizophrenia targeted to the general public; further links to other initiatives combating the stigma and discrimination associated with mental illness in general; and development of a newsletter to provide more ongoing communication and updates on activities in individual countries – with the goal of creating a central repository of information on best practices on educating about schizophrenia and fighting its stigma and discrimination.

Based on the experience with the programme website over the past seven years, we would make the following recommendations for other mental health initiatives developing a website:

- A brief, memorable URL address will help visitors remember your site;

- Use metatags and .pdf attachments to receive the highest relevancy scores with Internet search engines such as Google;

- Allow printable or downloadable options for content to allow users to review content offline;

- Writing for the web differs from writing for print media:

  - Long, scrolling screens of copy will not be read; if necessary, break the text into shorter paragraphs or sections;

  - Creation of hyperlinks within the document can allow readers to link to other sections of the website if a concept or term is unclear;

- Enquire at other websites with related or supplemental information, which might provide links to your website and similarly offer links to theirs.

In the ten years since the WPA Global Programme to Fight the Stigma and Prejudice because of Schizophrenia was launched, well over a million visitors have viewed the website. Many of these have returned more than once and others have contacted members of the Global Programme or individuals working on local initiatives in specific countries. In addition to providing information on schizophrenia, the website has assisted in building a network of committed individuals working together to a common goal of reducing the stigma and discrimination because of schizophrenia.

References

1. Sartorius, N. and Schulze, H. (2005) *Reducing the Stigma of Mental Illness*. Cambridge: Cambridge University Press.
2. Kissinger, M. (2005) Chat rooms' beacon of hope. *Milwaukee Journal Sentinel*, 1 August, G:3.
3. Griffiths, K.M., Christensen, H., Jorm, A.F., Evans, K. and Groves, C. (2004) Effects of web-based depression literacy and cognitive behavioural therapy interventions on stigmatizing attitudes to depression. *British Journal of Psychiatry* **185**, 342–349.

8 Building an evidence base for anti-stigma programming

Heather Stuart

Department of Community Health & Epidemiology, Queen's University, Kingston, ON K7L 3N7, Canada

Summary

This chapter discusses the importance of building evidence in support of anti-stigma programming in the current climate of evidence-based care and several key challenges faced by researchers in the field. Anti-stigma interventions are approached broadly from a public health perspective that emphasizes the burden associated with mental illness and the importance of population-based approaches designed to promote health and reduce disability. The multi-faceted nature of stigma, the overall complexity of many anti-stigma interventions, and the evolving nature of many anti-stigma interventions, makes them difficult to evaluate. Basing evaluations on explicitly defined theories of program change helps to focus attention on indicators that can be logically linked to program activities and extends knowledge about how and why a program works.

The burden of stigma and the rising popularity of stigma reduction activities

This chapter adopts a public health perspective to consider evidence-based approaches for anti-stigma activities. Public health is defined as *a set of efforts organized by society to protect, promote and restore the people's health through collective or social action* [1]. A public health perspective emphasizes the needs of the defined populations based on an ecological definition of health that recognizes broad social and political determinants of disease and disability, and the relationship of individuals to the social and physical environments in which they live. Activities included under a public health model are public education and communication; legislative, policy, and fiscal reform; social marketing of ideas and behaviors; community advocacy and development; and local community action. All of these approaches have been variously used in the fight to reduce stigma and discrimination because of mental disorders.

The public health importance of mental disorders is highlighted by the Global Burden of Disease Study. In 1990, five of the top ten leading causes of disability worldwide were mental disorders, accounting for 22% of the total years lived with a disability. Depression alone accounted for 10.7% of the years lived with a disability, making it the leading source of disability years – more than double that of the next leading contender (anemia with 4.7%) [2]. Considering productive years lost because of death and disability, neuropsychiatric conditions (and suicide) accounted for 15% of total burden of disease worldwide (25% in developed countries) – more than any other disease category [3].

Despite growing public health concern, mental disorders are not yet afforded the same policy or program priority as comparably disabling physical disorders. For example, the majority of the world's population still has little or no access to even the most basic mental health treatments. A third of the countries reporting to the World Health Organization's Mental Health Atlas Project in 2005, for example, had no specified budget for mental health programming, and one in five spent less than 1% of their total health budget on mental health [4]. Some two-thirds of the world's population have access to fewer than one psychiatric hospital bed per 10,000 population, and more than half of these beds remain in large custodial institutions. Such institutions have been widely associated with poor psychosocial and clinical outcomes (including human rights violations), and are not recommended for treatment of mental disorders [5]. Data from the World Health Organization's Mental Health Consortium Surveys tell a similar story. In developed countries, 35% to 50% of people with serious mental disorders living in the community did not receive any treatment in the year prior to the survey. In developing countries unmet need was as high as 76% to 85% [6].

Treatment gaps such as these can be traced back to a process of stigmatization that is fuelled by deeply held fears and prejudices – a process that limits access to adequate treatment and rehabilitation, social benefits, support and social and economic opportunities, and results in a cycle of disability and disadvantage [7, 8]. Modern mental health reforms, which are built on the notion of recovery, participation in normalized roles and relationships, and community integration, have been seriously undermined by public fear and intolerance. Discriminatory policies and practices are widely prevalent in both developed and developing countries, making psychiatric stigma the single most important barrier to mental health development worldwide [5, 9].

International public health efforts to reduce psychiatric stigma are gaining in presence and popularity. The first large-scale international anti-stigma effort was launched by the World Psychiatric Association in 1996 – a global program to reduce stigma and discrimination associated with schizophrenia. This program is now operating in over 20 countries [9, 10]. In 2001, at the 54th World Health Assembly, the World Health Organization called health ministers to action to redress mental health imbalances [11]. This was followed by a global advocacy program for mental health, initiated for World Health Day [12], and a global action program to raise awareness of the importance of mental health in 2003 [13]. In 2004, the World Association for Social Psychiatry, the World Psychiatric Association, the World Association for Psychosocial Rehabilitation, the World Federation for Mental Health and the Japanese Society for Social Psychiatry issued a joint statement urging the United Nations to recognize the importance of mental health problems and promote an anti-stigma movement to improve acceptance and treatment of people with mental disorders [14].

National public health support for stigma reduction is also evident in a growing number of official declarations, mental health system reviews, and action plans that highlight the disabling effects of stigma and the importance of reducing discrimination. In 2004, for example, the Council of European Ministers of Health pledged its support for anti-stigma activities in a special ministerial meeting convened by the Ministry of Health of Greece. In January of 2005, the WHO Ministerial Conference on Mental Health marked the occasion for the adoption of the Mental Health Declaration and the Mental Health Action Plan for Europe. Priorities for the next decade identified in the Declaration included collectively tackling stigma, discrimination and inequality, and empowering people with mental health problems and their families to be actively engaged in this process [15]. In 2003, the White House released the final report of the President's *New Freedom Commission* inquiry into mental health system functioning. The Commission was charged with conducting a comprehensive study and making recommendations for a transformed mental health system that would reduce fragmentation and focus on the needs of people with mental illnesses. The first goal of the Commission was to help Americans understand that mental health is essential to overall health. To accomplish this goal, they emphasized the importance of dealing with mental health with the same urgency as physical health problems and recommended a national campaign to reduce stigma and prevent suicide. Additional recommendations address the need to reduce disparities in access to quality care and improve research [16]. Almost five years earlier, the US Surgeon General's report had highlighted stigma as a key determinant of psychiatric disability and the importance of stigma reduction efforts [17]. Canada has undergone a similar national mental health review undertaken by the Standing Senate Committee on Social Affairs, Science, and Technology. This marks the first Parliamentary interest in mental health displayed in half a century. The interim report recognizes the enormous importance of fighting stigma and discrimination; the need for national leadership, a prolonged effort, and a multi-pronged approach including community-based education and action, media campaigns, professional awareness campaigns, and the elimination of structural discrimination [18]. The final report charges a newly developed national Mental Health Commission with the task of implementing programs designed to reduce stigma and discrimination [19].

Several nationally coordinated population-based anti-stigma initiatives have also emerged over the last decade. In 1995, for example, Australia initiated a *National Community Awareness Program* – an 8-million-dollar public advertising campaign to increase awareness about mental illness [20]. In 1996 New Zealand initiated the *Like Minds, Like Mine* program in an effort to create an environment that valued and included people with a mental illness [21]. In 1998, the Royal College of Psychiatry in the United Kingdom launched a 5-year *Changing Minds* campaign to improve understanding and reduce stigma and discrimination related to six mental illnesses: anxiety, depression, schizophrenia, dementia, alcohol and drug addiction, and eating disorders. Public views of stigma were found to differ across each of these groups [22]. In 2002, the Japanese Psychiatric Society changed the Japanese name of *schizophrenia*, meaning *split mind disorder*, to a term that is considered to be less prejudicial and more culturally palatable. The name change was intended to improve access to treatment and communication between doctors and patients regarding their diagnosis and treatment [23]. To date, few of these initiatives have been empirically evaluated and their impact on the quality of life of people with mental disorders (and their family members) is unknown.

Evidence-based practice and anti-stigma programming

Scholarly interest in anti-stigma programming and evaluation is increasing. The first international scientific conference on stigma and discrimination because of mental disorders was held in 2001 (Leipzig, Germany), followed by a second in 2003 (Kingston, Canada), and a third in 2006 (Istanbul, Turkey) [24]. In 2005, the World Psychiatric Association initiated a scientific section devoted to the study of stigma and mental disorders in the XIII World Congress of Psychiatry in Cairo, Egypt. A key goal of this section is to provide international scientific leadership designed to foster the production of evidence that can be used to diminish stigma and discrimination because of mental illness.

Despite these important initiatives, the evidence base to support best practices in the field of stigma reduction remains under-developed, incommensurate with the burden caused by stigma, and insufficient to support the growing public health interest in stigma reduction. For example, a review of the clinical literature (OVID Medline and PsychInfo) shows little scholarly interest in stigma or discrimination until the middle of the 1990s, when the number of publications began to rise. Although interest is increasing, current levels – approximately 100 publications a year with *stigma* or *discrimination* in the title or abstract – still reflect less than 2% of all publications focusing on mental disorders.

A key impetus to building a better evidence base for stigma reduction programs comes from the rise of evidence-based practice in general – a development that has been described as one of the more remarkable phenomena to emerge in modern medicine [25]. Although the principle of using external evidence to support clinical practice goes back several centuries, modern evidence-based medicine emerged only recently, during the 1990s. In this short time, it has transformed medicine from a predominantly descriptive discipline, based on careful clinical observation and experience, to one based on the direct application of the best available research evidence to clinical decision-making. Through research syntheses and the implementation of best practice guidelines, evidence-based practice attempts to reduce unjustified variations in clinical practice; promote the safest, most efficacious treatments; and reduce dissemination time to incorporate scientifically sound results into standard care. Clinicians now face unprecedented pressure to support their decisions with scientific evidence, and to develop the research and evaluation skills necessary to critically assess available scientific evidence for validity and applicability to their own practices [26, 27]. Indeed, the rise of the discipline of *clinical epidemiology* as the basic science of medical practice owes its success to the evidence-based revolution [28].

The rise of evidence-based medicine has prompted analogous transformations in health services management and policy-making. Although slower to emerge, the case for evidence-based policy and practice has been equally difficult to refute [29]. Referring to the British National Health Service, Charlton and Miles describe the evolution of an interlocking system of evidence-based activities – ranging from evidence-based medicine, through evidence-based education, research, nursing, public health and health policy – where all aspects of health service practice will be based upon standardized monitoring and interpretation of research and evaluation information [30].

Although psychiatrists have long used evidence to inform practice, the evidence-based paradigm is also playing an increasingly prominent role in mental health. The first paper to appear on evidence-based psychiatry appeared only about 10 years ago, and by 1998, there was a full journal dedicated to this topic. The inaugural editorial for this journal notes considerable unexplained variation in psychiatric practice (including diversity in the treatment of depression, use of electroconvulsive treatment, and use of prescription stimulants for the treatment of attention deficit disorder), suggesting that psychiatrists are not using the best available evidence and patients are not receiving the best available treatment [31]. As in other areas of medicine, psychiatrists are coming under increasing pressure to develop evidence-based skills and provide detailed instruction in research methods and critical appraisal skills to psychiatric residents. Such skills are now viewed as essential clinical tools required to provide the highest quality of care [32]. Teaching evidence-based skills is also considered to be essential preparation for a future managed by increasingly research-savvy and 'evidence-hungry' managers who will use the lack of evidence to restrict physician choice and limit patients' access to care [26, 30]. In this climate, unambiguous findings outlining best practices that are produced from rigorous evaluations and systematic reviews will be an important advocacy tool.

One of the major claims of the evidence-based approach is that it provides objective data about the effectiveness of interventions. By eliminating or restricting possibilities for subjective decision making and practitioner bias, the implicit promise of evidence-based practice is that it will result in greater fairness and reduce potentially discriminatory variations in practice. At the population level, findings from the evidence-based enterprise will be used to insure an effective distribution of services and greater overall equity. In this way, the use of evidence-based guidelines will promote equitable treatment for all those in need [33]. Not only will evidence supporting effective psychiatric interventions promote greater confidence among funders and other stakeholders, it will be instrumental in diverting program and research funding to mental health [34], making it increasingly difficult for future decision-makers to defend policies and practices that systematically disadvantage people with a mental illness or that are incommensurate with the burden of suffering caused by mental disorders.

While it is difficult to quarrel with the promise of evidence-based practice, its application has not gone without deep debate and criticism. A closer look at the nature of the evidence required, and the methods currently favored to generate it, yield several significant challenges for mental health researchers and advocates who would view evidence-based practice as an important anti-stigma tool. This is primarily because the evidence-based paradigm largely ignores the social and cultural forces that influence both the production of evidence and the distribution of health resources – failing to recognize that these processes may themselves be subject to significant bias.

It is now well recognized that the pervasive stigma associated with all aspects of mental illness has slowed the production of evidence in this field relative to other equally disabling conditions [35]. With fewer prospects for significant sustained funding, researchers gravitate to other areas, leaving the field with a lack of capacity to produce high-quality evidence. Even within psychiatry, there is a 'source of funding bias' as pharmaceutical companies provide a major share of funding and produce the lion's share of research data [36]. Currently, there is no equivalent, countervailing funding source for non-pharmaceutical research, particularly in the areas of social psychiatry or public mental health, and it is difficult to see how evidence-based practice will redress these historical imbalances. Developing a strong evidence base to support best practices in the delivery of high-quality mental health care – including best practices in anti-stigma programming – must remain a top priority.

A second challenge posed by the current evidence-based paradigm is that the rules governing the production of evidence favor interventions that can be studied using double-blind, randomized controlled trials and summarized using systematic reviews and meta-analyses. Because stigma interventions are often not oriented toward individual-level treatments and biological determinants of disease, they are rarely amenable to experimental designs. Often targeting entire nations, populations or communities, anti-stigma interventions are more appropriately studied using quasi-experimental and observational study designs. In some cases, specific legal or policy frameworks or organizational processes are the targets for change, which are best studied using case studies and other qualitative designs. A search of online databases (OVID Medline, PsychInfo, Healthstar) using controlled vocabulary terms (MeSH headings) such as 'Mental disorder' and 'Randomized controlled trial' combined with keywords such as 'stigma' and 'prejudice' yields only a smattering of controlled anti-stigma intervention studies (three from the US [37–39], one from Germany [40] and two from Australia [41, 42]; which is an insufficient evidence base to support anti-stigma programming.

Findings from quasi-experimental and qualitative approaches are currently excluded from traditional systematic reviews with the result that anti-stigma (and other public-health-oriented mental health research) will be systematically disadvantaged in the evidence pro-duction process as data from these studies will be considered of lower quality. Policy makers will be hesitant to support interventions based on inadequate evidence. However, there are many challenges inherent in combining the results of studies which have used diverse study designs [43]. Recognition of these problems has prompted calls for broader interpretations of 'evidence' including attempts to develop reporting standards for non-experimental studies so that their results can be systematically summarized to guide policy development [44–46]. The TREND statement, for example, recognizes that public health decisions will require evidence from non-randomized studies and provides a template to promote the 'transpar-ent reporting of evaluations with non-randomized designs" [45]. The MOOSE guidelines (meta-analyses of observational studies in epidemiology) provide a systematic process for combining and reporting the results from multiple studies so that findings may be system-atically combined to judge effectiveness [46]. Although these guidelines are relatively new and remain works in progress, anti-stigma researchers (and the field) would benefit from their widespread use.

Building better practices through theory-based evaluation

The complexities of the evidence based paradigm for anti-stigma programming notwith-standing, the allure of building better practices using systematically collected data and careful reflection remains. From a public health perspective, this means identifying the principles and procedures involved in successful anti-stigma programming in such a way that they can be meaningfully tested using a variety of research methods, and if found to be effective, widely disseminated. It does the field little practical good to know that gifted anti-stigma advocates can achieve good results locally; what is critical is that these inter-ventions can be clearly specified and taught [47]. From this perspective, understanding why a program works, or doesn't work, is as important as demonstrating that it produces change. Thus, a key element in building better practices is building generalizable theories of change.

Theory-based evaluation challenges program developers and evaluators to clearly articu-late the assumptions underlying the intervention about why the intervention is likely to work, then link program activities to these in explicit and logical ways. The aim of the evaluation is then to assess which assumptions hold, which break down and why, making it possible to determine which of the several theories underlying a program are best supported by the evidence. Theory-based evaluation asks practitioners to make their program assumptions explicit, link these to available knowledge, and achieve some consensus on what they are trying to do and why. Attention and resources may then be concentrated on the key aspects of the program. Finally, results from theory-based evaluation facilitates the accumulation of knowledge of best practices across programs into a broader theoretical base. The results from evaluations that test out the theoretical assumptions underlying program delivery are often more policy-relevant because they contribute to generalizable knowledge. Programs that appear to violate well-tested assumptions will then receive little support [48].

At a minimum, a theory of change should articulate the long-term program outcome(s) and the set of necessary and sufficient preconditions (or short- and medium-term outcomes) that need to be attained in order for the program to have the desired effect. Second, the assumptions that connect the preconditions for goal attainment and the long-term outcomes must be specified and, wherever possible, available research used to pre-test their plausibility. It is also useful to articulate the environmental constraints and barriers that may hinder or promote progress. Next, the set of interventions that are expected to bring about the change must be clearly specified. Finally, a set of performance indicators and thresholds of success must be articulated that outline the amount of change that must occur for a particular target population, over a specific time period, for the program to be declared successful [49].

Creating theories of change for complex, community-based anti-stigma programs will be a daunting task, particularly as there is little empirical evidence to draw on to support causal pathways or set plausible thresholds for success. It is not unusual for anti-stigma programs to be complex, working across several systems or sectors to bring about community-wide change (such as improvements in public attitudes toward people with a mental illness). A major assumption underlying these efforts is that changes at the level of the community will result in improvements in the circumstances of people with a mental illness, typically through some unspecified 'trickle-down' effect. Little is yet known about which components of the wider community are amenable to change, or the specific pathways through which community-level changes result in improvements in individual outcomes. There are also multiple contextual issues that can undermine specific anti-stigma efforts, such as media reporting of incidents involving someone with a mental illness. The global nature of the news and entertainment media means that it is virtually impossible to stem the flow of countervailing information and lay theories of mental illness.

To create plausible theories of change, anti-stigma programmers will confront difficult issues pertaining to the relationship between factual knowledge, attitude changes and discriminatory behaviors such as the extent to which social marketing campaigns can be expected to alter the nature of deeply entrenched discriminatory relationships experienced by people with a mental illness by increasing knowledge about mental illness or debunking a particular myth or stereotype. Secondly, because anti-stigma programs are often fuelled by the enthusiasm of volunteers and advocates, it can be difficult to curb the desire to 'do' long enough to develop a plausible theory of change and consider the evidence in support of the program's logic model. Having a clearly articulated program development process, such as the one articulated by the World Psychiatric Association's Global Anti-Stigma program, can channel energies into planning. Sites participating in the Global Anti-Stigma network must agree to develop a proposal with clearly articulated goals and objectives as well as follow a development, implementation and evaluation process that takes 18–24 months to complete [35].

Program developers and evaluators are increasingly using program logic models to help create testable theories of change. The logic model is used to link the program's resources to program activities, and the outcomes to be achieved. It is the road map that spells out how the program produces results. The process of developing a logic model typically involves multiple program stakeholders who work together to understand the underlying rationale for the program. Using available scientific evidence and logic, they articulate how and why a particular intervention will work; what series of steps needs to be implemented to meet short-, intermediate- and long-term objectives; how the objectives interrelate to produce an overall effect; and the broad conditions under which success is most likely. Building a program logic model requires clarity of thinking that can highlight areas where assumptions are tenuous, where service links are weak or missing or the elements in the broader social environment that need to be managed (if possible) to facilitate the program's success. The model is a focal point for discussion and consensus, and provides program staff with an important tool for describing their program to others. Most importantly, from an evaluation perspective, a logic model articulates the program's theory of change and highlights key process and outcomes that then become the focus of measurement and evaluation [50].

Ultimately, building better practices in anti-stigma programming will depend upon bridging the gap that often exists between the scientific and practitioner communities – not only for developing plausible program theories of change, or for evaluating program effects, but for insuring that these results become part of the body of 'best practice' evidence. Far too often, local programs are evaluated and found to be successful, only to have these results go no further than an agency annual report where they remain largely inaccessible to evidence-based reviews. A firm commitment to publish results – whether good, bad or ugly – will foster strategic alliances between anti-stigma programmers and the research community and enlarge the scope of evidence available to inform public policy.

Conclusions

Evidence-rich areas stand to gain the most in an evidence-based world. When the opportunity to produce evidence is limited, policy makers will continue to be swayed by public opinion favoring services that are more popular; particularly if these also appear to be scientifically credible [29]. Unfortunately, the evidence base required to support the expansion of stigma reduction initiatives remains under-developed. Though a number of approaches appear promising, position papers and systematic reviews are lacking. Clear demonstrations that anti-stigma programs are effective in reducing social inequities experienced by people with a mental illness are not yet available, and it is not yet possible to speak authoritatively about 'best practices' in the field [24]. Despite increasing public health recognition of the importance of stigma reduction, in the current climate of evidence-based care, anti-stigma interventions are at a significant disadvantage in terms of both sustaining policy attention and acquiring funding support.

Researchers interested in developing an evidence base to support anti-stigma interventions face a number of structural challenges beyond the effects of historical inequities that have undermined population-based mental health and social psychiatric research. The current evidence-based paradigm places a premium on data from randomized controlled trials and systematic summaries of these. Similar to many public-health-oriented programs, anti-stigma interventions are often not amenable to experimental approaches. Few randomized controlled trials exist and data from quasi-experimental studies remain outside of the current standard of 'evidence'. While there is increasing recognition that policy makers would benefit from a broader array of evidence – that many policy questions are too complex to be adequately studied using conventional randomized controlled trials – there are yet no widely accepted standards for standardized reporting observational studies, or for combining results from different and potentially disparate study designs, into systematic reviews to inform policy decisions. In building a stronger evidence base to support anti-stigma programming, these undoubtedly will stand as our greatest challenges. Anti-stigma programs can confront these challenges by ensuring that a steady supply of credible evaluation research reaches the scientific and policy literature – research that is focused on enlarging our understanding of what works, when, for whom, and why.

References

1. Last, J.M. (1998) *Public Health and Human Ecology* (2nd edn). Stamford, CT: Appleton & Lange. (p. 6).
2. Murray, C.J.L. and Lopez, A.D. (1996) *The Global Burden of Disease*. Geneva: World Health Organization.
3. Murray, C.J.L. and Lopez, A.D. (1997) Global mortality, disability, and the contribution of risk factors: global burden of disease study. *Lancet* **349**, 1436–1442.
4. World Health Organization (2005) *Mental Health Atlas 2005* (revised edition) Geneva: World Health Organization.
5. World Health Organization (2001) *The World Health Report 2001. Mental Health: New Understanding, New Hope*. Geneva: World Health Organization.
6. The WHO World Mental Health Survey Consortium (2005) Prevalence, severity, and unmet need for treatment of mental disorders in the World Health Organization World Mental Health Surveys. *JAMA* **291**(21), 2581–2590.
7. Goffman, E. (1963) *Stigma: Notes on the Management of Spoiled Identity*. Englewood Cliffs, NJ: Prentice-Hall.
8. Link, B. and Phelan, J.C. (2001) Conceptualizing stigma. *Annual Review of Sociology* **27**, 363–385.
9. Sartorius, N. and Schulze, H. (2005) *Reducing Stigma due to Mental Illness: a Report from a Global Program of the World Psychiatric Association*. Cambridge: Cambridge University Press.
10. Sartorius, N. (2004) The World Psychiatric Association Global Programme against Stigma and Discrimination because of Stigma. In A.H. Crisp (ed.) *Every Family in the Land* (pp. 373–375) (revised edition) London: Royal Society of Medicine Press.
11. World Health Organization (2001) *Mental Health: a Call for Action by World Health Ministers*. Geneva: World Health Organization.
12. World Health Organization (2001) *Results of a Global Advocacy Campaign*. Geneva: World Health Organization.
13. World Health Organization (2003) *Investing in Mental Health*. Geneva: World Health Organization.
14. Kobe Declaration (2004) World Association of Social Psychiatry. Available from www.wpanet .org/bulletin/wpaeb2103.html (accessed 28 February, 2005).
15. *Science and Care* (2004) Volume 4 (October–December), p. 12.
16. Druss, B.G. and Goldman, H.H. (2003) Introduction to the Special Section on the President's New Freedom Commission Report. *Psychiatric Services* **54**(11), 1465–1466.
17. US Department of Health and Human Services (1999) *Mental Health: A Report of the Surgeon General – Executive Summary*. Rockville, MD: US Department of Health and Human Services, Substance Abuse and Mental Health Services Administration, Center for Mental Health Services, National Institutes of Health, National Institute of Mental Health.
18. Standing Senate Committee on Social Affairs, Science, and Technology (2004) Mental Health, Mental Illness, and Addiction. Issues and Options for Canada. Ottawa: Interim Report of the Standing Committee on Social Affairs, Science, and Technology.
19. The Standing Committee on Social Affairs, Science and Technology. (2006) Out of the Shadows at Last: Transforming Mental Health, Mental Illness, and Addiction Services in Canada. Ottawa: The Parliament of Canada (available on the Parliamentary web site: www.parl.gc.ca).
20. Rosen, A., Walter, G., Casey, D. and Hocking, B. (2000) Combating psychiatric stigma: an overview of contemporary initiatives. *Australasian Psychiatry* **8**(1), 19–26.
21. Vaughan, G. and Hansen, C. (2004) Like Minds, Like Mine': A New Zealand project to counter the stigma and discrimination associated with mental illness. *Australasian Psychiatry* **12**(2), 113–117.
22. Crisp, A.H. (ed.) (2004) *Every Family in the Land* (revised edition). London: The Royal Society of Medicine.
23. Desapriya, E.B.R. and Nobutada, I. (2002) Stigma of mental illness in Japan. *Lancet* **359**, 1866.
24. Stuart, H. and Sartorius, N. (2005) Fighting stigma and discrimination because of mental disorders. In G.N. Christodolou. (ed.) *Advances in Psychiatry, Second Volume*. World Psychiatric Association (pp. 79–86).

25. Haynes, R.B. (2002) What kind of evidence is it that evidence-based medicine advocates want health care providers and consumers to pay attention to? *BMC Health Services Research* **2**(3), 1–7.
26. Sheldon, T. (2005) Making evidence synthesis more useful for management and policy-making. *Journal of Health Services Research and Policy* **10**(Suppl 1), 1–5.
27. Wiebe, S. (2000) The principles of evidence-based medicine. *Cephalalgia* **20** (Suppl 2), 10–13.
28. Sackett, D.L. (2002) Clinical epidemiology: what, who, and whither. *Journal of Clinical Epidemiology* **55**, 1161–1166.
29. Black, N. (2001) Evidence based policy: proceed with care. *British Medical Journal* **323**, 275–279.
30. Charlton, B.G. and Miles, A. (1998) The rise and fall of EBM. *Quarterly Journal of Medicine* **91**, 371–374.
31. Geddes, J., Reynolds, S., Streiner, D., Szatmari, P. and Haynes B. (1998) Evidence-based practice in mental health. *Evidence-based Mental Health* **1**(1), 4–5.
32. Bilsker, D. and Goldner, E. (1999) Teaching evidence-based practice in mental health. *Evidence based Mental Health* **2**, 68–69.
33. Rogers, W.A. (2004) Evidence-based medicine and justice: a framework for looking at the impact of EBM on disadvantaged groups. *Journal of Medical Ethics* **30**, 141–145.
34. Stuart, H. (2005) Evaluation of programs against stigma. In A. Okasha and C.N. Stefanis (eds) *Perspectives on the Stigma of Mental Illness*. Geneva: World Psychiatric Association (pp. 41–51).
35. Sartorius, N. and Schulze, H. (2005) *Reducing the Stigma of Mental Illness*. New York: Cambridge University Press.
36. Gupta, M. (2004) Evidence-based medicine: ethically obligatory or ethically suspect? *Evidence-based Mental Health* **7**, 96–97.
37. Corrigan, P.W., River, L.P., Lundin, R.K., Penn, D.L., Uphoff-Wasowski, K., Campion, J., Mathisen, J., Gagnon, C., Bergman, M., Goldstein, H. and Kubiak, M.A. (2001) Three strategies for changing attributions about severe mental illness. *Schizophrenia Bulletin* **27**(2), 187–195.
38. Penn, D.L. and Corrigan, P.W. (2002) The effects of stereotype suppression on psychiatric stigma. *Schizophrenia Research* **55**(3), 269–276.
39. Corrigan, P.W., Watson, A.C., Warpinski, A.C. and Gracia, G. (2004) Implications of educating the public on mental illness,violence, and stigma. *Psychiatric Services* **55**(5), 577–580.
40. Stengler-Wenzke, K., Beck, M., Holzinger, A. and Angermeyer, MC. (2004) [Stigma experiences of patients with obsessive compulsive disorders]. *Fortschritte der Neurologie-Psychiatrie* **72**(1), 7–13.
41. Griffiths, K.M., Christensen, H., Jorm, A.F., Evans, K. and Groves, C. (2004) Effect of web-based depression literacy and cognitive-behavioural therapy interventions on stigmatising attitudes to depression: randomised controlled trial. *British Journal of Psychiatry* **185**, 342–349.
42. Kitchener, B.A. and Jorm, A.F. (2004) Mental health first aid training in a workplace setting: a randomized control trial [ISRCTN13249129] *BMC Psychiatry* **4**, 1–8.
43. Mays, N., Pope, C. and Popay, J. (2005) Systematically reviewing qualitative and quantitative evidence to inform management and policy-making in the health field. *Journal of Health Services Research and Policy* **10**(1), 6–20.
44. Lavis, J., Davies, H., Oxman, A., Denis, J.L., Golden-Biddle, K. and Ferlie, E. (2005) Toward systematic reviews that inform health care management and policy-making. *Journal of Health Services Research and Policy* **10**(1), 35–48.
45. Des Jarlais, D.C., Lyles, C., Crepaz, N., the TREND Group (2004) Improving the reporting quality of nonrandomized evaluations of behavioral and public health interventions. The TREND Statement, *American Journal of Public Health* **94**(3), 361–366.
46. Stroup, D.F., Berlin, J.A., Morton, S.C., Olkin, I., Williamson, D.G., Rennie, D., Moher, D., Becker, B.J., Sipe, T.A., Thaker, S.B., for the Meta-analysis of Observational Studies in Epidemiology (MOOSE) Group. (2000) Meta-analysis of observational studies in epidemiology: a proposal for reporting. *JAMA* **283**, 2008–2012.
47. Chambless, D.L. and Crits-Christoph, P. (2005) What should be validated? The treatment method. In J.C. Norcross, L.E. Beutler and R.F. Levant (eds) *Evidence-based Practices in Mental Health* (pp. 191–218). Washington DC: American Psychological Association.

48. Weiss, C.H. (1995) Nothing as practical as good theory: exploring theory-based evaluation for comprehensive community initiatives for children and families. In J.P. Connell, A.C. Kubisch, L.B. Schorr and C.H. Weiss (eds), *New Approaches to Evaluating Community Initiatives* (pp. 65–92) Washington, DC: The Aspen Institute.
49. Anderson, A.A. (2004) Theory of change as a tool for strategic planning. A report on early experiences. The Aspen Institute Roundtable on Community Change. (Accessed from www.theoryofchange.org, 20 July, 2007).
50. McLaughlin, J.A. and Jordan, G.B. (1999) Logic models: a tool for telling your program's performance story. *Evaluation and Program Planning* **22**, 65–72.

9 Other people stigmatize … but, what about us? Attitudes of mental health professionals towards patients with schizophrenia

Alp Üçok

Professor, Istanbul Faculty of Medicine, Department of Psychiatry, Istanbul University, Istanbul, Turkey

In every layer of society, stigma affects the patient with mental illness and people close to the patient, at least as much as the illness. Patients with schizophrenia are the ones most affected by stigmatization. This situation is the case in many countries without regard to culture or geography. In society, the attitude towards patients with schizophrenia is worse than to those with depression [1, 2]. As stigma makes daily life more difficult for the patient with schizophrenia, the fear of labelling makes it more difficult for an ill person to seek help from professionals. We always complain that people find it hard to come to professionals because psychiatric clinics are associated with 'madness'. Then, let us ask ourselves, how is the situation on the 'inside'? Stigma related to mental illness is commonly attributed to the attitudes of the media or the mental health illiteracy of people. If mental health professionals have stigmatizing beliefs or behaviours, can we explain it by lack of knowledge, or lack of previous contact with a mentally ill person? The aim of this chapter is to review studies on the attitudes of psychiatrists, medical specialists outside of psychiatry, general practitioners, nurses, psychologists, staff and students towards schizophrenia.

General characteristics of the studies

Studies about attitudes of mental health professionals toward people with mental illnesses vary in terms of their target populaton, target illness and methodology. Some of them were carried out by face-to-face interviews while letters, e-mails or telephone calls were used in others. These studies are limited by the tendency to include cooperative respondents (volunteer bias). As response rates are relatively low, generalizability of the findings is limited. Moreover, the answers given may not assess actual behaviour, but should be considered more of a proxy measure of intended behaviour. Most of the studies we reviewed focused

Understanding the Stigma of Mental Illness: Theory and Interventions   Edited by Julio Arboleda-Flórez and Norman Sartorius
© 2008 John Wiley & Sons, Ltd

on either stereotypes which also commonly held by lay people, and/or feelings about social distance in mental health professionals. These two aspects of stigma have been questioned either directly by using questionaires or by means of case vignettes. Vignettes have been used since 1955 in the study of stigma of mental illness. Although the vignette approach has a lot of advantages, it is important to recognize that they are hypothetical and abstracted from 'real-life' experience. Moreover, the respondent is not in the presence of a real person, is not gleaning information from appearance and other non-verbal clues, and cannot assess the described person's responses to initial gestures that might affect reactions in 'real' situations [3]. Using a vignette to understand whether the respondents can differentiate a patient from a healthy person has a limited value when the target people are mental health professionals or students. Moreover, Nordt et al. [4] recently reported that surprisingly a quarter of the psychiatists have described a healthy person in vignette as a patient with mental illness (!).

As the majority of the questionaires were developed by the reserchers themselves it is not easy to compare the results across the studies. A large majority of the studies have been focused on schizophrenia and mood disorders. Some studies evaluated stigma related to one of these two disorders, while some others compared them. Findings of the studies seem to be affected by the type of facilities where the target mental health staff work. Stigma related to mental illness seems lower in those who work in community health services compared to those who work in 'revolving door' units. The most common locations where these studies have been conducted are in Europe and North America. However, there are some studies from eastern Asia and Middle Eastern countries. Some of the studies focused on specific professional groups like nurses or general practitioners, and some others compare the attitudes of different groups of professionals or compare professionals to lay people (see Table 9.1).

Table 9.1 Number and percentage of general practitioners whose answer is 'I agree' to items related with attitudes towards schizophrenia

	Pre-test (n = 106) (%)	Post-test (n = 54) (%)	p
1. Mentally ill can work	88 (83)	47 (87)	n.s.
2. Would oppose if one of his/her relatives would like to marry someone with schizophrenia	66 (64)	35 (64.9)	n.s.
3. Mentally ill could be recognized by his/her appearence	39 (37.5)	14 (25.9)	0.01
4. Schizophrenic patients are dangerous	29 (27.6)	11 (20.3)	n.s.
5. Would not like to have mentally ill neighbour	64 (62.1)	25 (46.2)	n.s.
6. Schizophrenic patients are untrustworthy	47 (46)	15 (27.7)	0.02
7. Schizophrenic patients could harm children	43 (41.3)	11 (20.3)	0.05
8. Mentally ill should be kept in hospitals	15 (14.7)	4 (7.4)	n.s.
9. Is worried or concerned about examining mentally ill patients	86 (83.5)	37 (68.5)	n.s.
10. Would be treated in the appropriate department of the general hospital	85 (81.7)	44 (81.4)	n.s.
11. Schizophrenia could be treated	73 (68.9	45 (83.3)	0.006
12. Mentally ill could not comprehend nor apply suggested treatment	34 (32.4)	8 (14.8)	0.007
13. Schizophrenia has chance of recovery	71 (67)	39 (72.2)	n.s.

Attitudes of psychiatrists towards schizophrenia

The stigma of mental illness also affects both mental health professionals and institutions. On the other hand, poor attitudes and behaviour of some mental health professionals towards individuals with mental illness and their families may in turn contribute to the poor public image of our profession and the stigma related to mental illness [5]. Ironically, these negative attitudes interfere with their own help-seeking behaviour for their personal problems [6]. In a recent paper, Sartorius [7] emphasized that psychiatrists should revise their own behaviour in order to convince other people that most people with mental illness retain many of their capacities and that their rights are often not respected. The attitude of psychiatrists plays a key role since it also affects the other members of the team, residents and/or students they have the responsibiity to train. This negative attitude varies from underestimating the effectiveness of psychosocial treatments to failing to inform the patients and their families about diagnoses [8].

Link et al. [3] stated that out of 109 empirical studies between 1995 and 2003, they found 20 studies focused on professional groups (e.g. mental health professionals, general prctitioners, medical students). We were able to consider some new studies from Japan [9], Australia [2], Singapore [10], Turkey [11, 12], Spain [13] France [14] and Switzerland [4], which were particularly focused on stigmatizing attitudes of psychiatrists. Although there are two studies which reported that psychiatrists' attitude was significantly more postive than that of the general population [15, 16], the majority of the studies showed that mental health professionals had more negative attitudes compared to that of the public [2, 10].

The proportion of mental health professionals advising the patients or their families about a diagnosis of schizophrenia is lower compared to other diagnoses [17]. A study from Switzerland [4], reported that only 7.3% of psychiatrists always informed their patients of the diagnosis of schizophrenia, and 51.9% of them informed on a case-by-case basis. The results also revealed that the Japanese term for schizophrenia influences a psychiatrist's decision to inform patients of the diagnosis and that, by changing the term to a less stigmatized one, the disclosure of information about schizophrenia to patients would be promoted.

Recently, we delivered questionnaries to psychiatrists assessing their attitudes in different parts of Turkey [11]. We found that 42.7% of 60 psychiatrists never informed patients of the diagnosis of schizophrenia and 40.7% informed on a case-by-case basis. The proportion is even higher than for delusional disorder which has a lot of similarities with schizophrenia in terms of both symptoms and treatment. The reason why psychiatrists avoid informing the patients or family members of the diagnosis was the idea that they could not understand the meaning (32.6%) or that they would drop out from treatment (28.3%). In another study, the authors came to similar findings [4] in that 88% of respondents thought the term 'schizophrenia' was used in a pejorative manner in public. Another group from Turkey [12] reported that 65% of psychiatrists believed that to mention the word 'schizophrenia' as diagnosis was inappropriate in official documents (e.g. expert reports sent to court) while 35% of non-psychiatric physicians shared the same opinion.

Bayle et al. [14] from France reported that approximately only one-third of psychiatrists deemed it appropriate to disclose a diagnosis of schizophrenia and two-thirds declared that they disclose it only occasionally. The main reasons for not disclosing the diagnosis were, first the 'reticence to give a diagnosis label' and secondly 'the functional incapacity of the patient to understand the concept'.

López-Ibor *et al.* [13] reported that it is not commonplace for psychiatrists to inform patients with schizophrenia about their diagnosis in Spain; they tend to disguise it under terms such as 'psychosis', 'disorder' or 'depression'. More interestingly, the results of a survey on 42 psychiatrists in Madrid reveal that they blame the patients for issues they should address like non-compliance to medication and the management of aggression. In this survey, some negative attitudes relating to social distance were reported. For example, 77% of the psychiatrists reported that they would not engage in a conversation with someone with schizophrenia, and 56% of them say they do not want to live in a hostal with someone with schizophrenia. However, 79% of the respondents reported that they would engage in a friendship with someone with schizophrenia. It seems that psychiatrists' attitude cannot be generalized, but differs depending on the context of the contact. Van Dorn *et al.* [18] reported that there were no statistically significant differences between psychiatrists, patients with schizophrenia, their relatives and members of the general public in the likelihood of violence or the desire for social distance. They reported that the patients tended to have the most negative views of the illness.

The latest study about the attitudes of psychiatrsts is from Switzerland [4]. In this study, 201 psychiatrists answered a telephone survey questioning attitudes about restrictions, stereotypes and social distance. Pychiatrists had significantly more negative stereotypes than psychologists, nurses or the general population. They had greater social distance toward the schizophrenia vignette than toward the depression vignette, but psychiatrists' social distance scores for both illnesses did not differ from those of the general public. There was less approval of legal restrictions (voting, driving licences) in the group of psychiatrists compared to the general population, but they had a more positive attitude toward compulsory admission.

The results of the above-mentioned studies demonstrate that it is too simple to assume that psychiatrists as mental health experts generally have more positive attitudes toward mentally ill people than do the general public.

Attitudes of general practitioners

Although the role of general practitioners in the health care system may vary internationally, they have an important role in the treatment of patients with an established diagnosis of schizophrenia as well as in the identification of people in the early stages of psychosis and referring them to psychiatrists. This role is more crucial in countries where the number of psychiatrists is insufficient. However, stigma was found to be barrier for psychiatric referrals by general practitioners [19].

The results of a recent study by Simon *et al.* [20], showed that general practitioners in Switzerland are involved in the treatment of approximately a quarter of patients with chronic schizophrenia. A total of 1089 general practitioners' responses to this postal survey suggest that their knowledge about the symptoms and the course of illness is enough, but they have some difficulties regarding treatment.

In a recent study in Turkey, 40% of the general practitioners reported that they were unable to make clinical decisions on patients with schizophrenia. On the other hand, despite their reservations about following up chronically mentally ill patients, general practitioners were willing to participate in training opportunities concerning schizophrenia [21]. Twenty-nine per cent of participants indicated that they had a positive attitude towards treatment outcomes of those patients with schizophrenia that they were treating, but 18% had a negative view of such effort and responded that these patients would not be able to recover

Table 9.2 Target populations of some recent studies focused on stigma in mental health professionals

	Psychiatrists	GPs	Nurses and students	Medical students	Staff	General population
Grausgruber et al. (2007) [46]			×		×	×
Nordt et al. (2006) [4]	×		×			×
Kingdon et al. (2004) [15]	×					
Lauber et al. (2004) [52]	×					
Mas and Hatim (2002) [36]				×		
Üçok et al. (2004) [11]	×					
Üçok et al. (2006) [22]		×				
Aydın et al. (2003) [23]			×		×	
Ono et al. (1999) [9]	×					
Llerena et al. (2002) [40]			×	×		
Yildiz et al. (2003) [21]		×				
Altindag et al. (2006) [27]				×		
Ay et al. (2006) [35]				×		
Fogel et al. (2006) [6]				×		
Van Dorn et al. (2005) [18]	×					×
Reddy et al. (2005) [37]				×		
Tay et al. (2004) [45]			×			

from schizophrenia. Recently, we studied the attitudes of general practitioners in two cities [22]. The study was a pre-test-post-test design, and 106 general practitioners from 71 health institutions responded to the questionnaire. In comparison to the earlier studies in Turkey with the lay public [1], and medical staff' attitudes [23], we found that the attitudes of general practitioners were slightly more negative than those of the public. Twenty-seven per cent of the lay public described the patients with schizophrenia as dangerous compared with 27.7% among general practitioners. The views of general practitioners show some similarities to the lay public view on schizophrenia particularly in issues of social context. In general, GPs responded more negatively to the questions on their attitudes in social settings than those which concentrated on their views within their professional roles (Table 9.2). This might be seen as a buffering effect of the professional role within the clinical context.

Medical students

Not surprisingly, 'tomorrow's doctors' share the same attitudes as psychatrists and the general population towards the mentally ill. The stigma of using mental health services hits the medical students themselves. The care of medical students as patients is complex because of problems associated with stigma and the dual role of trainee and patient in medical school [24]. Givens and Tija [25] reported that only 22% of the depressed medical students were using mental health services, and stigma was one of the reasons (30%).

In a recent study, Akdede et al. [26] studied the attitudes of young people (mostly medical students) toward psychotic disorders. In the first phase of the study, a case vignette about a young person who began to show psychotic symptoms was given to students, and their opinions were asked. At the second phase, after the diagnosis of the patient was given as schizophrenia, the same questionnaire was repeated. They found that the positive attitude of the whole group decreased meaningfully after they learned the diagnosis of the patient. There was no difference between the medical students and others.

Recently, we evaluated attitudes of first-year medical students' attitudes towards schizophrenia in Urfa, Turkey [27]. Before the anti stigma training programme, 68% of them believed that 'people with schizophrenia are violent', and 84% of them believed that 'persons with schizophrenia cannot make correct decisions about their own lives'. The effects of anti stigma education on these attitudes will be discussed later in this paper.

There have been some studies that have investigated the effects of mental illness education in medical students [28–30]. In Turkey, Yanik *et al.* [31] in a cross-sectional study surveyed the effects of medical education on attitudes towards mental illness. These authors concluded that the attitudes of medical students did not change favourably as they moved along in their medical education. Another study using case vignettes in Turkey reached a similar conclusion about patients with depression [32]. In a study from Samsun in Turkey, attitudes of 172 intern doctors attitudes were evaluated before and after a psychiatry training period. The researchers found no difference in attitudes between the beginning and the end of the training period [33]. In another study by Arkar and Eker [34], the authors found that after psychiatric training, there was no difference in social rejection toward patients with schizophrenia among fifth-year medical students, while there was a positive change toward depression. However, other studies have found more favourable results [28–30]. The largest study in Turkey was carried out among 452 students from all three public medical schools in Istanbul [35]. The scores for depression and schizophrenia scales among final year students were better compared with those of the second-years; however, the proportion of students who did not perceive schizophrenia as 'temporary' and 'curable' and the perceived likelihood of dangerousness for schizophrenia were higher among the last-year students compared with the second-years. The improvement in the attitude score between the second and the sixth years is considered a result of the students' contact and interaction with persons having mental disorders throughout their medical education. In a study with a similar design, a vignette and two dependent measures (social distance scale and dangerousness scale) were used to assess the attitudes of 108 first-year and 85 final-year medical students in Malaysia [36]. The first-year students did not have any prior psychiatric training. The final-year students who had knowledge and had had contact were less stigmatizing toward mentally ill patients. There were no significant differences in the attitudes towards mentally ill patient among the first-year students regardless of whether they had had previous contact with persons suffering from mental illness or not. The authors concluded that knowledge seems to have the effect of inculcating greater tolerance of mental illness. Contact by itself is not sufficient for attitude changes. In another study from Malaysia [37], it has been reported that there was a significant increase in the mean scores on both Attitudes towards Mental Illness and Attitudes towards Psychiatry scales following an eight-week psychiatric rotation among female medical students, but not among male students. Similarly, in Taiwan a study assessing medical students' change in attitude found a significant change after psychiatric internship [38]. Economou *et al.* have studied the effect of the psychiatric rotations on the attitudes of 157 medical students in their sixth year of study in Greece [39]. Results indicated that students' psychiatric training and contact with patients in psychiatric hospitals lead to the strengthening of students' negative beliefs concerning people with schizophrenia. These contradictory results imply that content and targets of psychiatric education and the conditions of psychiatric clinics may have an effect on the impressions of medical students.

Psychologists, nurses and other staff

Patients, particularly inpatients, have more contact with nurses and staff than with doctors. So, attitudes of these groups of mental health professionals have an impact on patients. Llerena *et al.* [40] from Spain, surveyed students of medicine and nursing during 2000 about their general knowledge of schizophrenia. Findings from these authors indicate that their subjects had a high awareness of mental illness, its onset, associated risk factors and manifestations and treatment; these authors did not find any significant difference between the two goups. On the other hand, both groups thought that people with schizophrenia never recover (50%), that they were or could be dangerous or violent (78%), and rejected or were ambivalent about whether to accept them in a social situation (40%). In addition, they did not feel they had enough information about schizophrenia (95%) and they did not know someone with this disorder (75%). Authors commented their findings as paradoxical and concluded that symptoms associated with the acute phase of schizophrenia create more stigma than the label of schizophrenia alone. Similarly, Ozyigit *et al.* [41] reported that while both nurses and nursing students have enough knowledge about the aetiology and clinical features of schizophrenia they had negative attitudes about social distance, like marrying or working in the same office with patients. However, compared to students, nurses reported lower social distance, and being acquainted with a mentally ill person was found to be related to lower social distance in this study. In a recent vignette study, the role of the psychiatric mental health nursing class and rotation were identified as improving stigmatizing attitudes and increasing help-seeking among nursing students in the United States [42]. However, in another study from the USA, researchers concluded that health education and experience did not significantly affect attitudes towards the mentally ill. Nursing students who had had a friend who was mentally ill prior to their school training showed a decrease in stigmatizing attitudes after being exposed to health education and experience whereas other students showed an increase in this study [43]. However, this factor was found unimportant in a study on students of nursing in Turkey [44]. The proportion of students who defined schizophrenia as a 'weakness of personality' was found to be lower in students with a personal history of psychiatric treatment in this study. Those who completed psychiatric training in a mental hospital were found to hold more pessimistic views about the treatability and outcome of schizophrenia, and also had more negative beliefs about 'dangerousness' compared to students who did not work in mental hospitals. In another study from Turkey, Aydın *et al.* [23] reported that attitudes of nurses who work in psychiatric inpatient units were more positive than non-psychiatric physicians, but worse than the support staff (e.g. driver, cook) in the same hospital. In contrast to others, the results of this study suggests a negative correlation between stigmatizing attitudes and education.

The findings of the studies suggest that study conditions affect the attitudes of the nurses. Tay *et al.* [45] reported that nurses working in short-stay wards had more positive attitudes than those working in long-stay wards. Similarly, in a study from Austria, researchers explained their findings of positive attitudes among nurses as resulting from characteristics of conditions of training among the participants [46]. In this study, a large number of staff came from extramural community-based institutions. They commented that this may have eliminated the well-known clinical observation bias, namely that staff in clinical services often see patients with a poorer prognosis, including 'revolving door' patients. Staff attitudes were found more positive particularly in items related to aetiology and treatability of illness compared to the general public in this study. Again, more than half of the lay respondents assumed that patients suffering from schizophrenia were more dangerous than average people, but only a quarter of the staff supported this belief.

Level of education seems to play a role in the attitudes of nurses and staff. Ucman [47] reported that mental health staff with a higher level of education had a more positive attitude toward patients with psychosis. Tay *et al.* [45] reported that a professional qualification of an advanced diploma in mental health nursing or a nursing degree or having a post-basic certificate was found to be related to a more positive attitude. Similarly, education was found as the only significant factor influencing social distance in staff in the study from Austria mentioned earlier [46].

Possible reasons of negative attitudes

It seems reasonable to explain the stigmatizing attitudes of lay people, police or journalists by lack of knowledge. Antistigma programmes focus on topics like the contribution of both biological and psychosocial factors, the effectiveness of treatment, accurate information about violence and mental illness, and myths about mental illness, and they aim at correcting wrong beliefs by substituting 'true' ones [48, 49]. On the other hand, as shown in this paper, most of the groups which are the topic of this paper have already got the 'true' knowledge during their professional education. What are the possible reasons for the negative attitudes of health professionals towards people with schizophrenia?

Corrigan [50, 51] states that protest, education and particularly contact with people with mental illness are the most effective approaches for diminishing social stigma. However, the findings of the above-mentioned studies show that 'classical' medical education and personal contact with a person with schizophrenia in a 'usual' psychiatric environment has no effect on reducing the stigma in health professionals and students. So it is worth having a look at the conditions in which mental health professionals and particularly students come face to face with patients with schizophrenia.

It has been reported that more knowledge about mental illnesses, especially schizophrenia, may increase social distance in lay people [52]. Findings among mental health professionals support this assumption. It seems that theoretical education is not enough to produce a more positive attitude and behaviour. The health professionals who approach the patients as professionally as possible in their white coats in hospital, are ordinary members of society as well. We can assume that a training period varying between a few weeks and a few years is not enough to remove the prejudices which are universal in society.

Contact with patients plays an important role both in developing and removing stigma. The personal impressions of health professionals who have worked in psychiatric services with patients with schizophrenia is generally limited to what they saw in inpatient units when they were students. The typical patient with schizophrenia that medical or nursing students meet in psychiatric wards is either a person who exhibits bizzare or impulsive behaviours in the acute phase of the illness or a chronic patient with severe disability in a mental hospital. Images absorbed during those short weeks of training in units or hospitals, when put together with the stereotype which is shown frequently in the media and movies [53], easily creates a 'patient image' that furthers stigmatization and discrimination.

The general conditions of psychiatric wards also contribute to the stigmatizing attitude of health professionals. Most psychiatric wards all over the world are far from being a therapeutic milieu even if they are not as bad as shown in movies. Psychiatric wards are in an unlucky situation compared to non-psychiatric inpatient units in terms of availability of leisure activities, psychosocial treatments, rehabilitation facilities and patient load. Patients have to share their use of beds with other patients because of lack of enough psychiatric beds, or stay in cage-like beds all day long in some countries. In addition, Corrigan [54] recently pointed out that many psychiatrists and other mental health professionals opt out of the public service system which serves people with the most serious psychiatric disorders in the USA. Salaries and benefits are better in the private health sector, where providers are more likely to treat relatively benign illnesses like adjustment disorders and relational problems. Hence, quality of services for people with serious mental illnesses like schizophrenia is often inferior to the quality of services for other psychiatric disorders. As a summary, general conditions in most of the psychiatry clinics are not good enough to remove the 'lunatic asylum' image most people have in mind. It seems logical to assume that this negative image affects the people who work or are being trained in these instutitions as well.

In the public's stereotype, schizophrenia is connected to the ideas of a 'split personality' or 'split mind'. Although mental health professionals know this is wrong, we may expect that the term itself may contribute to negative attitudes. Local terms which are used to define the illness are sometimes even more disturbing than the word 'schizophrenia' in some cultures. 'Seishin-bunretsu-byou' (splitting of the mind) in Japan, a general term 'mahalat nefesh' (disease of the soul) in Hebrew, and jing-shen-fen-lie-zheng (mind-split disease) in Chinese, are only some of them [55–58]. Opinions of psychiatrists about keeping or changing the term 'schizophrenia' vary in different countries. While both mental health professionals and the patients agreed that a substantial proportion of patients reject the current term, and the patients believed that the alternative term was less stigmatizing, mental health professionals accept the current term compared to patients in Israel [56]. In Japan, 'togo-shitcho-sho' (integration ataxic disorder), the alternative Japanese translation of schizophrenia was approved by the Japanese Society of Psychiatry and Neurology in 2002 [59]. The renaming was triggered by the request of an advocacy group. In a recent study, it was reported that after the change of name, the majority of psychiatrists (71%) prefer to use the new one; moreover 70% of the psychiatrists, especially the younger ones, informed their patients of their diagnosis [60]. However, it is not easy to say that just changing the term 'schizophrenia' to a more acceptable one, will reduce the negative attitudes of mental health professionals toward sufferers of schizophrenia.

What is being done to reduce the stigma, and what else can be done?

It is obvious that challenging the stigma of schizophrenia is going to require a multi-dimensional approach. Although it is impossible to consider the mental health professionals independent from the community in which they live, something can be done to change the stigmatizing attitudes of this group. The most important thing is to improve the quality of conditions with which mental health professionals and patients come face to face. This demand , which can be regarded as utopian in most parts of the world, actually means asking that we change the traditional approach to the patient with severe mental illness.

Another, more realistic, approach is to try to keep the stigma and discrimination towards patients with schizophrenia on the agenda of mental health professionals. The World Psychiatric Association started its Global Programme to Reduce the Stigma and Discrimination because of Schizophrenia in 1999. Local projects in the United States, Switzerland,

Germany, India, Spain, Slovakia, Romania, Brazil, Eygpt, Greece, Morocco, and Turkey chose general health practitioners as part of their target population in their communities [61]. Organizing meetings to discuss the issue in various congresses of mental health professionals, at least serves to confront these people with their own attitudes. The increasing interest has also stimulated research in this area. Angermayer and Holzinger reported that there is currently a boom of stigma research in psychiatry [62]. When 'stigma' and 'mental illness' were entered as key words in Pubmed search, there were 1093 papers about this topic (until April 2007), and more than half of them were published in the previous five years. Despite more research we are still far from understanding the stigma process in detail. This, however, is the prerequisite for developing successful anti-stigma interventions.

Another step to reducing stigma is to discuss the topic with specific target populations in smaller-size meetings. The content of these meeting should be tailored for each target group. Regardless of their attitudes, particularly general practitioners, nurses, staff and students report that they are willing to join training programmes in almost all of the studies. To discuss the myths related to schizophrenia can be helpful for all mental health professionals including psychiatrists and nurses. It can be helpful to update the basic information about the aetiology or treatment of schizophrenia for target groups whose contact with patients with schizophrenia is limited, like general practitioners or nursing and medical students. We present technical medical information about schizophrenia whenever we meet to discuss the myths and dynamics of stigma in meetings with general practitioners in Turkey. We also distributed the printed material about stigma and schizophrenia prepared by the WPA (Volume II) in these one-session meetings. We found significant, positive changes on five of the sixteen items in the post-test survey when compared to attitudes before training, including items about the treatability of schizophrenia, harmfulness and untrustworthiness of patients [22] (Table 9.2). In another meeting targeting medical students in 2004, in addition to the above-mentioned agenda, a patient with schizophrenia has spoken to students in an interactive manner, and the movie *A Beautiful Mind* was shown in the final part of the one-day meeting. Students' attitudes towards people with schizophrenia were assessed before and one month after the programme. Favourable attitudinal changes were observed in terms of 'belief about the aetiology', 'social distance to people with schizophrenia' and 'care and management of people with schizophrenia'. In contrast, no significant change was observed in the control group [27].

However, most of the above-mentioned efforts are based on one or a few sessions of intervention. When considering the pervasiveness of stigma because of schizophrenia, it seems crucial to organize such activites on a long-term basis. The WPA's anti stigma programme accelerated anti stigma activities targeting mental health professionals as well. If this programme lasts for a long period, it will make these efforts more permanent and effective.

References

1. Sagduyu, A., Aker, T., Ozmen, E., Ogel, K. and Tamar, D. (2001) Public opinion and attitude towards schizophrenia: an epidemiologic research. *Turk Psikiyatri Dergisi* **12**, 99–110 (in Turkish).
2. Jorm, A.F., Korten, A.E., Jacomb, P.A., Christensen, H. and Henderson, S. (1999) Attitudes toward people with a mental disorder: a survey of the Australian public and health professionals. *Australian and New Zeland Journal of Psychiatry* **33**, 77–83.

3. Link, B., Lawrance, H.Y., Phelan, J.C. and Collins, P.Y. (2004) Measuring mental illness stigma. *Schizophrenia Bulletin* **30**, 511–541.
4. Nordt, C., Rössler, W. and Lauber, C. (2006) Attitudes of mental health professionals toward people with schizophrenia and major depression. *Schizophrenia Bulletin* **32**, 709–714.
5. Walter, G. and Rosen, A. (1997) Psychiatric stigma and the role of the psychiatrist. *Australasian Psychiatry* **5**, 72–74.
6. Fogel, S.P., Sneed, J.R. and Roose, S.P. (2006) Survey of psychiatric treatment among psychiatric residents in Manhattan: evidence of stigma. *Journal of Clinical Psychiatry* **10**, 1591–1598.
7. Sartorius, N. (2002) Iatrogenic stigma of mental illness. *British Medical Journal* **324**,1470–1471.
8. Sartorius, N. (1998) Stigma: what can psychiatrists do about it? *Lancet* **352**, 1058–1059.
9. Ono, Y., Satsumi, Y., Kim, Y. *et al.* (1999) Schizophrenia: is it time to replace the term? *Psychiatry and Clinical Neurosciences* **53**, 335–341.
10. Kua, J.H., Parker, G., Lee, C. and Jorm AF. (2000) Beliefs about outcomes for mental disorders: a comparative study of primary health practitioners and psychiatrists in Singapore. *Singapore Medical Journal* **41**, 542–547.
11. Üçok, A., Polat, A., Sartorius, N., Erkoc, S. and Atakli, C. (2004) Attitudes of psychiatrists toward schizophrenia. *Psychiatry and Clinical Neurosciences* **58**, 89–91.
12. Mantar, A., Ozbey, D., Akdede, B.B. and Alptekin, K. (2004) Stigmatization level of psychiatrists toward schizophrenia. *Proceedings of 40th National Congress of Psychiatry, 28 September-3 October 2004, Kusadasi, Izmir, Turkey.* pp. 307–309.
13. López-Ibor, J.J., Cuenca, O. and Reneses, B. (2005) Stigma and health care staff. In A. Okasha and C. Stefanis (eds) *Perspectives on the Stigma of Mental Illness*, pp. 21–29, World Psychiatric Association.
14. Bayle, F.J., Chauchot, F., Maurel, M., Ledoriol, A.L., Gerard, A., Pascal, J.C., Azorin, J.M., Olie, J.P. and Loo, H. (1999) Survey on the announcement of schizophrenia diagnosis in France. *Encephale* **25**, 603–611 (in French).
15. Kingdon, D., Sharma, T. and Hart, D. (2004) What attitudes do psychiatrists hold towards people with mental illness. *Psychiatric Bulletin* **28**, 401–406.
16. Lauber, C., Anthony, M. and Ajdacic-Gross, V. (2004) What about psychiatrists' attitude to mentally ill people? *European Psychiatry* **19**, 423–427.
17. Schlosberg, A. (1993) Psychiatric stigma and mental health professionals (stigmatizers and destigmatizers). *Medicine and Law* **12**, 409–416.
18. Van Dorn, R.A., Swanson, J.W., Elbogen, E.B. and Swartz, M.S. (2005) A comparison of stigmatizing attitudes toward persons with schizophrenia in four stakeholder groups: perceived likelihood of violence and desire for social distance. *Psychiatry* **68**, 152–163.
19. Adeyemi, J.D., Olonade, P.O. and Amira, C.O. (2002) Attitude to psychiatric referral: a study of primary care physicians. *Nigerian Postgraduate Medical Journal* **9**, 53–58.
20. Simon, A.E., Lauber, C., Ludewig, K., Braun-Scharm, H. and Umricht S.D. (2005) General practitioners and schizophrenia: results from Swiss survey. *British Journal of Psychiatry* **187**, 274–281.
21. Yildiz, M., Onder, M.E., Tural, U., Balta, H.I. and Kocalim, N. (2003) General practitioners' attitudes towards psychotic disorders and their treatment in the primary health care system. *Turk Psikiyatri Dergisi* **14**, 106–115 (in Turkish).
22. Üçok, A., Soygur, H., Ataklı, C., Kuscu, K., Sartorius, N., Çetinkaya, Z., Polat, A. and Erkoç, S. (2006) The impact of anti-stigma education in general health setting on the attitudes of the general practitioners on schizophrenia. *Psychiatry Clinical Neurosciences* **60**, 439–443.
23. Aydın, N., Yigit, A., Inandi, T. and Kirkpinar, I. (2003) Attitudes of hospital staff toward mentally ill patients in a teaching hospital, Turkey. *International Journal of Social Psychiatry* **49**, 17–26.
24. Roberts, L.W., Warner, T.D. and Trumpower, D. (2000) Medical students' evolving perspectives on their personal health care: clinical and educational implications of a longitudinal study. *Comprehensive Psychiatry* **41**, 303–314.
25. Givens, J.L. and Tija, L. (2002) Depressed medical students' use of mental health services and barrires to use. *Academic Medicine* **77**, 918–921.
26. Akdede, B.B.K., Alptekin, K., Topkaya, Ş.O., Belkiz, B., Nazlı, E, Özsin, E., Piri, O. and Saraç, E. (2004) The level of stigma of schizophrenia among young people. *New Symposium* **42**, 113–117 (in Turkish).

27. Altindag, A., Yanik, M., Üçok, A., Alptekin, K. and Ozkan, M. (2006) Effects of an anti stigma program on medical students' attitudes towards people with schizophrenia. *Psychiatry and Clinical Neurosciences* **60**, 283–288.

28. Singh, S.P., Baxter, H., Standen, P. and Duggan C. (1998) Changing the attitudes of 'tomorrow's doctors' towards mental illness and psychiatry: a comparison of two teaching methods. *Medical Education* **32**, 115–120.

29. Mino, Y., Yasuda, N., Kanazawa, S. and Inoue S. (2000) Effects of medical education on attitudes towards mental illness among medical students: a five-year follow-up study. *Acta Medicana Okayama* **54**, 127–132.

30. Mino, Y., Yasuda, N., Tsuda, T. and Shimodera S. (2001) Effects of a one-hour educational program on medical students' attitudes to mental illness. *Psychiatry and Clinical Neurosciences* **55**, 501–507.

31. Yanik, M., Simsek, Z., Kati, M. and Nebioglu, M. (2003) Attitudes towards schizophrenia and influence of psychiatric training in medical students. *New Symposium* **41**, 194–199 (in Turkish).

32. Inandı, T., Aydın, N., Turhan, E. and Gultekin, D. (2006) Social distances of medical students towards a person in a depression vignette: cross-sectional comparative study. *Proceedings of Third International Conference: Together against Stigma, 5–8 October 2006, Istanbul, Turkey,* p. 59.

33. Aker, S., Alptekin, A., Boke, O., Dündar, C. and Peksen, Y. (2006) The attitudes of interns toward psychiatric illnesses and the role of psychiatric training period in changing these attitudes. *Proceedings of Third International Conference: Together against Stigma, 5–8 October 2006, Istanbul, Turkey,* p. 75.

34. Arkar, H. and Eker, D. (1998) Attitudes towards mental illness: effects of psychiatry rotation. *3P Journal* **6**, 263–270 (in Turkish).

35. Ay, P., Save, D. and Fidanoglu, O. (2006) Does stigma concerning mental disorders differ through medical education? A survey among medical students in Istanbul. *Social Psychiatry andPsychiatric Epidemiology* **41**, 63–67.

36. Mas, A. and Hatim, A. (2002) Stigma in mental illness: attitudes of medical students towards mental illness. *Medical Journal of Malaysia* **57**, 433–444.

37. Reddy, J.P., Tan, S.M., Azmi, M.T., Shaharom, M.H., Rosdinom, R., Maniam, T., Ruzanna, Z.Z. and Minas, I.H. (2005) The effect of a clinical posting in psychiatry on the attitudes of medical students towards psychiatry and mental illness in a Malaysian medical school. *Annals of Academic Medicine of Singapore* **34**, 505–510.

38. Yen, C. and Chong, M. (1998) Attitudes towards mental illness: a study of change during psychiatric internship. *Taiwanese Journal of Psychiatry* **12**, 64–72.

39. Economou, M., Kakavoulis, N., Seryianni, C., Yotis, L., Kolostoumbis, D. and Stefanis, C. (2006) Exploration of Greek medical students' beliefs and attitudes towards people with schizophrenia. *Proceedings of Third International Conference: Together against Stigma, 5–8 October 2006, Istanbul, Turkey,* p. 28.

40. Llerena, A., Caceres, M.C. and Penas-Lledo E.M. (2002) Schizophrenia stigma among medical and nursing undergraduates. *European Psychiatry* **17**, 298–299.

41. Ozyigit, S., Savas, H., Ersoy, M.A., Yuce, S., Tutkun, H. and Sertbas, G. (2004) Attitudes of nurses and nursing students towards schizophrenia. *New Symposium* **42**, 105–112 (in Turkish).

42. Halter, M.J. (2004) Stigma and help seeking related to depression: a study of nursing students. *Journal of Psychosocial Nursing and Mental Health Services* **42**, 42–51.

43. Sodow, D., Ryder, M. and Webster, D. (2003) Is education of health professionals encouraging stigma towards the mentally ill? *Journal of Mental Health* **11**, 657–665.

44. Taskin, E.O., Ozmen, D., Ozmen, E. and Demet M.M. (2003) Attitudes of school of health students towards schizophrenia. *Archives of Neuropsychiatry* **40**, 5–12 (in Turkish).

45. Tay, S.E., Pariyasami, Y., Ravindran, K., Ali, M.I. and Rowsudeen, M.T. (2004) Nurses' attitudes toward people with mental illnesses in a psychiatric hospital in Singapore. *Journal of Psychosocial Nursing and Mental Health Services* **42**, 40–47.

46. Grausgruber, A., Meise, U., Katschnig, H., Schöny, W. and Fleischhacker, W.W. (2007) Patterns of social distance towards people suffering from schizophrenia in Austria: a comparison between the general public, relatives and mental health staff. *Acta Psychiatrica Scandinavica* **115**, 310–319.

47. Ucman, P. (1983) Attitudes of psychiatric personnel and the therapeutic milieu. *Hacettepe Medical Journal* **16**, 191–197.

48. Thompson, A., Stuart, H., Bland, R.C., Arboleda-Flórez, J., Warner, R. and Dickson, R.A. (2002) Attitudes about schizophrenia from the pilot site of the WPA worldwide campaign against the stigma of schizophrenia. *Social Psychiatry and Psychiatric Epidemiology* **37**, 475–482.

49. Gaebel, W. and Baumann, A.E. (2003) Interventions to reduce the stigma associated with severe mental illness: experiences from the Open the Doors program in Germany. *Canadian Journal of Psychiatry* **48**, 657–662.

50. Corrigan, P.W. and Penn, D.L. (1999) Lessons from social psychology on discrediting psychiatric stigma. *American Journal of Psychology* **54**, 765–776.

51. Corrigan, P.W. (2004) Changing stigma through contact. *Advances in Schizophrenia and Clinical Psychiatry* **1**, 54–58.

52. Lauber, C., Nordt, C., Falcato, L. and Rossler, W. (2004) Factors influencing social distance toward people with mental illness. *Community Mental Health Journal* **40**, 265–274.

53. Stout, P.A., Villegas, J. and Jennings, N.A. (2004) Images of mental illness in the media. Identifying gaps in the research. *Schizophrenia Bulletin* **30**, 543–561.

54. Corrigan, P.W., Markowitz, F.E. and Watson A.C. (2004) Structurel levels of mental illness stigma and discrimination. *Schizophrenia Bulletin* **30**, 481–491.

55. Chung, K.F., Chan, J.H. (2004) Can a less pejorative Chinese translation for schizophrenia reduce stigma? A study of adolescents' attitudes toward people with schizophrenia. *Psychiatry and Clinical Neurosciences* **58**, 507–515.

56. Levav, I., Shemesh, A.A., Kohn, R., Baidani-Auerbach, A., Boni, O., Borenstein, Y., Dudai, R., Lachman, M. and Grinshpoon, A. (2005) What is in a name? Professionals and service users' opinions of the Hebrew terms used to name psychiatric disorders and disability. *Israeli Journal of Psychiatry and Related Sciences* **42**, 242–247.

57. Sugiura, T., Sakamoto, S., Tanaka, E., Tomoda, A. and Kitamura, T. (2001) Labeling effect of Seishin-bunretsu-byou, the Japanese translation for schizophrenia: an argument for relabeling. *International Journal of Social Psychiatry* **47**, 43–51.

58. Hirosawa, M., Shimada, H., Fumimoto, H., Eto, K. and Arai, H. (2002) Response of Japanese patients to the change of department name for the psychiatric outpatient clinic in a university hospital. *General Hospital Psychiatry* **24**, 269–274.

59. Sato, M. (2006) Renaming schizophrenia. A Japanese perspective. *World Psychiatry* **5**, 53–55.

60. Nishimura, Y. (2006) Is the informed consent for the individuals with schizophrenia being widely accepted among young psychiatrists after changing the name of the disease? Results of a 3-year study. *Proceedings of Third International Conference: Together against Stigma, 5–8 October 2006, Istanbul, Turkey*, p. 75.

61. The World Psychiatric Association. *Open the Doors. The Global Programme to Fight the Stigma and Discrimination because of Schizophrenia*, 2002 report.

62. Angermeyer, M.C. and Holzinger, A. (2005) Is there currently a boom of stigma research in psychiatry? *Psychiatric Praxis* **32**, 399–407 (in German).

10 Implementing anti stigma programmes in Boulder, Colorado and Calgary, Alberta

Richard Warner

Mental Health Center of Boulder County, Boulder, CO 80302, USA

Mental health professionals and sociologists focused attention on the problem of the stigma of mental illness in the 1950s and 1960s when many industrial world countries began to close psychiatric hospitals and to treat people with serious mental illness in the community. Researchers demonstrated that a high level of stigma existed [1–3] and unsuccessful attempts were made to reduce it [2]. There is no consensus about whether there has been much reduction in prejudice since that time [4, 5], but it is clear that stigma [6, 7], discrimination [8] and misconceptions about mental illness [9–13] continue to be very prominent. Citizen-driven 'not-in-my backyard' (NIMBY) campaigns continue to present obstacles to the placement of treatment or residential facilities in local neighbourhoods [14–16]. The US Surgeon-General's Report in 1999, cited stigma as one of the greatest obstacles to the effective treatment of mental illness [17].

Happily, in the last decade we have seen an increase in the will to combat the stigma of serious mental illness in many parts of the world, and the application of a new tool – social marketing – to this task. This chapter will describe how local communities can effectively combat the stigma of mental illness.

Social marketing

Social marketing campaigns have been used successfully around the world in AIDS prevention, reducing infant mortality, family planning, improving nutrition, smoking cessation and a variety of other causes [18]. Carefully designed campaigns can have substantial effects on behaviour [18]. Effectiveness is increased by 'audience segmentation' – partitioning a mass audience into sub-audiences that are relatively homogeneous and devising promotional strategies and messages that are relevant and acceptable to those target groups [19].

In developing such campaigns, it is useful to conduct a needs assessment that gathers information about cultural beliefs, myths and misapprehensions, and the media through which people would want to learn about the topic. The needs-assessment method may incorporate focus groups, telephone surveys and information from opinion leaders. A

Understanding the Stigma of Mental Illness: Theory and Interventions   Edited by Julio Arboleda-Flórez and Norman Sartorius
© 2008 John Wiley & Sons, Ltd

pre-testing mechanism is then established that allows the promotional strategy to be continuously refined [18]. Initially, specific objectives, audiences, messages and media are selected, and an action plan is drawn up. These messages and materials are pre-tested with specific audiences and revised. The plan is implemented and, with continuous monitoring of impact, a new campaign plan is developed and constantly refined.

Health promotion campaigns aim to heighten awareness and to provide information; the former is possible without the latter, but not the reverse. Awareness campaigns need to be supported by an infrastructure that can link people to sources of information and support – for example, a telephone number to call and trained people to respond to the caller. Ideally, the infrastructure should be a central organization with a local network. In the case of tackling the stigma of mental illness, a suitable organization would be a consumer advocacy group such as the National Alliance on Mental Illness (NAMI).

Implementing a local anti-stigma programme

The World Psychiatric Association (WPA) Programme to Reduce Stigma and Discrimination because of Schizophrenia, which was launched in the late 1990s [20], has established, to this date, 23 stigma-fighting projects in countries around the world. The author has been involved with the planning team for the global programme and worked closely with two of the local project sites, in Calgary, Alberta, Canada and Boulder, Colorado, USA. Much of the information in this chapter is taken from the experiences gained in these two sites. However, much more information and experience have been gained from the WPA programme as a whole. Information about this worldwide programme and materials that are useful to project organizers can be found at the programme's website www.openthedoors.com.

The WPA programme has established a simple process (which is available on the website) for setting up anti-stigma projects in local communities. Using social-marketing principles, the steps in creating a local programme include:

- setting up a local action committee;
- conducting a local survey of sources of stigma and types of discrimination;
- selecting target groups;
- choosing messages and media for these target groups;
- trying out interventions and testing their impact;
- broadening the scale of the intervention; and
- establishing some permanent changes.

Developing a local action committee

The composition of the action committee is a decisive element in establishing a local project. The committee members should include knowledgeable representatives of potential campaign target groups. The actual target groups to be selected will not be known at the time the action committee members are chosen, since this decision will be taken by the action committee itself. The initial planning group that selects action committee members, however, can select people from walks of life that may become target groups, such as: the police and judiciary; health service providers; high school students, teachers and school board members; employers; landlords; newspaper and mass media representatives; and the clergy. It is important to include people from advocacy groups, such as primary consumer groups or organizations like NAMI (in the US) or Rethink (in the UK). Building an alliance between different advocacy groups with a common interest is one of the potential long-term benefits of an anti-stigma campaign. Some of the most valuable members of the action committee will be consumers and their family members.

Action committee members should be people who are committed to the goals of the campaign and willing to devote substantial effort and time to it. Most of the work of the campaign will be unpaid volunteer effort performed by action committee members. It is also valuable to include on the action committee some prominent citizens with local name recognition (judges, city council members, etc.). When requesting a meeting with, say, the editorial board of the local newspaper, the presence of someone of prominence in the group will increase the interest of the target group members and the impact of the event. Such prominent individuals may not have much time to commit to the project; if so, they can be given advisory or affiliate status. If possible, a media or public relations expert should be included on the action committee. A media professional can help refine messages, design media materials and advise on cost-effective media outlets for the target groups in question.

The action committee should not be too small or the links to the community will be too restricted and the workload on individual members will be too great. Around 10 members would be a minimum. As many as 20 members is practicable; a group of this size should split into smaller task groups to refine the action plans for different target groups.

Effective programme participation

Regular communication with members of the action committee is important to maintain group cohesion and commitment. Initial meetings may involve wide-ranging discussions of relevant issues but, eventually, key target groups will be identified and specific objectives established. Action committees commonly meet monthly. Minutes are distributed to committee members soon after each meeting, and an agenda, sent prior to each meeting, helps focus the discussion and assists participants in preparing for the meeting. Regular attendance at meetings is important. The committee will monitor that action steps delegated to committee members are accomplished. Committee members should understand at the outset the importance of their individual contributions to the success of the campaign and the amount of time that is needed to carry out their assignments.

Involving consumers and family members

Involving people with mental illness (referred to as 'consumers' or 'users') and their family members is central to the success of an anti-stigma campaign. A goal of the campaign is to lead members of the community to see people with mental illness as people, like themselves, who happen to have a disability. Humanizing the condition, in this way, is best accomplished by introducing community members to people with mental illness who are willing to discuss their disabilities. People who know someone with mental illness are less likely to hold stigmatizing attitudes [21]. The action committee, therefore, should include consumers who can describe, first hand, the experience of mental illness and discrimination, and who are willing to speak at press conferences, be members of a consumer speakers' bureau, address the Chamber of Commerce, assist in police training, speak on the radio, attend meetings with the editorial board of the local newspaper, or help in similar ways.

Selecting target groups

It is useful to conduct a simple survey of local consumers, family members and other concerned figures, to determine where stigma is seen to be a significant problem in the community (for example, emergency rooms, employers, etc.). Using these data, the action committee will select a manageable number of target groups – three is a good number. It is not advisable to target the entire general population – to do so would be expensive and unlikely to have a measurable impact. The target groups need to be relatively homogeneous and accessible. Landlords, for example, are not a very accessible group in the US, since they do not meet as a group or use a common media outlet. In countries where most apartment renting is done by real-estate agents, however, it might be feasible to target this group. Employers also do not seem to be very accessible, but it may be possible to identify the few major employers who provide most of the employment in a district and to target the human resource departments of those businesses. High school students are a highly accessible group, as are the police (who receive regular in-service training) and the personnel of major news media outlets.

Assigning work responsibilities and monitoring progress

The action committee can split into task forces to develop action plans for each target group selected and report back to the action committee. For each target group the action committee will develop goals and objectives. These may include, in increasing order of difficulty, developing awareness, increasing knowledge, changing attitudes and changing behaviour (e.g. reducing discrimination in housing). For a target group such as high school students, the goals might be to increase awareness about the stigma of mental illness, to increase knowledge and understanding about schizophrenia, and to reduce stigmatizing attitudes.

To meet these goals, measurable objectives for high school students might include:

- make a presentation about stigma and schizophrenia to $X\%$ of the high school students in the district; and

- achieve an improvement in knowledge of $Y\%$ and a reduction in social distance of $Z\%$ with students who hear the presentation.

Based on these goals and objectives, the action committee or task group can establish some key messages and determine the media that will be used to put these messages across. Each message should be captured in a single short sentence.

The steps in putting this action plan into effect should be laid out by the action committee, specifying who will accomplish each step and by what date. For example, committee member A will develop a flyer for high school art teachers about the art competition by the end of December, and committee member B will organize a consumer speakers' bureau to address the school art classes by the end of January. The action committee will monitor whether these steps are accomplished. A simple 'programme planner' with such headings as: target group, communication goal, measurable objectives, key messages, media, action steps (task, person, time-line), can be used to track progress. Action steps are updated monthly.

Objectives for each target group should be realistic (e.g. a 10% improvement in social distance as measured on a pre-/post-test) so that group members are not disappointed by what they might otherwise imagine to be small gains. Local media exposure and project outcome research results are useful in demonstrating the success of the various phases of the campaign.

Accessing community opinion leaders

A small group of action committee members can meet with an opinion leader, such as the head of the Chamber of Commerce, or the newspaper editor, or the police chief, to discuss the campaign mission and the ways in which the opinion leader can advance the project goals. This consultation can lead to:

- gathering useful information about how to influence the target group in question;
- setting up events with, or the dissemination of information to, the target group;
- forging links with other people who do have time and knowledge to devote to the campaign.

Working with schools

High school students are a popular target group in the WPA global anti-stigma programme, having been selected by projects in Calgary, Alberta, Canada; Kent, UK; Leipzig, Hamburg and Munich, Germany; Innsbruck and Vienna, Austria; Ismailia, Alatrish and Port Said, Egypt; Boulder, Colorado, USA; and Brescia, Italy. The popularity of this target group has less to do with the likelihood that students will be a source of stigma and more to do with their ready accessibility and the opportunity to influence the attitudes and behaviour of a coming generation.

The task of working with schools is greatly simplified if a teacher, school board member and/or pupil is included in the action committee. To gain access to the target group, action committee members can meet with school principals and teachers to promote the concept of stigma reduction in mental illness as an important component in the acceptance of diversity. Many schools have priorities to provide training in this area. The point can also be made that mental illness is a sadly neglected area in health education.

Examples of messages that have been used in high school anti-stigma programmes include:

- No one is to blame for schizophrenia (a message about causes).
- People recover from schizophrenia (a message of hope).
- People with schizophrenia are *people* with schizophrenia (a message of compassion).
- Watch your language. (Don't use derogatory terms to refer to people with mental illness. An action message.)

Media that have been used include:

- a speakers' bureau of people with mental illness, family members and professionals;
- the WPA global anti-stigma project webpage (www.openthedoors.com) which has access doors for different types of users: teenagers, health professionals, and consumers and family members;

- a teaching guide on schizophrenia for teachers (such as the one developed for use in the Calgary project, which is available on the WPA project webpage);

- an art competition for high school students to produce anti-stigma materials, which has been used successfully in Calgary, Boulder and elsewhere.

To set up the art competition in Boulder, organizers obtained the approval of school principals, and the support of the district art teachers. A consumer speakers' bureau and a project coordinator with a visual arts background made presentations in art classes. (The presenters sometimes used role-playing, in which an interviewer asks questions of a student who is playing the role of a person hearing auditory hallucinations, while two other students, with scripts, play the role of his/her voices and speak simultaneously into both of his/her ears. The subsequent de-briefing of the student hearing voices reveals to the class some of the torment experienced by a person with mental illness.) The presenters announced a juried competition, with money prizes, for students to produce artwork dealing with the issue of stigma and mental illness. (Winning entries can be viewed at the web site of the Mental Health Centre of Boulder County, www.mhcbc.org.) Each year that the competition has been run, a public art show with an awards ceremony has been mounted, and the art exhibit has been displayed in participating high schools. After obtaining appropriate permission, winning art has been used in interior bus advertisements. The art show has been repeated annually.

In Colorado, interior bus advertisements reach a predominantly younger audience. The Boulder project took advantage of the opportunity for free public transportation interior advertising to display anti-stigma messages, including one designed around a piece of student art with the statement 'Sometimes those that are different are the most amazing'. Cinema patrons are also predominantly young people. For this reason, the Boulder project arranged to display slides promoting three selected anti-stigma messages along with the advertisements preceding the main feature in two local cinemas (with a total of 16 screens). Exit surveys revealed that this medium was cost-effective. Sixteen per cent of cinema patrons recalled the content of at least one of the three messages displayed. This means that, over the course of three months of displaying the slides, over 10,000 people could recall one of the messages two hours after seeing it – costing just pennies per person-message.

The outcomes from high school interventions have been positive throughout the WPA project. In Calgary, Alberta, substantial improvements in knowledge and attitudes were demonstrated by pre-/post-testing of students. The proportion of students expressing no social distance between themselves and someone with mental illness increased from 16% to 30%. The proportion with a perfect knowledge score increased from 12% to 28% [22]. In Gütersloh, Germany, the intervention produced a reduction in negative attitudes and prejudice [23], and in Vienna, Austria, positive changes in attitudes were evident 3 months after the intervention [24]. At three sites in Egypt, test scores of knowledge about schizophrenia and its treatment more than doubled, the proportion of students who regarded someone with schizophrenia as dangerous dropped from 81% to 26%, and the proportion who believed that someone with schizophrenia would be likely to commit a crime decreased from 56% to 29% [25]. In Leipzig, Germany, scores on attitudes towards someone with schizophrenia and willingness to enter social relationships with someone with the illness improved substantially over the course of a 3-month follow-up in the intervention group, while these scores declined slightly in a control group of students [26].

Working with the criminal justice system

Many mental health professionals regard criminal justice personnel as under-recognized partners in the treatment of people with mental illness. In the US, the police bring many people who are acutely disturbed into care or a protective setting. Jail officers have to arrive at management methods for people suffering from acute psychosis in an environment that is totally unsuited to this task. Judges wrestle with complicated issues around the disposition of people with mental illness who have committed crimes. Probation officers are often responsible for the supervision of mentally ill offenders in the community, without access to consultation around the probationer's capacity to respond to usual directives. Yet there are few examples of programmes that attempt to provide criminal justice personnel with the education necessary to perform these necessary parts of their job. For this reason, the Boulder anti-stigma project (and other WPA programme sites) selected criminal justice personnel as a target group.

With the primary goal of decreasing the number of people with mental illness in jail, the chief judge of the Boulder County district court organized a task force of heads of criminal justice elements (sheriff's department, probation, jail, district attorney's office), and the mental health and substance abuse treatment agencies. The task force requested that the Boulder anti-stigma project develop a series of mental health training programmes for the police, judges, attorneys and probation officers.

Police training

Mental health professionals, consumers and police officers collaborated in developing an 8-hour pilot training for officers in the Boulder City Police Department. The training was piloted twice, the first time with 15 seasoned officers and the second time with 15 rookies. Included in the training were lectures on mental illness by psychiatrists, a presentation on interviewing skills by a senior police officer, first-hand accounts of the effects of mental illness by consumers and family members, a role-playing exercise, and a talk on legal issues by the chief judge.

Applying lessons learned from the feedback and pre-/post-testing from the pilot training, the project undertook the training of the entire police department in Longmont, a nearby town with a population of 70,000. To minimize the disruption of police services to the community, the training was delivered as six identical 2-hour training sessions on adult disorders and six 2-hour sessions on child disorders, at change of shift in the afternoon or evening before the officers went on duty. The class size ranged from 10 to 30 participants. The presenters were psychiatrists, consumers and family members employing lectures, videotapes and discussion. The content included the features, course, treatment and outcome of psychotic disorders, common myths about schizophrenia, childhood disorders, and why people with psychosis should not be kept in jail. The class discussed suicide and suicide attempts, and why people with borderline personality disorder are often not admitted to hospital. This last point is an essential topic of discussion with police officers who, in any police department, are likely to complain about a patient whom they brought in for mental health evaluation after a suicide attempt, only to discover, as it is commonly phrased, 'She got home before I did!' Pre-/post-testing of the Longmont police officers was typical of results of similar training programmes conducted by the Boulder project. There was a 48% improvement in knowledge scores; the proportion of officers holding inaccurate beliefs about the causes of schizophrenia fell from 24% to 3%; and the proportion with an incomplete knowledge of acceptable grounds for involuntary treatment fell from 52% to 29%. But there was one misconception that proved unshakable. The proportion of officers holding a misconception about the usual behaviour of people with schizophrenia scarcely changed, falling from 82% to 71%. That is, after the training, 71% of officers still believed one or more of the following statements: people with schizophrenia are (a) always irrational, (b) much more likely to be violent than the average person, or (c) usually unable to make life decisions. This, despite the fact that the officers had all heard a presentation by a quietly eloquent, middle-aged woman with schizophrenia who was working full-time as a university library supervisor. As we puzzled over this finding, we realized that police officers are in an unusual situation. Their encounters with people with psychosis always occur when the person is acutely disturbed; they have little or no opportunity to meet people with schizophrenia who are working, happily married, or who have been out of hospital for years. We concluded that police training has to recognize this curious situation and to expose officers, even more than we had done to that point, to people who have recovered from serious mental illness if it is to effect a significant attitudinal change. A model programme using consumers to provide much of the police officer training has been established in the anti-stigma project in Kent in the UK [27].

To make mental health training available to police and probation officers across Colorado, the Boulder anti-stigma project collaborated with the US Department of Corrections to produce a training manual. This 8-hour training covers child, adult and elderly disorders, suicide and substance abuse, consumer and legal issues and police management techniques, and can be delivered by mental health professionals with a moderate level of expertise, consumers, family members and senior police officers. The manual and accompanying PowerPoint presentation are available from the author at rwarner@mhcbc.org. The legal information is specific to the Colorado mental illness statute, but the remainder of the training package is suitable for other North American or European settings.

Training of judges, attorneys, probation officers

In Boulder County, the chief judge requested training sessions for all district court judges, and the probation department and many private attorneys asked to attend the training. Psychiatrists, people with mental illness and family members provided four training sessions: three on adult disorders and one on child disorders. Topics included schizophrenia, depression, bipolar disorder, substance abuse, delirium and dementia, developmental disabilities, adult and childhood attention deficit disorder, and other childhood disorders. Outcomes were positive. For example, a pre-/post-test revealed that the judges' knowledge of schizophrenia improved from 47% accuracy to 74% accuracy, and some reported immediate changes in their sentencing practice for adults and juveniles. Subsequently the judges requested two more training sessions on juvenile disorders, which were provided by a child psychiatrist.

Working with journalists

The task of working with journalists will be greatly simplified if a journalist is included in the local action committee. It is feasible and productive for members of the action committee to meet with the editorial board of the local newspaper. This presents an opportunity to describe the goals and activities of the anti-stigma campaign and to increase the level of awareness of key staff of the newspaper about stigma and its consequences. For such a meeting, it useful to provide a one-page outline of the anti-stigma programme and the ways in which the newspaper could help realize the goals of the campaign. In Boulder County, meetings with the editorial boards of the two main local newspapers led to:

- the publication of editorials about stigma or about the campaign;
- invitations for members of the project to write guest opinions;
- project members learning what channels to follow to publish messages related to stigma and to the campaign (e.g. press releases and letters to the editor); and
- opportunities to communicate information to journalists about the ways in which the news media may inadvertently heighten stigma.

In both the Calgary and Boulder projects, journalists were provided with written suggestions on how to avoid stigmatizing references – for example, routinely associating of mental illness with violence, or using the term 'schizophrenic' to mean 'contradictory' or 'split personality'. Journalists in Boulder County also requested and received a resource list of consumers and experts who could be contacted to provide information for a story. Journalists are often writing to a tight deadline, and complain that they don't know whom to contact when they want to write a story about mental illness. It is useful to create a list of experts, with phone numbers, who can be contacted in such a situation, and to distribute the list to the local newspapers, radio stations and TV news channels. The list should include (a) people with mental illness and their family members (who have consented to be contacted), and (b) professionals. The list can be sorted by category (e.g. schizophrenia, suicide), and should be updated and redistributed at regular intervals. Even if the journalist cannot find the list of potential contacts when needed, it is useful if key people at the mental health agency or advocacy group have the list to hand, so that they can give names and phone numbers of useful informants to the reporter. The campaign should attempt to identify local journalists who are interested in the issue of mental illness and stigma and assist them in writing human-interest stories on this theme.

Both the projects in Calgary and in Boulder conducted analyses of column-inches of positive and negative coverage of mental illness in the local newspapers, before and after the initiation of the anti-stigma campaign. In neither case was there any demonstrable positive change. We drew the conclusion that so much of the news coverage in local papers is national in scope (for example, the Uni-bomber and the attempt by an armed man to enter the US Congress) that these news stories overwhelm any change in local coverage. In both cases, however, the projects established permanently improved relationships with the local media that continue to have ongoing benefits.

Setting up a consumer speakers' bureau

A speakers' bureau can be invaluable for addressing school classes, police, organizations of businesspeople, and similar groups. Commonly a speakers' bureau will comprise some people who have experienced mental illness, family members of mentally ill people and a mental health professional. An important function of the mental health professional is to answer questions of a factual nature (e.g. 'What causes schizophrenia?') that a consumer might not be able to answer.

People with mental illness can react to the stress of public speaking by experiencing an increase in symptoms shortly after the event. To minimize the likelihood of this reaction:

- consumers with a good stress-tolerance should be selected;
- consumers should be gradually introduced to the speaking experience by, first, observing, then speaking briefly, until they can participate fully without stress;
- speakers should be de-briefed after each presentation to see if they found the experience stressful;
- a substantial number of speakers should be trained so that the demand on any one person is not too great.

Consumer speakers will often describe the experience of illness, but their very appearance as public speakers will demonstrate the reality of recovery. They may describe problems of stigma and discrimination, but their presence is likely to evince feelings of compassion and an understanding that mental illness is a human problem that can affect anyone and everyone. They can talk about problems which are of particular interest to the community group to which they are speaking, for example, discrimination in employment, housing and law enforcement, but they should address such issues in a non-critical way which will not generate defensiveness in the audience.

A study conducted in Innsbruck [28] highlights the benefits of using consumers in addressing groups about mental illness. In this study, over 100 high school students, in 6 school classes, were assigned to one of two equal-size groups who were addressed on the topic of mental illness. One group was addressed by a psychiatrist and a consumer, the second by a psychiatrist and a social worker. Significant changes in social distance attitudes were evident in only the group that was addressed by the consumer.

It is important to have a coordinator for the speakers' bureau who will:

- be directly accessible to those in the community requesting speakers,
- maintain a diary of speaking engagements,
- select and contact speakers for each engagement,
- de-brief speakers after each engagement, and
- ask the person inviting the speakers to provide an assessment of the event.

The coordinator could be a consumer, family member, mental health professional or anyone else who is enthusiastic, well-organized and, preferably, carries a cellphone.

A successful consumer speakers' bureau, such as the Partnership Programme operated by the Calgary branch of the Schizophrenia Society, is likely to develop a strong sense of shared mission. This sense of community can be nurtured and maintained by establishing contact between all participants through regular meetings, and through celebratory events such as an annual banquet.

Setting up a media watch group

Local and national advocacy groups can lobby the news and entertainment media to exclude negative portrayals of people with schizophrenia. Such groups are known as 'stigma-busters' or 'media-watch' groups. The stigma-busting approach calls upon members to be alert to stigmatizing messages in any medium and to respond appropriately. At the local level, an anti-stigma project can establish the media-watch function in a number of ways. They can: (a) inform national media-watch organizations about negative portrayals with a national impact (for example, a two-faced action figure produced by Hasbro Toys that portrays an 'extreme paranoid schizophrenic' [29]), (b) respond to calls to action from national advocacy groups, and (c) contact local media outlets about stigmatizing messages in the local media. National media-watch bodies in the US have become very effective.

The National Stigma Clearinghouse, begun in 1990 by the New York State Alliance on Mental Illness collects examples of negative portrayals of people with mental illness from across the United States, from television, advertising, films and the print media. Members of the organization write or phone the responsible journalists, editors or others in the media, explaining why the published material is offensive and stigmatizing, and providing more accurate information about mental illness. The group also encourages local organizations to take local action and distributes a monthly newsletter summarizing recent negative media portrayals and the actions taken to inform people at the responsible media source. In this way the group educates other advocates about what kinds of media portrayals to look for and how to correct them [29].

An example of a successful stigma-busting intervention was the response coordinated by the National Stigma Clearinghouse to the advance publicity for the November 1992 issue of *Superman* comic reporting that the issue would reveal how Superman was to be killed by 'an escapee from an interplanetary insane asylum'. The Clearinghouse and other advocacy groups lobbied D.C. Comics, explaining that depicting the killer of the superhero as mentally ill would further add to the stereotype of mentally ill people as evil and violent. When the death issue hit the newsstands the killer was no longer described as an escaped mental patient or a 'cosmic lunatic', nor depicted wearing remnants of a strait-jacket [29].

The National Alliance on Mental Illness achieved similar success with a coordinated national response to the TV series *Wonderland*. In the initial episode of this 1999 TV series, set in a New York psychiatric hospital, mentally ill people were seen committing numerous violent acts, such as stabbing a pregnant psychiatrist with a syringe. Following a NAMI appeal disseminated by e-mail to advocacy groups across the nation, a mass mailing by concerned citizens to the network, the producers and the commercial sponsors led to the show being pulled from the air after two episodes, despite the fact that 13 shows had already been filmed.

Local action can also be effective. In Boulder County, a local newspaper carried an advertisement depicting a man with bulging eyes and distorted features accompanied by a legend which ran 'Driven crazy by your cramped housing?' and inviting readers to contact a rental company about relocating. A polite letter to the advertiser from a senior mental health professional on the action committee, with a copy to the editor of the local newspaper, led to immediate withdrawal of the advertisement and a letter of apology.

A media-watch group does not need to be large or complex. One or two people can be designated as coordinators. They will establish links, perhaps by e-mail, to a broader group of interested members of advocacy group members who will immediately report instances of stigmatizing news reporting or entertainment content, whether they be local or national in scope. The coordinators will discuss the issue and devise an appropriate response. They may forward items of national scope to a national stigma-busters group or respond directly to a local newspaper or business.

Stigma-busting groups have to tread a narrow line between educating the media about inaccurate, stigmatizing messages, on the one hand, and, on the other, coming across as intolerant nitpickers. The stigma-busters' response should not be so mild that editors and producers harbour the misconception that their media content is accurate and harmless, nor so fierce that they generate fears of censorship by a vociferous minority group. An approach of gradual escalation has shown itself to be effective. Begin with a polite request, perhaps including a suggestion that the stigmatizing reference must have been inadvertent. A positive response should be rewarded with a letter of thanks from the media-watch group. Often those guilty of such an offence are appropriately concerned and may later become supporters of the stigma-watch group. If the offender is unresponsive, increasing pressure can be brought to bear in gradual increments, such as a letter for publication in the local newspaper, escalating to consumer boycott of an offending business, if an appropriate response is not forthcoming.

Keeping track of resources

An estimate of the total funds likely to be available to the anti-stigma project should be made early in the project, and the campaign should be designed to fit within these budget constraints. For example, pre/post knowledge and attitude surveys of the general population are expensive. Broad-scale attempts to influence the general public through television or radio advertising is also very expensive and extremely unlikely to prove effective unless very large amounts of money are invested. On the other hand, many effective target group interventions, such as police training and presentations to high school students, can be conducted and assessed with modest expense. Accurately anticipating the available resources will significantly influence the design of the project.

Low-cost media outlets, such as public service announcements in the press, on buses and on television and radio can be explored. Their value should be estimated in terms of the amount of exposure to be gained. Public service announcements on television, for example, are often aired at times when few people are watching.

The project director or programme treasurer will maintain a balance sheet, and expenditures and revenues entered as they occur. The project balance should be reviewed monthly by the project director and presented regularly to the action committee.

Planning for sustainability

The campaign cannot run for ever (in fact, a three-year project is a reasonable goal) but some more permanent structures and partnerships can be developed. Based on the experience in Boulder and Calgary and elsewhere, these might include:

- a change in the local high school health curriculum to include mental illness;
- adapting 'diversity' education programmes in local high schools to include the mentally ill with other discriminated groups, such as ethnic and sexual-preference groups;
- the formation of a consumer speakers' bureau;
- the creation of a media-watch group within a local advocacy organization;
- the establishment of alliances between diverse advocacy groups and agencies with a common interest in stigma reduction;

- the reinforcement of the stigma-fighting mission of established advocacy groups;

- a change in institutional or health-service policy (such as establishing new local or national emergency-room procedures for the evaluation and treatment of people with mental illness).

If an opportunity presents itself to create a permanent change in the health or science curriculum of the school district to include serious forms of mental illness, or to influence the routine training of police officers, these should be grasped eagerly. Such opportunities may develop as project personnel forge enhanced working alliances with school board members, police chiefs and others in key organizations.

The project director should evaluate which components of the campaign will require ongoing funding (for example, speakers' fees for consumer speakers, or prizes for an annual art show) and look for ongoing support for these elements. The required support may be quite limited. Local advocacy groups or agencies may be willing to assume the responsibility for different components of the project.

Conclusions

To implement an effective local anti-stigma project it is necessary to establish an effective action committee, and it is useful to conduct a survey of perceived stigma. The action committee should select a few homogeneous and accessible target groups, and not aim to impact the general public. Messages for these target groups and the media to reach them should be carefully selected, tested and refined. Throughout the campaign the organizers should be on the lookout for valuable changes which can become permanent. If these guidelines are followed, the project does not have to cost much.

References

1. Star, S. (1955) in National Association for Mental Health meeting, Chicago, Illinois, 1955.
2. Cumming, E. and Cumming, J. (1957) *Closed Ranks: An Experiment in Mental Health Education.* Harvard University Press, Cambridge, MA.
3. Nunally, J.C. (1961) *Popular Conceptions of Mental Health: Their Development and Change.* Holt, Rinehart and Winston, New York.
4. D'Arcy, C. and Brockman, J. (1976) Changing public recognition of psychiatric symptoms? Blackfoot revisited. *Journal of Health and Social Behavior* **17,** 302–310.
5. Cockerham, W.C. (1981) *Sociology of Mental Disorder.* Prentice-Hall, Englewood Cliffs, NJ.
6. Hall, P., Brockington, I.F., Levings, J. and Murphy, C. (1993) A comparison of responses to the mentally ill in two communities. *British Journal of Psychiatry* **162,** 99–108.
7. Brockington, I.F., Hall, P., Levings, J. and Murphy, C. (1993) The community's tolerance of the mentally ill. *British Journal of Psychiatry* **162,** 93–99.
8. Sayce, L. (1998) Stigma, discrimination and social exclusion: What's in a word? *Journal of Mental Health* **7,** 331–343.
9. O'Grady, T.J. (1996) Public attitudes to mental illness. *British Journal of Psychiatry* **168,** 652.
10. Borenstein, A.B. (1992) Public attitudes towards persons with mental illness. *Health Affairs* Fall, 186–196.
11. Weiner, B., Perry, R.P. and Magnusson, J. (1988) An attributional analysis of reactions to stigmas. *Journal of Personality and Social Psychology* **55,** 738–748.
12. Schony, W.: personal communication, 1999.
13. López-Ibor, J.J.: personal communication, 1999.
14. Boydall, K.M., Trainor, J.M. and Pierri, A.M. (1989) The effect of group homes for the mentally ill on residential property values. *Hospital and Community Psychiatry* **40,** 957–958.

15. Robert Wood Johnson Foundation (1990) *Public Attitudes toward People with Chronic Mental Illness*. The Robert Wood Johnson Foundation Program on Chronic Mental Illness, New Jersey.
16. Repper, J., Sayce, L., Strong, S., *et al.* (1997) *Tall Stories from the Backyard: A Survey of 'Nimby' Opposition to Mental Health Facilities, Experienced by Key Service Providers in England and Wales*. Mind, London.
17. US Department of Health and Human Services (1999) Mental Health: A Report of the Surgeon General. US Department of Health and Human Services, Substance Abuse and Mental Health Services Administration, Center for Mental Health Services, National Institutes of Health, National Institute of Mental Health, Rockville, MD.
18. Rogers, E.M. (1995) *Diffusion of Innovations*. Free Press, New York.
19. Rogers, E.M. (1996) The field of health communication today: an up-to-date report. *Journal of Health Communication* **1**, 15–23.
20. Sartorius, N. (1997) Fighting schizophrenia and its stigma: a new World Psychiatric Association educational programme. *British Journal of Psychiatry* **170**, 297.
21. Penn, D.L. Guynan, K., Daily, T. *et al.* Dispelling the stigma of schizophrenia: what sort of information is best? *Schizophrenia Bulletin* **20**, 567–575.
22. Stuart, H. (2002) Stigmatisation: leçons tirées des programmes de réduction. *Santé Mentale au Québec* **28**, 37–53.
23. Gonther, U., Milse, T., Küster, H-W. and Börner, I. (2001) Secondary school students regularly meet the patients of a psychiatric hospital; does this help alter stereotypes? Presented at the conference Together against Stigma, Leipzig, 2–5 September.
24. Ladinser, E. (2001) Students and community psychiatry: changes in attitudes towards people with mental illness and community psychiatry from an anti-stigma programme in schools. Presented at the conference Together against Stigma, Leipzig, 2–5 September.
25. El-Defrawi, M.H., El-Serafi, A. and Ellaban, M. (2001) Medical students' involvement in health education about schizophrenia: a campaign in secondary schools in Ismailia, Egypt. Presented at the conference Together against Stigma, Leipzig, 2–5 September.
26. Schulze, B., Richter-Werling, M., Matschinger, H. and Angermeyer, M.C. (2001) Crazy? So what! Effects of a school project on students' attitudes towards people with schizophrenia. Presented at the conference Together against Stigma, Leipzig, 2–5 September.
27. Pinfold, V. (2001) Working with police to reduce the stigma of mental illness. Presented at the conference Together against Stigma, Leipzig, 2–5 September.
28. Meise, U., Sulzenbacher, H., Kemmler, G. and De Col, C. (2001) A school programme against stigmatization of schizophrenia in Austria. Presented at the conference Together against Stigma, Leipzig, 2–5 September.
29. Wahl, O.F. (1995) *Media Madness: Public Images of Mental Illness*. Rutgers University Press, New Brunswick, NJ.

11 Stigma measurement approaches: conceptual origins and current applications

Lawrence H. Yang[1], Bruce G. Link[1] and Jo C. Phelan[2]

[1]*Department of Epidemiology, Columbia University, New York, NY 10032, USA*
[2]*Department of Sociomedical Sciences, Columbia University, New York, NY 10032, USA*

Introduction

The US Surgeon General's 1999 Report on Mental Health identifies a strong consensus that "our society no longer can afford to view mental health as separate and unequal to general health" (page vii, Executive Summary, [1]). The report goes on to indicate the central place that stigma plays in the sustenance of this unequal treatment, such as its effects in 'reducing patients' access to resources and opportunities (e.g. housing, jobs) and leading to low self-esteem, isolation, and hopelessness" (page 6, [1]). In order to address the pernicious outcomes associated with stigma, a diverse set of initiatives focused on combating stigma has emerged in the United States and globally. The World Health Organization has implemented a broad-based campaign to counteract stigma and discrimination due to mental illness. In September 2001, a broad range of National Institutes of Health partners sponsored the first international conference focused on stigma and global health. It is thus clear that there exists substantial interest in addressing the stigma of mental illness. The effectiveness of any efforts to address stigma, however, will rest on an understanding of the processes stigma implies, the factors that produce and sustain it, and the mechanisms that lead from stigmatization to its negative outcomes.

Essential to the scientific understanding of stigma is our capacity to observe and measure it. We endeavour to advance the measurement of stigma of mental illness through two papers. In a previous paper entitled "Measuring mental illness stigma" [2], we reviewed 123 articles focused on the stigma of mental illness that were published between 1995 and June 2003 and examined the measures employed in them. This review enabled us to characterize the breadth of methods currently employed in studying stigma, the kinds of study populations that have been assessed, the geographic location of the study sites, and the coverage of stigma concepts that the investigations achieved. Following this review, we described the content of selected measures, discussed evidence for reliability and validity, and indicated particular strengths or shortcomings of each measure. This previous paper

Understanding the Stigma of Mental Illness: Theory and Interventions   Edited by Julio Arboleda-Flórez and Norman Sartorius
© 2008 John Wiley & Sons, Ltd

also addressed three additional measurement topics: (1) the use of vignettes, (2) the use of behavioural measures in experimental and non-experimental studies and (3) the use of qualitative assessment.

While the earlier paper focused more on an empirical examination of the stigma literature, in the present chapter we provide an in-depth description of the evolution of each major stigma measurement perspective to achieve several purposes. First, we wish to provide readers a fuller context to understand how each major approach came into being. Second, we trace the development of each perspective to provide examples of how measures were derived from their theoretical origins, and how these measures subsequently were constructed, piloted and validated using empirically sound strategies. Lastly, we describe the development of measures from their origins to current usages and adaptations. We do this in an attempt not only to aid readers in locating current measures, but also to spur further innovation and development within these measurement paradigms. In this vein, we will also suggest novel adaptations of these stigma approaches derived not only from stigma measurement in particular, but from other areas of psychological research more generally.

Conceptualizing stigma

As a starting point, we return to the stigma concept and in particular to three influential theoretical frameworks. We do so as a basis for judging whether current measurement corresponds to the full range of stigma conceptualizations. These three conceptualizations were all developed by considering not just mental illnesses but multiple circumstances in which stigma arises. We believe this enriches the conceptualization of stigma by highlighting important components that might otherwise be overlooked. Note that other authors have offered conceptual frameworks for stigma [3–5]; hence, none of these conceptualizations alone should be viewed as definitive.

Goffman

Goffman [6] is widely cited for his insightful exposition of the stigma concept, and his formulation continues to be relevant today. A very common definition cited from Goffman is that of an "attribute that is deeply discrediting" and that reduces the bearer "from a whole and usual person to a tainted, discounted one" [6 p. 3]. Elsewhere, Goffman defines stigma as the relationship between an "attribute and a stereotype". Many of Goffman's ideas have been applied to the recent conceptualization and measurement of stigma. His distinctions between the "discredited" and the "discreditable" are evident in subsequent conceptualizations of the "visibility" dimension of stigma [7] and in attention paid to "secrecy" as a potential coping mechanism [8]. Similarly, Goffman's concepts of the "own" (those similarly stigmatized) and the "wise" (those who know about and accept the stigma) are apparent in efforts to measure withdrawal as a stigma coping mechanism [8].

Jones and colleagues' dimensions of stigma

Following Goffman's insights, a second conceptual framework was developed by Jones et al. [7]. Jones et al. use the term "mark" to encompass the range of conditions considered deviant by a society that might initiate stigmatization. Stigma takes place when the mark links the identified person via attributional processes to undesirable characteristics that in turn discredit him or her. The mark is thus highlighted as an integral part of the individual's identity that dominates others' perceptions. This process then results in barriers in interaction, typically disrupting the observer's emotions, cognitions and behaviours upon encountering the stigmatized individual.

Jones et al. identify six separate dimensions of stigma. *Concealability* is a dimension of a mark that indicates how detectable the characteristic is to others. Those able to conceal their condition (such as many people with mental illness) often do so to avoid negative social consequences. However, such actions may lead to shame over the undisclosed mark and fear of discovery. *Course* is a dimension that indicates whether the stigmatizing condition is reversible over time, with perceptions of irreversibility tending to elicit more negative attitudes. People's beliefs about a condition's future alterability are likely to influence the degree of stigma, especially for conditions not visible to the eye (like mental illness) for which observable changes are difficult to perceive. *Disruptiveness* indicates to what degree a mark strains or obstructs interpersonal interactions.

The dimension of *aesthetics* reflects what is pleasing to one's perceptions, and concerns the degree to which a mark elicits disgust. The aesthetic qualities of marked conditions in part determine subsequent experiences of rejection. *Origin* refers to how the condition came into being. One aspect of origin – perceived responsibility for the condition – has been found to greatly influence whether others will respond with negative attitudes and/or behaviour towards the target person. The final dimension, *peril*, refers to perceptions of danger or threat that the mark induces in others. Threat can either refer to a fear of actual physical danger (e.g., from a communicable disease like leprosy) or exposure to uncomfortable feelings of vulnerability (e.g., guilt due to watching a disabled person negotiate a flight of stairs). These six dimensions, although described separately, often exert influence upon one another. For example, stigmas that are genetically caused (origin) may tend to be relatively inflexible to future change (course).

Link and Phelan's components of stigma

A third conceptualization, provided by Link and Phelan [9], was formulated in response to recent criticisms of the stigma concept. A major critique of previous formulations of stigma is that the language used locates "stigma" in the target individual. For example, the "mark" in Jones et al.'s conceptualization refers to an attribute of a person rather than a designation conferred on the person. Furthermore, stigma research has largely focused on the cognitive processing of information, and far less on any discrimination a stigmatized person may experience, which would place equal attention on the producers of rejection and exclusion.

In an attempt to be attentive to such criticisms, Link and Phelan offer a definition of stigma that links interrelated components under a broad umbrella concept. According to Link and Phelan [9 p. 367] stigma occurs, "when elements of labelling, stereotyping, separation, status loss and discrimination co-occur in a power situation that allows them to unfold". Link and Phelan's set of stigma components are useful in identifying a possible domain of content for stigma measures. In addition, we expanded this conceptualization to include a component of emotional responses [2]. It also should be noted that each component can occur to a matter of degree; e.g., the linking of labels to a negative stereotype for a particular condition can be relatively strong or weak.

Distinguishing and labelling differences

The vast majority of human differences (e.g., finger length) are not considered to be socially relevant. However, certain differences, such as skin colour, are currently awarded a high degree of social salience. But both the selection of salient characteristics and the creation of labels are highly arbitrary. Regarding the latter, consider the degree of oversimplification required to create the categories of "black" and "white" when there is no clear demarcation on "defining" criteria such as skin colour, parentage or facial characteristics.

Associating differences with negative attributes

In this component, the labelled difference is associated with negative stereotypes. For example, a person who has been hospitalized for mental illness may be linked to stereotyped beliefs about people with mental illness being dangerous and unpredictable.

Separating "us" from "them"

A third aspect of the stigma process occurs when social labels connote a separation of "us" from "them". For example, certain ethnic groups [10] may be considered fundamentally different types of people from "us". Note that stereotyping and separating work hand in hand – the linking of labels to undesirable attributes becomes the rationale for believing that negatively labelled persons are fundamentally different.

Emotional responses

Underrepresented in previous formulations of stigma and added recently by Link et al [2] are the emotional responses stigma entails. Emotional responses to stigma may occur in the stigmatizer (e.g. disgust) and the stigmatized (e.g., shame). The emotions felt by the stigmatizer are likely to be important for at least two reasons. First, an overt emotional response can provide an important indication of a stigmatizer's response to a person who is stigmatized. For example, a person who manifests anxiety in the presence of a person with mental illness might signal to the person with mental illness that he/she is being perceived as dangerous and/or unpredictable. Second, emotional responses of the stigmatizer may shape subsequent behaviour toward the stigmatized person or group. Attribution theory and its application to stigmatizing conditions in general [11] and to mental illnesses in particular [12] emphasize the importance of emotional responses in the stigma process. Angermeyer and Matschinger [13] have also studied the stigmatizer's emotional reactions by employing large-scale surveys of the general public to identify the prevalence of emotions associated with vignette descriptions of people with mental illness.

From the vantage point of the person who is stigmatized, emotions of shame, embarrassment, humiliation, fear, alienation or anger are possible. Scheff [14] has, for example, argued that the emotion of shame is central to stigma. Stigma-related emotions may be particularly important because they may provide a critical link between stigma experiences and psychological outcomes such as self-esteem, mastery orientation and depressive symptoms [15]. Emotions associated with stigma have been found to be associated with biological mechanisms that may underlie such a relationship – for example, the emotional effects of rejection are found to trigger biological correlates in the brain that signal physical pain [16]. For these reasons, we include emotional responses in the conceptualization of stigma.

Status loss and discrimination

When people are labelled, set apart and linked to undesirable stereotypes, a rationale is constructed for devaluing, rejecting and excluding them. The most obvious example of this is individual discrimination, such as when labelling and stereotyping leads a person to refuse to rent an apartment to a person with a mental illness. However, discrimination may also take place through more subtle mechanisms. One of these is structural discrimination, in which institutional practices disadvantage stigmatized groups even in the absence of purposeful discrimination by individuals. For example, mental illnesses receive less insurance coverage when compared with physical conditions [17]. Another subtle form of discrimination works through status loss. Negatively labelled persons become connected to undesirable characteristics that reduce the respect accorded them in everyday interactions. Finally, once cultural stereotypes are in place, they can also have negative consequences that operate through the stigmatized person him- or herself via processes specified in modified labelling theory [8], stereotype threat [18] and stigma consciousness [19]. These processes can result in negative outcomes such as strained social interactions [20], constricted social networks [8], and unemployment and income loss [21, 22].

The dependence of stigma on power

A unique contribution of Link and Phelan's [9] conceptualization is the idea that stigma depends on social, economic and political power. Lower-power groups (e.g., psychiatric patients) may label, stereotype and cognitively separate themselves from higher-power groups (e.g., psychiatrists), but members of lower-status groups do not have the social power to attach serious discriminatory consequences to these cognitions. Thus, it is within this context of power that the negative consequences of stigma occur.

Stigma measurement approaches: history and current developments

We now describe each of the major measurement perspectives that have developed to assess stigma, beginning with a definition of its concepts, followed by a history of its early development, then concluding with a discussion of its evolution towards present-day use. The review is organized by first considering measurement perspectives applicable to: (1) members of the general public followed by (2) consumers of mental health services. We categorize the approaches into these two domains because the assumptions of these measurement perspectives share commonalities based on their target population. Within each domain, we review the measurement perspectives in chronological order of the citation that marks the measure's first use in studying the stigma of mental illness. We also include one separate section focused on the use of vignettes due to their prominent use in stigma research.

Stigma measurement approaches applicable to the general public

Social distance

One measurement perspective that has an extensive history of use is that of "social distance". Measures of social distance seek to assess a respondent's willingness to engage with a target person in relationships that vary in closeness. The idea is to find out how close an association the respondent will allow with the target person. For example, the original social distance scale developed in 1925 by Bogardus [23] included acceptance to close kinship through marriage at one pole and exclusion from the country at the other.

The concept of social distance emerged from the Chicago School of Sociology and its efforts to understand urban ecology. One of their core propositions was the idea that groups, as defined by race/ethnicity and class, competed for desirable space. Within this ecology of the urban environment, the sentiments of the groups towards one another became a critical issue, thus creating the concept of "social distance". Robert Park [24], one of the leaders of the Chicago School, in 1925 defined this as "the grades and degrees of understanding and intimacy which characterize pre-social and social relations generally". The first social distance scale was developed by Bogardus [23] and was used to describe social distance by race/ethnicity. The first published use of this scale with mental illnesses occurred in 1957 during Cumming and Cumming's [25] classic effort to change public attitudes. Shortly thereafter, in 1959 Whatley [26] administered an eight-item agree-disagree social distance scale to 2001 persons in 17 counties in Louisiana to assess attitudes towards people with mental illness as a group. To our knowledge, Phillips [27] in 1963 was the first to employ a social-distance scale in the context of a vignette experiment. His influential experiment showed that a person described in a vignette was rejected more strenuously if the help source involved psychiatric contact (mental hospital, psychiatrist) than if it did not (general practice physician, clergy or no help-source at all). These earlier studies (e.g., [26, 27]) evaluated the scales using Guttman criteria and generally found that social distance fit criteria for a uni-dimensional scale (coefficients of reproducibility of .9 or better). Since these initial studies, variants of the scale have frequently been used in stigma research and particularly in combination with vignettes.

Close scrutiny of the literature reveals remarkable variability in the operationalization of social distance. The specific format of items employed varies from study to study – response formats are sometimes "yes/no", other times "agree/disagree", and still other times "willing/unwilling". In addition, the chosen target is sometimes "mental patients" (or some other group referent) and at other times an individual described in a vignette. Fortunately, the concept appears robust, and it is likely true that the above variations are not a major problem in interpreting studies. Still, measurement has evolved, and there are some principles we recommend for this very commonly used measure. First, there is little reason to restrict the format to a dichotomy. Crocetti and Spiro [28] conducted the first study we know of to begin using a "definitely willing/probably willing/probably unwilling/definitely unwilling" response format. Since this study, such an approach has become much more common, perhaps because it allows more variability of response. Further, if the investigator wishes, these response categories can be recoded into dichotomous 'willing/unwilling' responses during later analyses. One recent study included an "unsure" category as a neutral response [29], an option that future researchers may want to consider. The tendency to provide socially desirable responses is such a substantial problem that allowing respondents to indicate that they are "not sure" allows a less-than-fully-positive response without endorsing a rejecting response. Second, recent social distance scales have addressed a weakness in previous scales that stems from the hypothetical nature of some of the items. Early scales included items like "would you discourage your children from marrying someone like X". The problem is that potential respondents may not have children, rendering questions like these excessively hypothetical. Because of this, we decided to use social-distance items that are potentially relevant to the respondent when we conducted a nationwide study of homeless people with mental illnesses [30, 31] and the MacArthur Module of the 1996 General Social Survey [32, 33]. For example, the item regarding "discouraging your children from marrying" was changed to "How willing would you be to have X marry into your family" so as to allow people without children or whose children might already be married to answer the question without imagining a situation outside their real experience.

Semantic differential and related measures

The Semantic Differential is a measurement technique that directly assesses stereotyping-i.e., the tendency to link a label like "mental patient" with negative characteristics (9). The respondent is presented with labels and then asked to evaluate the degree to which those labels are associated with various characteristics. Specifically, respondents are asked to rate the concept on a number of seven-point scales, each bounded by a pair of polar adjectives such as "safe–dangerous" and "valuable–worthless." Respondents are then asked to rate one or more additional concepts (e.g., "average person" or "me") using the identical response scales to provide a point of comparison. Semantic Differential instruments have typically been given as a self-administered measure, but an interview format has also been used [34]. See Nunnally [35], Olmsted and Durham [36] and Crisp et al. [34] for sample stimulus concepts and adjective pairs.

The Semantic Differential was developed in 1957 by Osgood et al. [37] as a general technique aimed at quantitatively measuring the psychological meaning that concepts have for people. Through a series of factor analyses of Semantic Differential ratings, Osgood et al. identified evaluation (e.g., good–bad), potency (e.g., hard–soft) and oriented activity (e.g., active–passive) as the factors that accounted for the largest amount of variability in respondents' ratings towards a variety of concepts. Nunnally in 1958 [35, 38] applied the Semantic Differential to assess public conceptions of people with mental illnesses and the professionals who treat them. Nunnally identified understandability as an additional factor that was particularly important for judgements of mental illness. To assess evaluations of people with mental illnesses, Nunnally asked respondents to rate concepts including "neurotic woman/man", "average woman/man", "insane woman/man", "mental patient", "psychiatrist", "old man", "child", "me", "mother" and "father" on 17 scales of adjective pairs. Subsequent uses of the Semantic Differential with mental illness concepts include a study by Olmsted and Durham [36] in which they compared the responses of college students to seven mental-health and comparison concepts on 12 of Nunnally's adjective pairs. More recently in 2000, Crisp et al. [34] used a similar approach by asking respondents to characterize seven mental disorders on response scales anchored by short phrases such as "dangerous to others – not dangerous to others" and "hard to talk to – easy to talk to".

A variant of the Semantic Differential that has been developed more recently is the Social Response Questionnaire (SRQ) [39]. The SRQ is similar to the Semantic Differential in that it provides a stimulus concept that is rated on a set of 32 adjectives. However, the stimulus concept is an actual individual and is rated by him-herself and by a significant other such as a family member. The SRQ thus assesses different aspects of stereotyping a psychiatric patient may encounter, including expectations of family or friends and self-stereotyping. Another difference from the Semantic Differential is that respondents are asked to rate adjectives (e.g., weak, reliable) as "like the subject", "somewhat like the subject" and "not like the subject" rather than the scales being anchored by opposite adjectives. Adjectives were derived from a literature review regarding the images of 'the sick role' for people with mental illness. Higher scores indicate greater levels of negative stereotyping by the individual or by the significant other.

One technique related to the Semantic Differential that to our knowledge has not been applied to the issue of mental illness - the Implicit Association Test (IAT; [40, 41]) – deserves mention. This approach was designed to measure unconscious prejudice, specifically the extent to which individuals implicitly evaluate some groups or concepts as good or bad.

In one example, the words "African American" and "European American" are paired on a computer screen with the words "good" and "bad". For one series of responses, "European American" and "good" are paired on the left side of the screen, with "African American" and "bad" paired on the right. Then a series of positive and negative words such as "friend", "pleasure", "war" and "horrible", interspersed with photographs of black and white faces, are flashed on the screen one by one, and the respondent must choose as quickly as possible whether the word or photograph is associated with the words on the left ("European American or good") or on the right ("African American or bad"). In a second series of responses, "African American" and "good" are paired on the left side of the screen, with "European American" and "bad" paired on the right. The outcome measure is the speed and accuracy with which positive words are identified as being associated with "good" and negative words with "bad". If respondents more quickly associate positive words with "good" when "good" is paired with "European American", this suggests that it is easier for the respondent to think of "European American" and "good" as being associated and is considered to indicate implicit prejudice against black people. This innovative measurement approach also could be easily adapted to study implicit prejudice towards people with mental illness. One obvious advantage is that social desirability bias is likely to be minimized.

Opinions about Mental Illness (OMI) and Community Attitudes toward Mental Illness (CAMI)

This scale was developed in the early 1960s by Cohen and Struening [42] and Struening and Cohen [43] and continues to be used extensively. The scale came into being because treatment developments at the time were based on the idea that social context, both in treatment settings and in wider society, affected recovery from mental illness. At that time, the pioneering work of Cumming and Cumming [25] and of Gilbert and Levinson [44] were limited to uni-dimensional assessments of attitudes towards mental illnesses. To provide more than a single dimension of measurement, Cohen and Struening [42] sought the "adequate conception and objective measurement of attitudes towards mental illness (p. 349)" through a multidimensional scale. The Opinions about Mental Illness Scale (OMI) was therefore developed in two large psychiatric hospitals using the responses of 1194 hospital workers.

To construct the scale, Cohen and Struening [42] in 1962 developed approximately 200 items based on quotes from case conferences and casual conversations in the hospitals they studied and paraphrases of common ideas about mental illness. These items were reviewed by a group of experts, edited and narrowed down to 55 items. These 55 items were then supplemented by 15 items taken from the Custodial Mental Illness Ideology Scale (CMI), the California F-Scale and Nunnally's work on popular conceptions of mental health. This final 70-item instrument was then factor-analysed, and five dimensions were identified: (A) authoritarianism – that obedience to authority is essential and that persons with mental illness require coercive handling; (B) benevolence – a paternalistic view of people with mental illnesses based on humanism and religion rather than science; (C) mental hygiene ideology – the notion that mental illness is like any other illness and that a rational, professional approach is essential for effective treatment; (D) social restrictiveness – that people with mental illnesses should be restricted in important social domains such as marriage and employment; (E) interpersonal aetiology – the belief that mental illnesses result from interpersonal experiences, in particular not having a loving home environment.

Struening and Cohen [43] subsequently examined whether the five factors remained consistent across independent samples of psychiatric hospital employees. The original 70 items were reduced to 51 by retaining only items referring to mental illness. The evidence suggested similar factor structures amongst personnel of three newly sampled hospitals. One factor, mental hygiene ideology, showed poor internal consistency in the three hospitals ($Alpha = .29$ to $.39$). However, authoritarianism (.77 to .80), benevolence (.70 to .73), restrictiveness (.71 to .77) and interpersonal aetiology (.65 to .66) had good internal consistency. It is this 51-item version of the OMI [43] that is used today (see [45]).

In 1979, Taylor, Dear and Hall [46] and Taylor and Dear [47] created the Community Attitudes toward Mental Illness (CAMI) measure to analyse the public's attitudes towards community-based treatment for people with mental illness. They used concepts within the OMI as a model, seeking to regenerate three of five factors (authoritarianism, benevolence and social restrictiveness) and to create a new factor assessing community mental health ideology. The scale includes 40 items, 10 for each of the proposed factors. Eleven of the items were taken from previous scales, with 29 items newly written.

The CAMI was tested using a community sample of 1090 persons from households in Toronto, Canada [47]. The sample was stratified by socioeconomic status, location, and whether a community mental health facility was in the area. The four a priori scales had $Alpha$ ranging from .68 for authoritarianism to .88 for community mental health ideology, with benevolence (.76) and social restrictiveness (.80) lying in between. Taylor and Dear also found the scales to be very highly correlated. A subsequent exploratory factor analysis [47] showed that many of the items placed a priori on one scale had substantial loadings on other factors. Because the items in the authoritarianism and social restrictiveness domains loaded highly on the same factor, the reallocation of items to other scales could result in a compact three-factor scale measuring authoritarian restrictiveness, benevolence and community mental health ideology.

The CAMI has continued to be used in recent studies (e.g. [48, 49]). The CAMI's main contribution lies in its assessment of attitudes towards community mental health treatment facilities. One other advantage of the scale was that it was developed by sampling community groups as opposed to the OMI which was created by sampling people who worked in mental hospitals.

Attributional measures

Attribution theory [50] proposes that an observer's causal attributions of why a stigmatizing condition occurs, in particular the target person's perceived ability to control the event, will shape subsequent emotions and behaviours toward the target. Since Weiner's [11] first application of attribution theory to stigma in 1988, researchers have focused on the causal domains of controllability and stability. The target person's perceived responsibility for the condition is hypothesized to predict either anger and punishing behaviour (if perceived to be controllable), or pity and helping actions (if perceived to be uncontrollable). Causes that are seen as changeable over time (unstable) generate beliefs that recovery is achievable, while causes that are perceived as unchangeable (stable) elicit beliefs that the condition is irreversible.

In 2000, Corrigan [12] provided a social cognitive model adapted from Weiner's [11] work. Corrigan proposed that signals of mental illness (e.g., "that person saying bizarre things is crazy") lead to stereotypes ("crazy people are impulsive") that produce behavioural reactions including discrimination ("I am going to avoid that person"). In this conceptualization, stereotypes of people with psychiatric illness represent cognitive knowledge structures that mediate behavioural responses. Corrigan also defined circumstances in which behaviours are not mediated by causal attributions, which he deems a variation of Weiner's [51] theory of primary appraisal [52]. This occurs, for example, when signals of dangerousness lead directly to an emotional response of fear, which in turn produces behavioural avoidance or discrimination.

Weiner et al.'s [11] original attribution measure was composed of eight questions about 10 illnesses (5 mental-behavioural and 5 physical). These eight questions consisted of: (a) three items assessing the responsibility, blame and changeability of each illness and (b) five items about the subject's liking, pity, anger, charitable donations, and personal assistance towards each illness. Three separate indices – controllability, positive emotions and a helping variable – were generated by adding single-item scores together (*Alpha* ranging from .67 to .90 (see [11]).

The Attribution Questionnaire (AQ), developed by Corrigan [52] and derived from Weiner's [11] instrument and 11 items from Reisenzein [53], assesses key constructs from his social cognitive model. Corrigan's AQ consists of 21 items using a nine-point response set (1 = not at all, 9 = very much) to measure six constructs: (1) *personal responsibility*, (2) *pity*, (3) *anger*, (4) *fear*, (5) *helping/avoiding behaviour* and (6) *coercion-segregation* (each construct composed of three to four items). Internal consistency of the subscales ranged from *Alpha* = .70 to .96 [52].

Another instrument that assesses causal attributions is the Revised Causal Dimension Scale (CDSII; [54]) adapted from the Causal Dimension Scale (CDS; [55]). The CDSII assesses attributional leanings about one's own personal behaviours or performance. This scale consists of: (1) a *locus of causality scale*, which assesses whether the cause is internal or is external to the person making the attribution, and (2) a *stability dimension*, which gauges whether the cause is fixed or variable over time. The remaining two scales consist of: (3) *personal control,* or how controllable the cause is by the actor, and (4) *external control,* or whether the cause is controllable by outside others. Three items, each rated on a nine-point scale, compose each CDSII attributional domain. *Alpha* ranges from .60 to .92 for these four subscales. To assess stigma, the CDSII has been adapted to measure an observer's causal attributions about a stigmatized individual [56].

These attribution measures have typically been administered as surveys, either with or without a vignette, to study the general population's emotional and behavioural reactions to people with mental illness. Several studies have also utilized the AQ to measure subjects' affective and behavioural responses in quasi-experimental conditions, in which an independent variable, such as exposure to an education condition, was experimentally manipulated.

Measures associated with the "modified labelling theory"

Perceived devaluation-discrimination

To test hypotheses associated with "modified labelling theory", Link [21] devised a perceived devaluation-discrimination measure. Rather than assessing a person's own beliefs about people with mental illnesses, the instrument measures a person's perception of what *most other people* believe. According to modified labelling theory [8, 21, 22], people develop conceptions of mental illness as part of their socialization [13, 57]. These conceptions then become a "lay theory" whereby people form expectations as to whether most people will reject or devalue an individual with mental illness [58, 59]. For most people, these beliefs are innocuous because they concern how someone else – someone labelled as mentally ill – will be treated. But for a person who develops a serious mental illness, these beliefs of possible devaluation and discrimination now become personally relevant. Internalizing such beliefs can have potent consequences. First, the person may feel personally disheartened and demoralized [60]. Second, expecting and fearing rejection, labelled individuals may act less confidently and more defensively, leading to impaired social performance [20]. Third, efforts to protect oneself from feared rejection, such as through social withdrawal, may lead to diminished social networks and fewer work, housing and marital opportunities [8, 61].

To test this theory, Link [8, 21, 60, 62, 63] developed a 12-item perceived devaluation-discrimination measure (utilizing a six-point format) that assesses whether respondents agree with statements indicating that most people will devalue or discriminate against psychiatric patients. Items about devaluation include seeing people with mental illness as failures or as individuals whose opinions need not be taken seriously. The scale also assesses perceived discrimination by enquiring whether most people would reject people with mental illness in respect of jobs, friendships and love relationships.

Although the scale has mostly been administered to people in treatment for mental illnesses, it has been used with the general public as well. Information from the general public is also crucial to testing modified labelling theory. First, the theory says that each society member, whether labelled with mental illness or not, forms conceptions about how people with mental illness will be treated by others. For example, if members of the public believed that devaluation and discrimination towards people with mental illness was generally absent, a person with newly developed mental illness would not face an internalized threat of rejection. But Link et al. [8] found extremely few members of the public who did not believe that people with mental illness would face devaluation and discrimination. Second, because the theory indicates that conceptions about devaluation and discrimination form through socialization via a uniform set of cultural influences, then scale scores should be quite similar across patient and community groups. Supporting this idea, no significant differences between several patient and community groups were found in two studies. Further, nearly equal means in scale scores across groups helps to rule out the influence of psychopathology potentially elevating discriminatory perceptions by the patient group [8, 21]. Finally, modified labelling theory predicts that perceived devaluation-discrimination should have no impact on social or psychological functioning in people who suffer from psychiatric impairment but have never been officially labelled with mental illness. Consistent with this prediction, when administered to persons who were never officially labelled, there were no significant associations between scale scores and earnings, unemployment, social network ties or psychological demoralization [21]. The internal consistency of this scale has been reported as .73 in a community-based non-patient population.

Stigma measurement approaches applicable to mental health consumers

Measures associated with the "modified labelling theory"

Perceived devaluation-discrimination

In addition to utilization among the general public, the most common use of the devaluation-discrimination measure has been in groups of mental health consumers. From the consumer's perspective, one's perception of future devaluation-discrimination of persons labelled with mental illness becomes personally relevant once one comes into contact with this official label. This sense of internalized rejection then may lead the labelled individual to adopt coping orientations which may lead to negative psychological and social outcomes. A recent study by Link et al. [60] reported that beliefs of anticipated discrimination are prevalent among mental health consumers (see also [8, 64]); 74% agreed that employers will discriminate against former psychiatric patients; 81% and 66% similarly expected rejection in dating relationships and close friendships respectively; and 67% that their opinions will be taken less seriously. The variation in scale scores mostly ranged between perceptions of extreme and moderate rejection. *Alpha* values were reported as ranging from .82 to .86 [63].

Recently, Struening et al. [65] adapted Link's devaluation-discrimination scale to assess whether family caregivers endorse that most people devalue families that include a person diagnosed with serious mental illness. This seven-item scale contains statements about what "most people would think" rated on a four-point scale ("strongly agree" to "strongly disagree"). Factor analysis identified three related factors. The Community Rejection factor, explaining 33% of the total variance, was defined by four items assessing beliefs that most people would avoid social contact with family members of a person with mental illness. The second factor, titled "Causal Attribution", explained 21% of the variance. This factor was defined by two items, the more prominent item being "beliefs that most people would blame parents for their child's illness". The Uncaring Parents factor, explaining 17% of the total variance, was defined by one item – that most people believe that parents of children with a mental illness are just as caring as other parents. The seven-item scale has shown good internal consistency (*Alpha* = .71 to .77) across two different diagnostic samples.

Experiences of rejection

In addition to beliefs of anticipated rejection, people labelled with mental illness may also suffer from experiences of rejection. To measure this, Link et al. [62] constructed a 12-item measure (*Alpha* = .80) to assess rejection experiences among dually diagnosed persons with serious mental illness and substance abuse. This scale makes an important contribution by assessing stigma associated specifically with drug use. Second, it includes new measures of experiences of rejection, as distinguished from expectations of rejection, for both drug use and mental hospitalization. However, subsequent to this scale's creation, Wahl [66] constructed a more complete set of items measuring rejection/discrimination experiences for people with mental illness in general (see below) which we recommend for use.

Measures of coping orientations and stigma-related feelings

This anticipation of status loss and discrimination may cause a person to seek to avoid such negative outcomes by adopting one of several potential coping orientations. While such coping orientations can protect a person from rejection, they may also cut off opportunities and reinforce the experience of feeling different from others. Negative consequences ensue in a broad range of outcomes, from self-esteem to social networks and jobs. To evaluate these potential coping actions, Link et al. [8] developed measures of the coping orientations of *secrecy*, *education* and *withdrawal*, and more recently [67] expanded these coping styles to include *distancing* and *challenging* behaviours.

Secrecy measures the degree to which respondents endorse concealment in order to avoid rejection. An earlier version of the scale [8] included five items (*Alpha* = .71). Link et al. [67] have since revised and added new items to create a nine-item scale (*Alpha* = .84).

Withdrawal measures the degree to which people endorse avoidance in order to protect themselves from potential rejection. This idea focuses on the tendency to limit social interaction to those who know about and accept one's stigmatized circumstance. The original seven-item version [8] (*Alpha* = .67) was recently modified and expanded to a nine-item scale (*Alpha* = .70) [67].

Educating assesses respondents' orientation to educating others in order to reduce the possibility of rejection. The idea originated from Schneider and Conrad [68] and their ideas about "preventive telling". The earlier five-item version [8] (*Alpha* = .71) was recently revised into a three-item scale (*Alpha* = .67). The new scale consists of fewer items because questions from the original version were used to create a new coping-orientation measure of "challenging" (see below).

Challenging measures people's orientations to confronting prejudice and discrimination. Link et al. [67] created a five-item scale (*Alpha* = .72) to assess how likely respondents are to challenge stigmatizing behaviour when it occurs or to disagree with people who make stigmatizing statements.

Distancing is a recently created three-item scale [67] (*Alpha* = .63) that assesses the extent to which people cope with stigma by indicating that their problems are very different from and that they have little in common with other people with mental illness.

Stigma-related feelings

An additional step in the measurement of modified labelling theory is an assessment of the feelings that stigma creates in the people exposed to it. To begin to address this, Link et al. [67] introduced two scales of stigma-related feelings – feeling *misunderstood by others* and feeling *different and ashamed*. These new measures provide a more fully elaborated set of empirical assessments that can be used to test modified labelling theory. Feeling **Misunderstood** assesses the degree to which people feel that their experience of mental illness has been misunderstood by others (*Alpha* = .62). The second scale, feeling **Different and Ashamed** is a four-item measure (*Alpha* = .70) assessing the degree to which people's experiences of mental illness and psychiatric hospitalization cause them to feel different from other people and ashamed.

Mental health consumers' experience of stigma

Although not itself a measurement perspective, the rejection that people with mental illness encounter represents a critical element of stigma integral to many of the above measurement approaches. The most comprehensive measure of mental health consumers' experience of stigma was developed by Wahl [66]. Common stigma experiences were identified from first-person accounts of mental illness such as those in *Schizophrenia Bulletin*, from consumer members of the research team and from representatives of the National Alliance for the Mentally Ill. The questionnaire, designed to be self-administered, includes nine statements concerning "stigma experiences" such as being treated as less competent and being advised to lower one's expectations. There are 12 items concerning discrimination experiences that include being denied a job, educational opportunities, housing or health insurance when consumer status was revealed, as well as avoiding indicating consumer status on written applications for fear of discrimination. Items are rated as occurring "never", "seldom", "sometimes", "often" or "very often". Data on reliability are not reported.

Dickerson et al. [69] adapted the instrument for a sample of schizophrenia outpatients by supplementing the term "consumer" with the term "persons with mental illness". They did so because pilot interviews indicated that many respondents did not associate the term "consumer" with consumers of mental health services. They also administered the survey in face-to-face interviews rather than via questionnaire. These authors did not report internal consistency reliability estimates, although they found that all nine stigma items were significantly correlated with the total Stigma score, and six of the 12 discrimination items were significantly correlated with the total Discrimination score.

The use of vignettes in research on stigma

Because vignettes are one of the most common methodological approaches used in tandem with stigma measurement perspectives, we include a discussion of their history and current usages. The approach was first used in 1955 by Star [70] to examine stigma in a study of public attitudes towards mental illnesses conducted on a nationwide basis in the United States. Star constructed vignettes portraying anxiety neurosis, paranoid schizophrenia, simple schizophrenia, alcoholism, juvenile character disorder and compulsive phobia and administered them to over 3000 U.S. residents in 1950. After each vignette, Star assessed the respondent's judgement about the seriousness of the vignette condition and whether the vignette character had a form of mental illness. Star's pioneering data revealed that the public was very unlikely to view the described disorders as mental illnesses. Only the vignette of paranoid schizophrenia which included a description that "a couple of times now he has beaten up men who didn't even know him, because he thought they were plotting against him" was identified as "mental illness" by a majority (75%) of respondents. Subsequent studies using Star's vignettes showed that the proportion of the general public identifying the vignettes as mental illnesses dramatically increased in the 1960s and 1970s, perhaps due in part to public education campaigns [71].

A critical development in the use of vignettes came in 1963 when Phillips [27] utilized the Star vignettes in a survey experiment. Phillips manipulated five vignette disorders (four from Star and a "normal" man) and five sources of help (no help source, clergy, physician, psychiatrist and mental hospital) in a classic Greco-Latin square experimental design. Phillips's study showed that help source significantly influenced respondents' levels of social distance from the vignette character, suggesting that rejection might result from seeking mental-health treatment. From a measurement perspective, Phillips's innovation ensured the future utilization of vignettes by combining their use with the experimental method. Since then, investigators have randomly varied other features of vignette descriptions, such as symptoms, behaviours, labels, causal attributions and sociodemographic variables.

The Star vignettes themselves are rarely used now, having been replaced by vignettes utilizing explicit criteria for diagnosing mental disorders derived from DSM-III (and subsequently DSM-III-R and DSM-IV). A group at Columbia University (Link, Phelan, Bresnahan and Stueve) specifically developed vignettes depicting six major mental disorders according to DSM-IV criteria. A "troubled person" vignette that did not meet any DSM-IV criteria was also created as a baseline for understanding responses to the other vignettes. Subsequently, four of these vignettes (alcoholism, major depression, schizophrenia and troubled person) and an additional vignette describing cocaine abuse were administered as part of the MacArthur Mental Health Module of the 1996 General Social Survey to a nationally representative sample of 1444 persons. The exact wording of these vignettes is available in Link et al. [32] and Pescosolido et al. [33]. Vignettes depicting disorders according to the International Classification of Diseases have also been developed by Angermeyer and Matschinger [72] and Jorm et al. [73] to study public attitudes in Germany and in Australia, respectively.

Following a vignette description, a variety of measures can be applied. Such measures may utilize the stigma components discussed earlier regarding the various conceptualizations of stigma. For example, using Link and Phelan's conceptualization, people can be asked to suggest labels for the described behaviour – e.g., "Is it some kind of mental illness?" Possible stereotypes such as dangerousness or incompetence as well as the respondent's emotional reactions (e.g., anger or pity) can be assessed. Finally, intentions to discriminate can be measured by social-distance questions that assess the respondent's willingness to engage in various types of social relationships with the described person.

There are two major reasons for why vignettes continue to have a prominent position in research on the stigma of mental illness. First, vignettes present a more elaborate stimulus to respondents than simply asking people about "mental illness", or "mental health consumer". Sometimes investigators may wish to study stereotypes associated with such general concepts, but vignettes afford great flexibility in allowing researchers to construct stimuli to test specific ideas about stigma processes. For example, in testing attribution theory, an investigator may wish to present a person whose illness emerged from a situation he or she could not control versus a person who may have created his or her problem. A second reason vignettes are popular is that they can be administered via random assignment, which brings the power of the experimental method to hypothesis testing. Further, vignette experiments can be administered to randomly selected general population survey samples, which in turn improve external validity.

Conclusion

In this chapter, we have reviewed the main measurement perspectives that have arisen to study the complex construct of stigma. Beginning with a discussion of several major conceptualizations regarding the stigma construct itself, we then traced the development of each main stigma measurement approach from its theoretical origins to its current applications. We believe this historical and methodological overview will be useful to researchers intending to use these stigma measurement approaches by providing a fuller context of the foundations of each perspective. Further, we believe researchers developing new stigma measures can draw valuable lessons from how prior measurement traditions developed from solid theoretical bases and robust psychometric testing. Lastly, we intend for this review to form a basis for further innovation and growth in developing new measurement paradigms to advance the study of stigma.

References

1. U.S. Department of Health and Human Services SAMHSA, Center for Mental Health Services, National Institutes of Health, National Institute of Mental Health. Mental Health: A Report of the Surgeon General. Washington, D.C.: U.S. Government Printing Office; 1999.
2. Link, B.G., Yang, L.H., Phelan, J.C. and Collins, P.Y. (2004) Measuring mental illness stigma. *Schizophrenia Bulletin* **30**(3), 511–541.
3. Crocker, J., Major, B. and Steele, C. (1998) Social stigma. In: D.T. Gilbert and S.T. Fiske (eds). *The Handbook of Social Psychology*. Boston, MA: McGraw-Hill.

4. Fine, M. and Asch, A. (1988) Disability beyond stigma: social interaction, discrimination, and activism. *Journal of Social Issues* **44**, 3–22.
5. Sayce, L. (1998) Stigma, discrimination and social exclusion: What's in a word? *Journal of Mental Health* **7**(4), 331–343.
6. Goffman, E. (1963) *Stigma: Notes on the Management of Spoiled Identity*. Englewood Cliffs, NJ: Prentice-Hall.
7. Jones, E., Farina, A., Hastorf, A., Markus, H., Miller, D.T. and Scott, R. (1984) *Social Stigma: the Psychology of Marked Relationships*. New York: W.H. Freeman and Company.
8. Link, B.G., Cullen, F.T., Struening, E.L., Shrout, P.E. and Dohrenwend B.P. (1989) A modified labeling theory approach to mental disorders: an empirical assessment. *American Sociological Review* **54**(June), 400–423.
9. Link, B.G. and Phelan J.C. (2001) Conceptualizing stigma. *Annual Review of Sociology* **27**, 363–385.
10. Morone, J.A. (1997) Enemies of the people: the moral dimension to public health. *Journal of Health Politics, Policy and Law* **22**(4), 993–1020.
11. Weiner, B., Perry, R.P. and Magnusson, J. (1988) An attributional analysis of reactions to stigmas. *Journal of Personality and Social Psychology* **55**(5), 738–748.
12. Corrigan, P.W. (2000) Mental health stigma as social attribution: implications for research methods and attitude change. *Clinical Psychology: Science and Practice* **7**(1), 48–67.
13. Angermeyer, M.C. and Matschinger, H. (1996) The effect of personal experience with mental illness on the attitude towards individuals suffering from mental disorders. *Social Psychiatry and Psychiatric Epidemiology* **31**(6), 321–326.
14. Scheff, T.J. (1998) Shame in the labeling of mental illness. In: P. Gilbert and B. Andrews (eds). *Shame: Interpersonal Behavior, Psychopathology, and Culture*. New York: Oxford University Press, pp. 191–205.
15. Link, B.G., Yang, L.H., Phelan, J.C. and Collins P.Y. (2004) Measuring mental illness stigma. *Schizophreria Bulletin* **30**(3), 511–541.
16. Eisenberger, N.I., Liberman, M.D. and Williams K.D. (2003) Does rejection hurt? An fMRI study of social exclusion. *Science* **302**, 290–292.
17. Angermeyer, M. and Matschinger, H. (2003) The stigma of mental illness: effects of labelling on public attitudes towards people with mental disorder. *Acta Psychiatrica Scandinavica* **108**, 304–309.
18. Steele, C.M. and Aronson, J. (1995) Stereotype vulnerability and the intellectual test performance of African Americans. *Journal of Personality and Social Psychology* **69**, 797–811.
19. Pinel, E.C. (1999) Stigma consciousness: the psychological legacy of social stereotypes. *Journal of Personality and Social Psychology* **76**(1), 114–128.
20. Farina, A., Allen, J.G. and Saul, B. (1968) The role of the stigmatized in affecting social relationships. *Journal of Personality* **36**, 169–182.
21. Link, B.G. (1987) Understanding labeling effects in the area of mental disorders: an assessment of the effects of expectations of rejection. *American Sociological Review* **52**, 96–112.
22. Link, B.G. (1982) Mental patient status, work and income: an examination of the effects of psychiatric label. *American Sociological Review* **47**, 202–215.
23. Bogardus, E.M. (1925) Measuring social distance. *Journal of Applied Sociology* **9**, 299–308.
24. Park, R.E. (1925) The concept of social distance. *Journal of Applied Sociology* **8**, 339–344.
25. Cumming, J. and Cumming, E. (1957) *Closed Ranks*. Cambridge, MA: Harvard University Press.
26. Whatley, C.D. (1959) Social attitudes toward discharged mental patients. *Social Problems* **6**, 313–320.
27. Phillips, D.L. (1963) Rejection: a possible consequence of seeking help for mental disorders. *American Sociological Review* **28**, 963–972.
28. Crocetti, G. and Spiro, H. (1973) *Contemporary Attitudes towards Mental Illness*. Pittsburgh, PA: University of Pittsburgh Press.
29. Schulze, B., Richter-Werling, M., Matschinger, H. and Angermeyer M.C. (2003) Crazy? So what! Effects of a school project on students' attitudes towards people with schizophrenia. *Acta Psychiatrica Scandinavica* **107**(2), 142–150.
30. Phelan, J.C., Link, B.G. and Moore R.E. (1997) The stigma of homelessness: the impact of the label 'homeless' on attitudes toward a poor person. *Social Psychology Quarterly* **60**, 323–337.

31. Link, B.G. and Schwartz, S. (1995) Public knowledge, attitudes, and beliefs about homeless people: evidence for compassion fatigue? *American Journal of Community Psychology* **23**, 533–555.

32. Link, B.G., Phelan, J.C., Bresnahan, M., Stueve, A. and Pescosolido B.A. (1999) Public conceptions of mental illness: labels, causes, dangerousness, and social distance. *American Journal of Public Health* **89**(9), 1328–1333.

33. Pescosolido, B.A., Monahan, J., Link, B.G., Stueve, A. and Kikuzawa, S. (1999) The public's view of the competence, dangerousness, and need for legal coercion of persons with mental health problems. *American Journal of Public Health* **89**(9), 1339–1345.

34. Crisp, A.H., Gelder, M.G., Rix, S., Meltzer, H.I. and Rowlands O.J. (2000) Stigmatisation of people with mental illnesses. *British Journal of Psychiatry* **177**, 4–7.

35. Nunnally, J.C. (1961) *Popular Conceptions of Mental Health*. New York: Holt, Rinehart, and Winston.

36. Olmsted, D.W. and Durham, K. (1976) Stability of mental health attitudes: a semantic differential study. *Journal of Health and Social Behavior* **17**, 35–44.

37. Osgood, C.E., Suci, G.J. and Tannenbaum P.H. (1957) *The Measurement of Meaning*. Urbana, IL: University of Illinois Press.

38. Nunnally, J.C. and Kittross, J.M. (1958) Public attitudes toward mental health professions. *American Psychologist* **13**(September), 589–594.

39. Beiser, M. and Waxler-Morrison, N. (1987) A measure of the 'sick' label in psychiatric disorder and physical illness. *Social Science and Medicine* **25**(3), 251–261.

40. Fazio, R.H. and Olson, M. (2003) Implicit measures in social cognition research: their meaning and uses. *Annual Review of Psychology* **54**, 297–327.

41. Greenwald, A.G. and McGhee, D.E. (1998) Measuring individual differences in implicit cognition: the implicit association test. *Journal of Personality and Social Psychology* **74**, 1464–1480.

42. Cohen, J. and Struening, E.L. (1962) Opinions about mental illness in the personnel of two large mental hospitals. *Journal of Abnormal and Social Psychology* **64**, 349–360.

43. Struening, E.L. and Cohen, J. (1963) Factorial invariance and other psychometric characteristics of five opinions about mental illness factors. *Educational and Psychological Measurement* **23**(2), 289–298.

44. Gilbert, D.C. and Levinson, D.J. (1956) 'Custodialism' and 'humanism' in staff ideology. In D.J. Levinson and R.H. Williams (eds). *The Patient and the Mental Hospital*. Glencoe, IL: Free Press.

45. Madianos, M.G., Economou, M., Hatjiandreou, M., Papageorgiou, A. and Rogakou, E. (1999) Changes in public attitudes towards mental illness in the Athens area (1979/1980–1994). *Acta Psychiatrica Scandinavica* **99**(1), 73–78.

46. Taylor, S.M., Dear, M.J. and Hall GB. (1979) Attitudes towards the mentally ill and reactions to mental health facilities. *Social Science and Medicine* **13D**, 281–290.

47. Taylor, S.M. and Dear, M.J. (1981) Scaling community attitudes towards the mentally ill. *Schizophrenia Bulletin* **7**(2), 225–240.

48. Wolff, G., Pathare, S., Craig, T. and Leff, J. (1996) Community attitudes to mental illness. *British Journal of Psychiatry* **168**(2), 183–190.

49. Sevigny, R., Yang, W., Zhang, P., Marleau, J.D., Yang, Z., Su, L., et al. (1999) Attitudes toward the mentally ill in a sample of professionals working in a psychiatric hospital in Beijing (China). *International Journal of Social Psychiatry* **45**(1), 41–55.

50. Weiner, B. (1986) *An Attributional Theory of Motivation and Emotion*. New York: Springer-Verlag.

51. Weiner, B. (1995) *Judgments of Responsibility: a Foundation for a Theory of Social Conduct*. New York: Guilford Press.

52. Corrigan, P.W. (2003) An attributional model of public discrimination towards persons with mental illness. *Journal of Health and Social Behavior* **44**, 162–179.

53. Reisenzein, R. (1986) A structural equation analysis of Weiner's attribution-affect model of helping behavior. *Journal of Personality and Social Psychology* **50**, 1123–1133.

54. McAuley, E., Duncan, T.E. and Russell, D.W. (1992) Measuring causal attributions: the revised causal dimension scale (CDSII). *Personality and Social Psychology Bulletin* **18**(5), 566–573.

55. Russell, D.W. (1982) The causal dimension scale: a measure of how individuals perceive causes. *Journal of Personality and Social Psychology* **42**, 1137–1145.

56. Boisvert, C.M. and Faust, D. (1999) Effects of the label "schizophrenia" on causal attributions of violence. *Schizophrenic Bulletin* **25**(3), 479–491.
57. Scheff, T.J. (1964) The societal reaction to deviance: ascriptive elements in the psychiatric screening of mental patients in a Midwestern state. *Social Problems* **11**(Spring), 401–413.
58. Angermeyer, M. and Matschinger, H. (1994) Lay beliefs about schizophrenic disorder: the results of a population study in germany. *Acta Psychiatrica Scandinavica* **89**, 39–45.
59. Furnham, A. and Bower, P. (1992) A comparison of academic and lay theories of schizophrenia. *British Journal of Psychiatry* **161**, 201–210.
60. Link, B.G., Struening, E.L., Neese-Todd, S., Asmussen, S. and Phelan, J.C. (2001) Stigma as a barrier to recovery: the consequences of stigma for the self-esteem of people with mental illnesses. *Psychiatric Services* **52**(12), 1621–1626.
61. Perlick, D.A., Rosenheck, R.A., Clarkin, J.F., Sirey, J.A., Salahi, J., Struening, E.L., et al. (2001) Stigma as a barrier to recovery: adverse effects of perceived stigma on social adaptation of persons diagnosed with bipolar affective disorder. *Psychiatric Services* **52**(12), 1627–1632.
62. Link, B.G., Struening, E.L., Rahav, M., Phelan, J.C. and Nuttbrock, L. (1997) On stigma and its consequences: evidence from a longitudinal study of men with dual diagnoses of mental illness and substance abuse. *Journal of Health and Social Behavior* **38**(2), 177–190.
63. Link, B.G., Mirotznik, J. and Cullen, F.T. (1991) The effectiveness of stigma coping orientations: can negative consequences of mental illness labeling be avoided? *Journal of Health and Social Behavior* **32**, 302–320.
64. Rosenfield, S. (1997) Labeling mental illness: the effects of received services and perceived stigma on life satisfaction. *American Sociological Review* **62**(August), 660–672.
65. Struening, E.L., Perlick, D.A., Link, B.G., Hellman, F., Herman, D. and Sirey, J.A. (2001) Stigma as a barrier to recovery: the extent to which caregivers believe most people devalue consumers and their families. *Psychiatric Servicees* **52**(12), 1633–1638.
66. Wahl, O.F. (1999) Mental health consumers' experience of stigma. *Schizophrenia Bulletin* **25**(3), 467–478.
67. Link, B.G., Struening, E.L., Neese-Todd, S., Asmussen, S. and Phelan J.C. (2002) On describing and seeking to change the experience of stigma. *Psychiatric Rehabilitation Skills* **6**(2), 201–231.
68. Schneider, J.W. and Conrad, P. (1980) In the closet with illness – epilepsy, stigma potential and information control. *Social Problems* **28**, 32–44.
69. Dickerson, F.B., Sommerville, J., Origoni, A.E., Ringel, N.B. and Parente, F. (2002) Experiences of stigma among outpatients with schizophrenia. *Schizophrenia Bulletin* **28**(1), 143–155.
70. Star, S. (1955) The public's ideas about mental illness. In: Annual Meeting of the National Association for Mental Health, 1955, Indianapolis, Indiana.
71. Brockman, J. and D'Arcy, C. (1978) Correlates of attitudinal social distance toward the mentally ill: a review and re-survey. *Social Psychiatry* **13**, 69–77.
72. Angermeyer, M.C. and Matschinger, H. (1997) Social distance towards the mentally ill: results of representative surveys in the Federal Republic of Germany. *Psychological Medicine* **27**(1), 131–141.
73. Jorm, A.F., Korten, A.E., Jacomb, P.A., Christensen, H., Rodgers, B. and Pollitt, P. (1997) "Mental health literacy": a survey of the public's ability to recognise mental disorders and their beliefs about the effectiveness of treatment. *Medical Journal of Australia* **166**(4), 182–186.

Appendix Inventories to measure the scope and impact of stigma experiences from the perspective of those who are stigmatized – consumer and family versions

Heather Stuart, Michelle Koller and Roumen Milev

Queen's University, Kingston, Canada

Understanding the needs of people who live with a mental disorder is essential if anti-stigma programmes are to be appropriately targeted and evaluated against criteria that are meaningful for those who bear the greatest burden of stigma. This technical appendix is written for researchers and programme evaluators to assist them in measuring the scope and impact of mental-health-related stigma from the perspective of people who have a mental illness ('consumers') and their family members. Information on the development, reliability and factor structure of the two inventories (consumer and family versions) is provided.

Conceptualization of stigma

Modern conceptualizations of stigma, based on Goffman's seminal work [1], recognize a feature or attribute – in this case a mental illness – that serves to morally and socially taint the bearer. Members of stigmatized groups are depicted in inaccurate and stereotypical ways, but at the core of stigma are prejudicial attitudes that often find expression in discriminatory behaviours.

In developing inventories to assess stigma from the perspective of consumers (of mental health services) and family members, respondents were asked to conceptualize stigma in terms of 'negative feelings that people may have toward those with a mental or emotional

Understanding the Stigma of Mental Illness: Theory and Interventions   Edited by Julio Arboleda-Flórez and Norman Sartorius
© 2008 John Wiley & Sons, Ltd

disorder'. To capture a range of stigma experiences, both inventories contain a frequency and an intensity scale. In each case, the 'Stigma Experiences' scales measure the frequency of stigma experienced. The total score reflects the pervasiveness of stigma that was experienced across a variety of life domains. The 'Stigma Impact' scales measure the intensity of the psychosocial impact of stigma on major life domains such as quality of life, family relations, social contacts and self-esteem. The two approaches produce results that are modestly correlated, indicating that the frequency and impact of stigma experiences are separate but related phenomena.

Item development

In each case, items were developed to capture the central features of the stigma experienced by consumers and family members as depicted in the theoretical, empirical and qualitative literature. Stigma experiences characterizing particular sub-groups of people (such as those who were employed or those who were hospitalized) were avoided in favour of experiences that would be potentially relevant to all respondents. Early versions of the instruments were reviewed by local experts: people who have a mental illness, family members and mental health professionals. Questions were refined for content and flow, then formally field-tested. Results of the two field tests are reported below. Both field tests received ethics clearance from Queen's University, Faculty of Health Sciences, Research Ethics Board.

Internal consistency of the inventory of stigma experiences – consumer version

Field test sample

People who had been clinically diagnosed with a serious mental illness and who were living in the community were the target population for this field test. A total of 88 volunteers were recruited from hospital-based outpatient programmes, community clinics, and local mental health advocacy groups. The Stigma Experiences scale (the frequency scale) was developed and field-tested first on 30 subjects. A review of the open-ended comments collected revealed the necessity of differentiating the frequency or breadth of experiences from their psychosocial impact. An impact scale was subsequently developed and tested on an additional 58 respondents. More detailed information on the development and testing of this inventory is published elsewhere [2].

The characteristics of the consumer test sample are presented in Table A.1. Sixty percent were female and the average (median) age was 46 years. Almost two thirds had a college or university education, but only a third were employed in any capacity. Two-thirds were un-married. A third were living with a spouse or partner and a small proportion (approximately one in ten) were living with parents. A third were living alone. The most common current diagnoses were depression, schizophrenia, anxiety and manic-depressive illness. Forty per cent thought their mental health had improved over the previous year and a third thought that it had become worse. One in ten reported that their symptoms had emerged prior to 10 years of age and another third reported first symptoms during adolescence (11–19 years). Over half waited more than a year to receive treatment and almost one in five waited over ten years. One in five received treatment during adolescence. Almost 80% had been ill for more than ten years at the time of the survey. Most (over 80%) had come to accept their di-agnosis and had done so for a number of years. Most reported past admissions to psychiatric

Table A.1   Characteristics of the consumer test sample ($N = 88$)*

Characteristic	% (N)
Gender	
• Male	40.9 (36)
• Female	59.1 (52)
Age group	
• 20–29	13.1 (11)
• 39–39	10.7 (9)
• 40–49	34.5 (29)
• 50–59	25.0 (21)
• 60–69	11.9 (10)
• 70–79	4.8 (4)
Highest education	
• Public school or less	1.1 (1)
• High school	35.2 (31)
• College or technical training	36.4 (32)
• University	27.3 (24)
Employment status	
• Employed	32.2 (28)
• Not employed	67.8 (59)
Marital status	
• Single	63.6 (56)
• Married/common law	36.4 (32)
Living situation	
• Alone	34.5 (30)
• Spouse/Partner	36.8 (32)
• Parents	11.5 (10)
• Other	17.2 (15)
Current diagnosis	
• None	2.4 (2)
• Schizophrenia	27.0 (22)
• Manic-depressive illness	24.4 (20)
• Depression	47.6 (39)
• Anxiety	26.7 (22)
• Substance abuse	3.7 (8)
• Other	14.7 (12)
Mental health now compared to a year ago	
• Better	40.7 (35)
• About the same	26.7 (23)
• Worse	32.6 (28)
Age that symptoms were first noticed	
• 10 or under	8.6 (7)
• 11–19	32.1 (26)
• 20–29	28.4 (23)
• 30–39	20.1 (17)
• 40–49	6.2 (5)
• 50–59	3.7 (3)
Age at first treatment	
• 13–19	20.5 (17)
• 20–29	34.9 (29)
• 30–39	24.1 (20)
• 40+	20.5 (17)

(Continued)

Table A.1 *(Continued)*

Number of years between symptoms and first treatment	
• Under 1 year	43.8 (35)
• 1–2 years	15.0 (12)
• 3–5 years	11.3 (9)
• 6–10 years	11.3 (9)
• 10+ years	18.8 (15)
Number of years ill (as of 2005)	
• 10 or under	23.1 (18)
• 11–19	21.8 (17)
• 20–29	24.4 (19)
• 30–39	18.0 (14)
• 40–49	11.5 (9)
• 50–59	1.3 (1)
Have come to accept diagnosis	
• No	15.2 (12)
• Yes	84.8 (67)
Years diagnosis has been accepted	
Not accepted	16.7 (12)
• 1–5	26.4 (19)
• 6–10	19.4 (14)
• 11–15	11.1 (8)
• 16–20	11.1 (8)
• 21–25	9.7 (7)
• 25+	5.6 (4)
Hospital use	
• Ever hospitalized for mental illness or suicide attempt	70.1 (61 of 87)
• Ever hospitalized in a provincial psychiatric institution	62.3 (38 of 61)
• Ever hospitalized in a general hospital psychiatric unit	73.8 (45 of 61)
• Ever committed under provincial mental health legislation	32.2 (19 of 59)
• Ever remanded to a forensic unit under federal legislation	2.1 (1 of 47)
Service use in the last year	
• Hospitalized as a voluntary patient	19.6 (12 of 61)
• Hospitalized as an involuntary patient	4.9 (3 of 61)
• Use of outpatient community mental health programme	50.0 (43 of 86)
Frequency of outpatient treatment ($N = 42$)	
• Weekly	47.7 (20)
• 2–3 times per month	31.0 (13)
• Monthly	4.8 (2)
• Every 2–3 months	11.9 (5)
• 1–2 per year	4.8 (2)

*Missing data for some items will mean that frequencies may not total to 88.

institutions and general hospital psychiatric units, and a third had been committed under mental health legislation. The majority were actively involved in outpatient community mental health programmes at the time of the survey.

Scoring

The 10 items making up the Stigma Experiences Scale – Consumer Version are shown in Table A.2. The first two items refer to expectations of stigma and are scored on a 5-point Likert-type scale using the response categories of never, rarely, sometimes, often

Table A.2   Reliability coefficients for the Stigma Experiences Scale – Consumer Version

Scale item	% endorsed (out of 70)	Item-rest correlation ($N = 70$)
Do you think that people think less of you if they know you have a mental illness?	52.8%	.35
Do you think that the average person is afraid of someone with a serious mental illness?	67.1%	.39
Have you ever been teased, bullied or harassed because you have a mental illness?	41.4%	.44
Have you felt that you have been treated unfairly or that your rights have been denied because you have a mental illness?	44.3%	.51
Have your experiences with stigma affected your recovery?	47.1%	.54
Have your experiences with stigma caused you to think less about yourself or your abilities?	60.0%	.50
Have your experiences with stigma affected your ability to make or keep friends?	41.4%	.69
Have your experiences with stigma affected your ability to interact with your family?	57.1%	.43
Have your experiences with stigma affected your satisfaction or quality of life?	64.3%	.60
Do you avoid situations that may be stigmatizing to you?	61.4%	.58

Kuder–Richarson coefficient of reliability (KR-20) = .83

and always. These responses were recoded into a binary variable, with 1 reflecting a high expectation of stigma (often and always), and zero reflecting no or low expectation (never, rarely, sometimes). The remaining eight items used three response categories: no, unsure and yes. These were also recoded into binary categories reflecting the presence (yes) or absence (no and unsure) of each experience. To create the index, scores were summed across all items for a maximum scale score of 10. Aggregated scores showed good dispersion across the entire range of possible values, with a median of 4.5 and an interquartile range of 2.5-7.5.

The seven items comprising the Stigma Impact scale are shown in Table A.3. These were rated on an 11-point scale ranging from 0 (reflecting no impact) to 10 (reflecting the highest amount of impact). Items were summed to give a scale score ranging from 0 to 70 with a median of 35, a mean of 32 and a standard deviation of 19.3.

Internal consistency (reliability) of scale scores

Table A.2 reports the percentage of the sample that positively endorsed each item on the Stigma Experiences Scale, the item-rest correlation (showing the correlation between each individual item and the remaining scale score with that item removed) and the Kuder–Richarson coefficient of reliability to measure the internal consistency of the scale scores when the data are binary. Positive endorsements for items were generally in the desired range, from 41.4% to 67.1%. The average for the scale was .50, above the conventional .40 threshold. The item-rest correlations for both items dealing with expectations of stigma fell slightly below the .40, suggesting they may be candidates for removal. However, eliminating these items did not improve the overall internal consistency of the scale scores so they were

Table A.3 Reliability coefficients for the Stigma Impact Scale – Consumer Version

Scale item	Median (N)	Item-rest correlation
On a ten point scale, where 0 is the lowest possible amount, and 10 is the highest possible amount, how much as stigma affected you personally?		
Quality of life	4 (59)	.77
Social contacts	6 (58)	.82
Family relations	5.5 (48)	.82
Self-esteem	4 (58)	.61
On a ten-point scale where 0 is the lowest possible amount, and 10 is the highest possible amount, how much has stigma affected your family as a whole?		
Quality of life	3.5 (55)	.69
Social contacts	2.5 (54)	.69
Family relations	4 (55)	.73

Cronbach's alpha reliability coefficient = .91

retained on the strength of their theoretical relevance. The Kuder–Richarson coefficient of reliability was .83, indicating high internal consistency of the scale scores.

Reliability coefficients for the Stigma Impact Scale are presented in Table A.3, along with the median score for each item. Median scores ranged from 2.5 to 6. Item-rest correlations ranged from .61 to .82, yielding a high scale reliability coefficient of .91. The self-esteem item was the weakest (with an item-rest correlation of .61); however, eliminating it from the scale had little effect on the overall reliability, so it was retained.

Spearman's rank order correlation was used to assess the association between the two scales. A statistically significant but moderately low correlation of .47 ($p = .001$), indicated that the two scales share some common variance, but measure somewhat different constructs.

Internal consistency of the inventory of stigma experiences – family version

Test sample

Parents of children with a serious mental illness, such as schizophrenia or depression, and who attended family-oriented advocacy groups, family network meetings or family conferences were the target population for this field test.

Sixty-six parents completed the inventory. Their characteristics are presented in Table A.4. The majority were female and the average (median) age was 59 years. Three quarters were mothers and the majority were college- or university-educated. Most were living with a spouse or partner and just over half were employed. Half reported that their mentally disabled relative lived with them.

Table A.5 describes the characteristic of their disabled relative. Over sixty per cent were male and the average (median) age was 34 years. The most frequently reported diagnoses were schizophrenia, depression, bipolar disorder and misuse of alcohol or street drugs. Almost half had received more than one diagnosis since the inception of their illness and almost half were reported to be improving. Half had been ill for more than ten years. Almost half first noticed symptoms during adolescence (11 to 19 years); however, less than a third

Table A.4   Characteristics of the family test sample ($N = 66$)

Characteristic	% (N)
Gender	
• Male	24.2 (16)
• Female	75.8 (50)
Age group	
• 20–39	12.4 (8)
• 40–49	9.1 (6)
• 50–59	25.8 (17)
• 60–69	25.8 (17)
• 70–89	18.2 (12)
Relationship	
• Mother	54.5 (36)
• Father	9.1 (6)
• Sibling	9.1 (6)
• Spouse/partner	18.2 (12)
• Other	9.1 (6)
Highest education	
• Public school or less	1.5 (1)
• High school	12.1 (8)
• College or technical school	43.9 (29)
• University	42.4 (28)
Living situation	
• Alone	12.1 (8)
• Spouse/partner	78.8 (52)
• Other	9.1 (6)
Employment status	
• Employed	53.0 (35)
• Not employed	47.0 (31)
Does your relative live with you?	
• Yes	50.0 (33)
• No	50.0 (33)

*Missing data for some items will mean that frequencies may not total to 66.

received their first treatment during this time and a third waited more than three years before receiving treatment (17% waited over ten years). The majority had been hospitalized at some point in the past and half had been involuntarily committed under mental health legislation. Approximately one third had been hospitalized in the year prior to the survey and almost half were involved in the community outpatient treatment system – most receiving weekly treatment.

Scoring

The seven items making up the Stigma Experiences Scale – Family Version are shown in Table A.6. The first four items are scored on a 5-point Likert-type scale using the response categories of never, rarely, sometimes, often and always. These responses were recoded into a binary variable, with 1 reflecting the presence of stigma (often and always), and zero reflecting the absence of stigma (never, rarely, sometimes). The remaining eight items used three response categories: no, unsure and yes. These were also recoded into binary categories reflecting the presence (yes) or absence (no and unsure) of each experience. To

Table A.5   Characteristics of mentally ill relatives ($N = 66$)

Gender	
• Male	62.1 (41)
• Female	37.9 (25)
Age of relative	
• 20–29	40.9 (27)
• 30–39	16.7 (11)
• 40–49	24.2 (16)
• 50–59	10.6 (7)
• 60+	7.5 (5)
Diagnosis of relative (multiple responses accepted)	
• Schizophrenia	48.5 (32)
• Manic depression/bipolar	24.2 (16)
• Depression	33.3 (22)
• Anxiety disorder	16.7 (11)
• Misuse of alcohol or street drugs	24.2 (16)
• Personality disorder	9.1 (6)
• Other	9.1 (6)
Number of diagnosis	
• 1	54.5 (36)
• 2	28.8 (19)
• 3	13.6 (9)
• 4	3.0 (3)
Mental health now compared to a year ago	
• Better	48.5 (32)
• About the same	37.9 (25)
• Worse	13.6 (9)
Number of years ill (as of 2005)	
• Under 5	16.7 (11)
• 5–10	30.3 (20)
• 11–19	15.2 (10)
• 20–29	19.7 (13)
• 30–39	10.6 (7)
• 40–49	4.5 (3)
• 50–59	1.5 (1)
Age that symptoms were first noticed	
• 10 or under	9.1 (6)
• 11–19	48.5 (32)
• 20–29	27.3 (18)
• 30–39	7.6 (5)
• 40+	6.0 (4)
Age at first treatment	
• 5–19	30.3 (20)
• 20–29	43.9 (29)
• 30–39	15.2 (10)
• 40+	7.6 (5)
Number of years between symptoms and first treatment	
• Under 1 year	39.4 (26)
• 1–2 years	22.7 (15)
• 3–5 years	15.2 (10)
• 6–10 years	3.0 (2)
• 10+ years	16.7 (11)

Table A.5   (*Continued*)

Hospital use	
• Ever hospitalized for mental illness or suicide attempt	78.8 (52 of 66)
• Ever hospitalized in a provincial psychiatric institution	48.1 (25 of 52)
• Ever hospitalized in a general hospital psychiatric unit	86.5 (45 of 52)
• Ever hospitalized in a forensic unit	17.4 (8 of 46)
• Ever personally involved in commitment process	50.0 (26 of 45)
Service use in the last year	
• Hospitalized in the past year	31.8 (21 of 66)
• Hospitalized as a voluntary patient	18.2 (12 of 66)
• Hospitalized as and involuntary patient	24.2 (16 of 66)
• Use of outpatient community mental health program	43.9 (29 of 64)
Frequency of outpatient treatment (N = 28)	
• Weekly	60.7 (17)
• 2–3 times per month	7.1 (2)
• Monthly	10.7 (3)
• Every 2–3 months	7.1 (2)
• 1–2 per year	14.3 (4)

*Missing data for some items will mean that frequencies may not total to 66.

create the index, scores were summed across all items for a maximum scale score of 7. Aggregated scores showed good dispersion across the entire range of possible values, with a median of 2 and an interquartile range of 1–4.

The seven items of the Stigma Impact scale are shown in Table A.7. These were rated on an 11-point scale ranging from 0 (reflecting no impact) to 10 (reflecting the highest amount of impact). Items were summed to give a scale score ranging from 0 to 70 with a median of 28, a mean of 27 and a standard deviation of 19.6.

Internal consistency (reliability) of scale scores

Table A.6 reports the percentage of the sample that positively endorsed each item on the Stigma Experiences Scale, the item-rest correlation (showing the correlation between each individual item and the remaining scale score with that item removed) and the Kuder–Richarson coefficient of reliability to measure the internal consistency of the scale scores

Table A.6   Reliability coefficients for the Stigma Experiences Scale – Family Version

Scale item	% endorsed (N = 61)	Item-rest correlation
Do you think that people think less of those with a mental illness?	70.5%	.29
Do you think the average person is afraid of someone with a mental illness?	52.5%	.35
Has your relative been stigmatized because of their mental illness?	42.6%	.59
Have you felt stigmatized because of your relative's mental illness?	19.7%	.69
Has stigma affected your family's ability to make or keep friends?	27.9%	.46
Has stigma affected your ability to interact with your other relatives?	42.6%	.45
Have your experiences with stigma affected your family's quality of life?	52.5%	.53

Kuder–Richarson coefficient of reliability for binary data (KR-20) = .76

Table A.7   Reliability coefficients for the Stigma Impact Scale – Family Version

Scale item	Median (*N*)	Item-rest correlation
On a ten-point scale, where 0 is the lowest possible amount, and 10 is the highest possible amount, how much as stigma affected you personally?		
Quality of life	3.5 (54)	.80
Social contacts	2.0 (54)	.85
Family relations	4.0 (54)	.73
Self-esteem	1.0 (55)	.69
On a ten-point scale where 0 is the lowest possible amount, and 10 is the highest possible amount, how much as stigma affected your family as a whole?		
Quality of life	4.0 (53)	.87
Social contacts	3.0 (52)	.84
Family relations	4.0 (52)	.75

Cronbach's alpha reliability coefficient = .93

when the data are binary. Positive endorsements for items were generally in the desired range, from 19.7% to 70.5%. The average for the scale was .44, above the conventional .40 threshold. The item-rest correlations for both items dealing with expectations of stigma fell slightly below the .40, suggesting they may be candidates for removal. However, eliminating these items did not improve the overall internal consistency of the scale scores, so they were retained on the strength of their theoretical relevance. The Kuder–Richarson coefficient of reliability was .76, indicating high internal consistency of the scale scores.

Reliability coefficients for the Stigma Impact Scale are presented in Table A.7, along with the median score for each item. Median scores ranged from 1.0 to 4.0. Item-rest correlations ranged from .69 to .87, yielding a high scale reliability coefficient of .93. The self-esteem item was the weakest (with an item-rest correlation of .67); however, eliminating it from the scale had little effect on the overall reliability, so it was retained.

Spearman's rank order correlation was used to assess the association between the two scales. A statistically significant but moderately low correlation of .66 ($p = .001$) indicated that the two scales share some common variance, but measure somewhat different constructs.

Factor structure – stigma impact scales

In order to be valid and interpretable, factor analysis requires interval-level data. While it has often been used with dichotomous items, the practice is highly suspect and often leads to anomalous results [3]. The requirement for interval-level data, therefore, excludes the possibility of testing the factor structure of the Stigma Experiences Scales as these were composed of dichotomous variables. However, as the Stigma Impact Scales are numeric, it is possible to assess the extent to which the various items load on a single factor, indicating whether variables are assessing a single, underlying dimension.

Table A.8 shows the results of the factor analysis, using a principal factor approach, for both the consumer and family versions of the Stigma Impact Scale. Results from the analysis of the consumer version yielded a single factor with an eigenvalue well above

Table A.8 Factor loadings for the Stigma Impact Scales – Consumer and Family Versions

	Factor loadings	
Item	Factor 1	Factor 2
CONSUMER VERSION		
How stigma has affected you personally with respect to:		
• Quality of life	.80	.34
• Social contacts	.77	.38
• Family relations	.81	.12
• Self-esteem	.62	.51
How stigma has affected your family as a whole		
• Quality of life	.79	−.44
• Social contacts	.79	−.43
• Family relations	.85	−.37
FAMILY VERSION		
How stigma has affected you personally with respect to:		
• Quality of life	.82	−.30
• Social contacts	.88	−.25
• Family relations	.77	.53
• Self-esteem	.69	.006
How stigma has affected your family as a whole		
• Quality of life	.90	−.22
• Social contacts	.87	−.17
• Family relations	.80	.45

1 (4.3), which represented 82% of the variation in the data. All items loaded strongly (.62 to .85) on a single factor, as expected. A principal factor analysis using the seven items making up the Stigma Impact Scale – Family Version yielded similar results. Items loaded strongly on a single factor (.69 to .90) with an eigenvalue of 4.7, representing 86% of the variation in the data.

A comment on reliability and validity

Neither reliability (defined as the reproducibility of a measure), nor validity (defined as the extent to which a psychometric instrument measures what it was designed to measure) are inherent characteristics of a scale. Both vary with the purpose for which it is used, the characteristics of the individuals being assessed, and the environmental context in which the assessment takes place. This makes it difficult to declare any scale or inventory to be generally 'reliable' or 'valid' [3, 4].

In our applications, consumer and family experts who reviewed the inventories and helped to revise the questions considered that the scales had good face validity. The content of the questions appeared to address the most salient features of their own stigma experiences and the constructs appeared to map well onto those depicted in the theoretical literature. In addition, the scale scores demonstrated good internal consistency. Finally, the Stigma Impact Scales demonstrated a factor structure consistent with a single underlying construct. All of these results suggest that in our application, these scales yielded reliable and valid data. However, users are strongly encouraged to confirm the reliability and factor structure of the scales in their own applications.

A final comment on utility

According to scale development literature, reliability coefficients in the range of .70 to .85 are likely to yield scale scores that are (a) sufficient to describe the distribution of the characteristic of interest in a sample and (b) differentiate groups of people on the basis of high and low scores (discriminant validity). Our coefficients for the Stigma Experiences Scales were well within this range: .76 and .83 for consumer and family versions, respectively. These results suggest that the experiences scales are ideal for developing population benchmarks and distinguishing groups of people with high and low stigma experiences – knowledge that is helpful in targeting anti-stigma programmes [5].

The reliability coefficients for the stigma impact scales were higher: .91 and .93 for consumer and family versions, respectively. Thus, in addition to adequately distinguishing between groups on the basis of extreme scores, these scales may also be helpful in differentiating between or within individuals, so may be more useful in evaluating the impact of anti-stigma programmes over time [5].

Understanding the frequency and scope of stigma experienced by people who live with a mental disorder will be essential for targeting anti-stigma programmes to where they are needed most. Further, as reducing the psychosocial impact of stigma on people with mental disorders and their families becomes an ever more important public health goal, having the capacity to measure changes over time will be critical to evaluating programme success. The scales described in this appendix are new additions to a field that is currently lacking such measurement options. Subsequent research will be needed to assess their full utility. In the meantime, they are offered to promote the development of an evaluation base in support of best practices in the field of stigma reduction.

Acknowledgements

Funding for this project was provided through an Ontario Premier's Research Excellence Award and a research grant provided by the Schizophrenia Society of Ontario.

References

1. Goffman, E. (1963) Stigma: Notes on the Management of Spoiled Identity. Englewood Cliffs, NJ: Prentice-Hall.
2. Stuart, H., Milev, R. and Koller, M. (2005) The inventory of stigmatizing experiences: its development and reliability. World Psychiatry 4, S1, 35–39.
3. Aiken, L.R. (1997) Questionnaires and Inventories. New York: John Wiley & Sons (pp. 145–172).
4. Streiner, D.L. and Norman, G.R. (1995) Health Measurement Scales. A Practical Guide to their Development and Use (2nd edn). Oxford: Oxford University Press.
5. McDowell, I. and Newell, C. (1987) Measuring Health: a Guide to Rating Scales and Questionnaires. New York: Oxford University Press.

Index

Understanding the Stigma of Mental Illness: Theory and Interventions   Edited by Julio Arboleda-Flórez and Norman Sartorius
© 2008 John Wiley & Sons, Ltd